The author on the Dagala Trek with his family

About the Author

Bart Jordans has been exploring treks and trekking peaks in the Himalayas, Karakorams, Hindu Kush and European Alps since 1984. He has led treks in Bhutan since 1994, and grasped the opportunity of getting to know the Bhutan Himalayas in greater depth when he lived in the country with his wife and two small children for more than four years from 1999. His familiarity with all aspects of the overwhelming beauty of the Bhutan Himalayas and its people has encouraged him to write a trekking guidebook to share his great love for this part of the eastern Himalayas. Bart may be contacted on **info@bhutantreks.com** (see **www.bhutantreks.com**).

BHUTAN
A TREKKER'S GUIDE

by
Bart Jordans

CICERONE

2 POLICE SQUARE, MILNTHORPE, CUMBRIA LA7 7PY
www.cicerone.co.uk

Second edition 2008
ISBN-13: 978 1 85284 553 7

© Bart Jordans 2005, 2008

First edition 2005
ISBN 1 85284 398 5

British Library Cataloguing-in-Publication Data. A catalogue record for this book is available from the British Library.

Photographs by Bart Jordans unless stated. Flower sketches on pages 34 to 36 by Dr A.K. Hellum. Illustrations on page 42 from *Birds of Bhutan*, used with permission.

**To the friendly, colourful and magical people of Bhutan
and Helene, Laura and Max with love**

Warning

All mountain activities contain an element of danger, with a risk of personal injury or death. Treks described in this guidebook are no exception. Under normal conditions wandering the trails of Bhutan will be neither more nor less hazardous than walking among big mountains anywhere in the world, but trekking involves physically demanding exercise in a challenging landscape, where caution is advised and a degree of stamina is often required, and it should be undertaken only by those with a full understanding of the risks, and with the training and experience to evaluate them. Trekkers should be properly equipped for the routes undertaken. Whilst every care and effort has been taken in the preparation of this guide, the user should be aware that conditions can be highly variable and change quickly. Rockfall, landslip and crumbling paths can alter the character of a route, and the presence of snow and the possibility of avalanche must be carefully considered, for these can materially affect the seriousness of a trek.

Therefore, except for any liability which cannot be excluded by law, neither Cicerone Press nor the author accepts liability for damage of any nature (including damage to property, personal injury or death) arising directly or indirectly from the information in this guide.

Readers are warned that trekkers are sometimes badly injured by passing yaks; a few unfortunates die of hypothermia or acute mountain sickness; while some simply lose their balance and fall from the trail due to a momentary loss of concentration. Since there is no organised mountain rescue service in Bhutan, such as exists in some mountain regions of Europe and the USA, if an accident occurs self-help may be your only option.

Front cover: Tsho Phu lakes and Jitchu Drake (6850m), seen on Trek 4, day 6

CONTENTS

Map Key

～～～	ridge
··············	trek
～～～	road
---------	dirt track/feeder road
—·—·—·—	national boundary
●	habitation/village/town/gompa
⅄	col/pass/la
▲	summit
▥▥▥▥	ropeway
～～～	river
⬭	lake
?	unknown area
¥	hot spring/tsachu
→	direction arrow
⌂	bridge
⊕	international airport
5043	height in metres

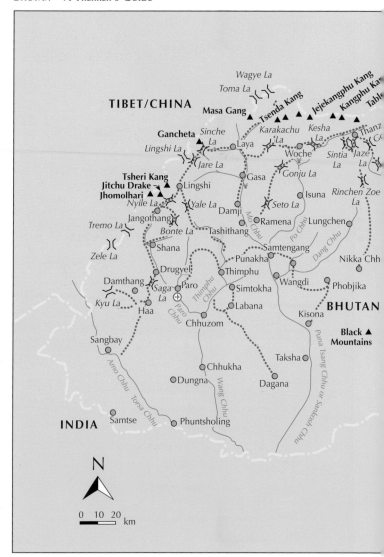

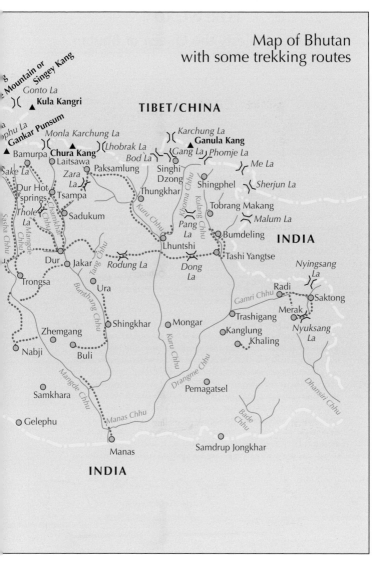

Map of Bhutan
with some trekking routes

TIBET/CHINA

Mountain or Singey Kang

Gonto La

Kula Kangri

phu La

Gankar Punsum

Monla Karchung La

Karchung La

Ganula Kang

Bamurpa **Chura Kang**

Lhobrak La

Gang La

Phomje La

Sake La

Laitsawa

Paksamlung

Bod La

Singhi Dzong

Me La

Zara La

Shingphel

Sherjun La

Dur Hot springs

Tsampa

Thungkhar

Tobrang Makang

Thole La

Sadukum

Pang La

Malum La

Sasha Chhu

Mangde Chhu

Chamkhar Chhu

Lhuntshi

Bumdeling

INDIA

Dur

Jakar

Tang Chhu

Rodung La

Dong La

Tashi Yangtse

Nyingsang La

Trongsa

Bumthang Chhu

Ura

Radi

Saktong

Shingkhar

Mongar

Trashigang

Merak

Nyuksang La

Zhemgang

Buli

Kanglung

Khaling

Gamri Chhu

Nabji

Kuru Chhu

Mangde Chhu

Drangme Chhu

Dhansiri Chhu

Samkhara

Pemagatsel

Gelephu

Manas Chhu

Bada Chhu

Manas

Samdrup Jongkhar

INDIA

9

FOREWORD
by Her Majesty the Queen of Bhutan

TASHICHHODZONG
THIMPHU, BHUTAN

October 16th 2004

Foreword

HER MAJESTY THE QUEEN

I welcome Bart Jordan's guidebook focusing exclusively on trekking routes based on his experiences as a guide for nearly ten years in Bhutan. The guidance provided by this book starts to come into use where travellers leave their cars behind and use their legs instead. There is useful information on woods, passes, rivers, and villages on what a walking-traveller will come across in the numerous enchanting treks described in this book. Some of the routes are described for the first time and adds more insights into the beautifully serene reaches of the land. At the same time, the book should inspire readers to visit other places in Bhutan beside the more popular trekking routes, and help sustain the uses of relatively more obscure routes.

The trekking routes detailed in this book are but a fraction of the footpaths and mule tracks connecting different localities in Bhutan, both near and far flung. I have travelled most of the routes included in this guidebook and have realised how important the routes are to the pattern of positive relationships amongst our communities. The tracks on which people and livestock trod for centuries were a testimony of their meaningful interdependent relationships. People in each locality were drawn into interaction both at the personal as well as economical levels along such tracks. Trade and exchange amongst our mountain people, though cut off from the rest of the world, was forged with the continual use of trekking routes. The reorientations of traffic towards motor highways bring changes that make hundreds of footpaths and mule tracks obsolete, pushing the locations of the smaller and remoter communities to become unviable and causing their residents to migrate. Bhutan is marked by countless networks of trekking routes that could still benefit the communities that grew along them as they did in the past with more appreciative trekkers seeking out these near forgotten routes.

Dorji Wangmo Wangchuck
Her Majesty the Queen of Bhutan

PREFACE TO THE FIRST EDITION

Bhutan – a trekking destination beyond imagination

The Kingdom of Bhutan is a landlocked country comprised of mountains and forest and offering all the beauties of the Himalayas. The Bhutanese people have travelled through their country on foot for centuries, developing many routes through valleys and over passes. Over time these routes witnessed many different faces from many different places, each with their own story to tell. The majority are still in use; however, the building of roads to access more and more remote places in the Kingdom has caused the disappearance of several routes (only a few decades ago there were no roads in Bhutan).

Having had the unique opportunity of living in Bhutan for more than four years (1999–2003), and leading treks there since 1994, I felt that it was time to write a trekking guidebook for Bhutan. When we approached Paro airport in 1999 my daughter Laura (then 2½ years old) looked out of her window and said, 'Look, papa's mountains'. This book is intended to share my love and respect for the Bhutan Himalayas and its hospitable people.

The information given is as accurate as possible, but with many different – and sometimes hard to access – sources, details are always changing. Deriving details from local people, reading different maps, studying various (old) sources didn't make the process easier, but it was very interesting. Accuracy is important in a guidebook, but as more information comes in I am sure that changes will need to be made, names re-spelled, and so on. I always welcome comments and updated information from readers.

This guidebook unfolds many routes throughout the Kingdom in detail. Some routes have been described earlier in other sources (such as in accounts from explorers); some routes are described here for the first time, with perhaps a lesser degree of detailed information. Every trek description starts and finishes where transport is left behind or met.

The book should inspire the reader to visit places away from the more popular routes, and opens up some remote valleys. Travel around with respect so as not to spoil the environment for either the people living there or for future visitors. Many valleys have hardly been visited by foreigners and are pretty well unmapped. You may feel that writing a guidebook might give the adventurer too much information, but don't worry: there is plenty left! I collected material for more than 65 treks – and probably many more routes exist throughout this mountainous country.

One of my favourite treks, the Ramena trail leading to Lunana, couldn't make this edition. I have to apologise to everybody who contributed text and can't find it here, especially seven-year-old Beth Dutson. Be assured that your contributions will be handed out as background information to trekkers joining me – a special treat.

Bhutan has been closed to outsiders until recently, with a few exceptions; the first paying tourist group visited the country in 1974. Trekking started in western Bhutan in 1978, and in central Bhutan in 1982, and the trekkers make up only 10 percent of total tourist numbers (just over 7500 tourists in 2000). The Bhutanese believed for a long time that a thunder dragon protected the country and its people from any trespassers or evil spirits. The independence Bhutan has

11

known for so long is highly treasured. For generations past the country has isolated herself from the outside world in her attempt to preserve successfully her civilisation. Only a few foreigners visited the country.

This book is written for both the experienced and inexperienced trekker. Treks at both levels are described. After some practical information the treks are described, following a general line through Bhutan from the west to the centre and finally the east.

Treks in Bhutan are guided: from arrival until departure the visitor is accompanied by a Bhutanese guide (sometimes assisted by one from outside the country). Treks are accompanied by a group of staff. Overnight accommodation is in tents, with luggage carried by pack animals.

Bhutan offers other activities too such as whitewater rafting, mountain biking, rock climbing, family trekking, birdwatching, meditation and retreat centres, textile tours, festivals, stone baths, motor-bike tours and golf, or the chance to just relax and do nothing at a pleasant place like Bumthang. Activities which could develop include high-altitude trekking (including crossing technical passes), border-crossing treks, paragliding and ballooning. Mountaineering is not permitted at the present time, since the mountain people petitioned the king to put a stop to it, for fear of disturbing the mountain deities. There could also be mushroom tours, traditional medicine tours and cooking courses. Skiing has been attempted but the terrain is not really suitable.

GPS measurements are not included in this book because repeatedly measuring and getting different results on the same trek led me to conclude that they are not yet very useful (for me!). Swiss altimeter and altimeter watches work perfectly but you do need references, which are hardly available for Bhutan. The altitudes quoted in this book must be taken with a pinch of salt: there are simply too many different altitudes derived from different sources and measurements.

Detailed trekking maps of Bhutan are still unavailable. Missionaries and diplomatic missions visiting the country in the past have produced some maps; more recently, data has been collected, but maps not yet been printed. For more recent maps that are available see page 21. The maps used in this book are based on my own sketch maps, and whatever I could glean from the Survey of Bhutan. It has not been an easy process, but the outcome should be reasonable. Names of places, rivers, mountains and so on are spelled in endlessly different ways, making it almost impossible to arrive at one uniform spelling. These uncertainties just add to the level of adventure!

Bhutan receives less than 1000 trekkers each year. You will be well looked after, and the country has a good infrastructure to back this up. However, bear in mind that due to factors outside your control – a delayed flight, impassable road, high passes blocked with snow, unreliable pack animals – itineraries will have to be altered. This can be frustrating, but also brings new surprises. Pack a flexible attitude in your luggage and I am sure you will have an experience to remember for the rest of your life.

Tashi Delek! – good luck!
Bart Jordans, 2005

PREFACE TO THE SECOND EDITION

Since the first edition of this book was published (2005), economic development in Bhutan has continued to expand at a rapid rate. Physical infrastructure is improving, with more roads and bridges (mainly for farmers) being constructed, and talks taking place about possible additional airstrips and even a domestic airline. More tour operators (281 in 2006), hotels and restaurants have opened for business. The tourism sector in general is growing (9249 tourists in 2004, 13,626 in 2005, and 17,344 in 2006), although the number of trekking visitors has remained stable over the last few years (in 2006 766 visited Bhutan exclusively for trekking and another 1723 combined their cultural itinerary with a short trek).

The pace of development is a challenge to Bhutan's environmental managers and, along with climate change and its possible impact on glacial retreat, is one of the main threats that the country's policy-makers are well aware of. All tourists need to keep the unique environment in mind when they come to Bhutan.

In this second edition of the book, new roads and bridges are taken into account as well as an outline of the international border change (from 2006). The latter change does not actually affect the trekking routes described in this guidebook, since none is located near the border area in question.

There are some minor changes to the treks, such as where new feeder roads are replacing some parts of trekking routes. Some treks described in the first edition have been left out because they have either still not been opened or have been substantially changed. In four cases they have been replaced by new treks, as described below.

In western Bhutan the trekking/rafting route (Haa – Amo Chhu – Phuentsholing) has been replaced by a newly opened trek in Haa (Trek 2). The Gangte trek (Trek 12) – which is slowly being replaced by a feeder road – has been summarized in the book, and a new trek in the area has been added (there are plans to make the original Gangte trek the first lodge-based trek in Bhutan).

In central Bhutan, the new Nabji–Korphu route (Trek 13) has been included. This trek has been designed so that local communities obtain benefit from it. Finally a trek in the far east of Bhutan (Brangzungla Alpine Trek) has been replaced in the second edition by a route in central Bhutan, called the Royal Heritage Trek (Trek 22), which follows the route travelled by the royal family between Bumthang and their winter palace south of Tongsa.

My heartfelt thanks go to those who helped me with updating this new edition. I have mentioned their names in the acknowledgement section of the book.

I would like to finish this preface by congratulating the Kingdom of Bhutan on reaching 101 years of monarchy in 2008. I wish the country all the best for the forthcoming coronation, the first democratic parliamentary elections and implementation of the constitution.

Bart Jordans
Hanoi – autumn 2007

Near Laya village 3800m

INTRODUCTION

THE THRILL OF BHUTAN

The Himalayan Kingdom of Bhutan – located between the two huge neighbouring countries of China and India – has, throughout most of its history, survived as a result of its independence. There is little information available regarding the history of the country, most documents having been destroyed by fire or other catastrophes.

According to legend Bhutan was, up to the 7th century, part of the Tibetan empire, after which it became part of North India, but since the 10th century onwards the country has not apparently been occupied by any foreign power. Bhutan was comprised of a couple of small kingdoms before the 17th century, when Shabdrung Namgyal (1594–1651) started to unify the country. In 1651 he enlisted the help of Je Kenpo as spiritual leader, and Druk Desi as leader for non-religious issues. In 1907 the monarchy was established.

Bhutan is located on roughly the same latitude as Cairo. It is roughly 10 percent smaller than Switzerland. It is a mountainous country with an extensive natural border formed by high mountains to the north, rising to over 7000m, and virtually impassable jungle to the south. The country has been closed to foreigners for centuries, with only a handful allowed across the border. Bhutan has always been a place of mystery, its lack of contact with and influence from the outside world resulting in a unique culture. This culture, and the untouched nature of the country and its people, gives Bhutan its unique appeal. Recently the country has started to open up, allowing more visitors in.

TREKKING

According to the Oxford dictionary a trek is 'a long hard walk lasting several days or weeks, especially in mountains'. The word originates from the Dutch for 'promenade', and was refined to its current meaning by the Boer (farmer) emigrants to South Africa who went on difficult walks during their search for new land.

Trekking has a meditative effect on both mind and body: you are surrounded by nature with few materialistic disturbances. Being pampered by a local staff gives you time to concentrate on other things such as a good walk, a good meal, and a very good night's sleep under the stars. Trekking is the ultimate experience of a quiet, healthy and active holiday, and once a trekker – always a trekker.

The Bhutanese don't necessarily have the same idea about trekking as foreigners; for them it means a trip to their home village, a pilgrimage to a monastery high in the mountains, placing prayer flags on mountaintops, visiting one of the country's hot springs, or (for those in remote areas) a visit to the market to buy supplies.

Rinpung Dzong – Paro

Trekking in Bhutan is different from other regions in Asia. You are trekking in a country steeped in Buddhist traditions and culture, even high up in the mountains. Bhutan Himalaya, with a forest/ shrub cover of around 80 percent and plenty of rain in the monsoon months, provides an enormously rich flora and fauna, unlike anywhere else in this region. There are fewer villages in the high mountains of Bhutan than there are in places such as Nepal, and villagers often gaze at trekkers because they see so few. The daily altitude gain in Bhutan Himalaya is typically more than in other Himalayan countries, and trekking in the northern part often involves crossing more than one high pass of 5000m. Trekking in Bhutan is also more costly then in most other Himalayan destinations. Part of the daily rate (government tax about $US70) is indirect development aid.

Every trek is led by a qualified Bhutanese guide (without a support group of Sherpas as in Nepal). Trekking in the Bhutan Himalayas does not require any special technical skills. The mountains are covered with a network of trails but, because of the sparse population, these are not heavily travelled. The trails are generally in good condition, and fit, experienced walkers should have no difficulty navigating them, although natural obstacles such as snowfall and landslides can require a change of plan. There are also very few trekkers to encounter (600–1000 each year, the majority of whom are on the Jhomolhari trek).

Meals on trek are as good as anywhere in the Himalayas. Lunch is not like the typical Nepalese extended break where a hot lunch is cooked; in Bhutan a hot lunch is prepared at breakfast time and carried in thermos flasks and pots. Animals such as mules and yaks will transport your luggage. Sometimes – on the first day yaks are used – they may arrive late at the start or end of the day (or not arrive at all because they have turned round and gone home!). It therefore makes sense to carry dry (and warm) clothing in your daypack, just in case you reach camp before the luggage arrives.

No food is sold along the trail, so trekking in Bhutan involves a lot of luggage. A party of eight trekkers will typically have four members of staff, four yak herders or horsemen, and more than 20 yaks or small but sturdy horses.

There are few burglary or safety problems while trekking or camping. Campfires are generally not permitted, but at certain villages locals are allowed to sell firewood.

Trekking in the Himalayas is often thought to be the preserve of the super-fit, but there are treks catering for all different fitness levels: easy to tough, short to long, and from lower to higher altitude. Of course, it helps to be fit and prepared for a trek. Make sure you choose a trek that is not too difficult or hard. It is never fun to have to give up and turn back, or to exhaust yourself and so be unable to finish the trek. The most important thing is that you are happy to walk for several days, and that you enjoy camping.

Trekking grades can be confusing. Each commercial operator uses their own

After crossing Bonte La (Trek 4, day 6)

17

Monk students in Rinpung Dzong – Paro

grading systems, so check them out carefully. A good trek description should enable you to make the right choice.

In general trekking in Bhutan includes long days with several ascents and descents each day. Bhutan's valleys are steeper then in neighbouring Nepal. The trails are less used simply because the population is at a much lower level in Bhutan.

TREKKING GRADES USED IN THIS GUIDE

- **Easy**: lower altitude, good trails, shorter days, short treks, suitable for most people
- **Moderate**: a mix between low and high altitude and shorter and longer days, not always on a good trail, basic fitness required
- **Demanding**: travelling at altitude, some high passes to be crossed, trails not always in the best state, possible river crossings, some longer days, higher level of fitness required
- **Strenuous**: high altitude, high passes, high camping, difficult trails, possible river crossings, long days, long treks, only for well-prepared trekkers (previous experience recommended).

CLIMATE AND TREKKING SEASONS

The most popular period for trekking in Bhutan is spring and autumn. However, with climate change the seasonal patterns are becoming less predictable. The country, located in the eastern part of the Himalayas, receives a good deal of rain. The valleys experience strong winds, and each one has its own weather. Mountains tend to create their own weather patterns with storms, hail, snow and thunder. Be

FOUR CLIMATIC SEASONS

- **Winter:** very nice dry/sunny period with cold nights/warm days; more or less cloudless; good views and snow on the high passes; good season for low-altitude trekking. Impossible to find pack animals willing to cross high passes due to snow conditions. Watch for avalanches
- **Spring:** more rain/precipitation; clear early in the morning; around 10.00/11.00hr the first clouds build up, accompanied by strong wind. When the sun shines it can be very hot. Bring good sun protection/sunhat; people have fainted on the first day of a trek due to heat. Can be unpredictable with blue sky/sun in the morning and storm/rain/hail/thunderstorms in the afternoon. Thunderstorms normally blow in very fast and can be tricky at high altitude. Depending on winter snowfall some passes are impassable. Watch for avalanches.
- **Summer:** warm with some rain during the day or several overcast days in a row. Rain does not necessarily travel up into the high mountains, but rivers can fill up fast during monsoon rains. Be prepared to get wet/muddy/attacked by leeches for the first couple of days. Drier conditions will be found higher up the mountains. Summer is brief in the high mountains, but full of life. As unpredictable as the summer and the monsoon can be, there can be periods of nice weather and clear views. Trekking in the monsoon is probably one of the last challenges in the Himalayas, but for every rain drop a flower blooms in the mountains!
- **Autumn:** some rain showers, not as heavy as in summer. Rain might become snow at altitude but can easily melt off during the day. Clear views.

Average temperature (°F/°C) and rainfall (mm) for Thimphu (7708ft/2350m) and Paro (7480ft/2280m)

Note that for every 1000m height increase the temperature drops about 7°C.

	Jan	Feb	Mar	Apr	May	Jun	Jul	Aug	Sep	Oct	Nov	Dec
Max	37/3	45/7	57/14	61/16	64/18	68/20	77/25	77/25	68/20	64/18	57/14	45/7
Min	27/–3	30/–1	41/5	45/7	47/8	54/12	57/14	50/10	47/8	43/6	36/2	32/0
Rain	25	25	25	51	51	76	355″	304″	127	76	25	0

aware of wind and rain, which can have a major effect on temperature.

Note: When flying in and out of the country count on extra days because precipitation and overcast conditions may cause the airport to be closed.

ORGANISING A TREK

A visit to Bhutan has to be booked and organised through an international and/or Bhutanese tour operator. (A tour operator outside Bhutan will use a local company to handle most services.) Visa, flights, transportation, permits, accommodation, meals, guiding, trekking support, etc, are all organised (in advance) by a Bhutanese company supported by official authorities and international tour operators.

Your stay in Bhutan is therefore managed from beginning to end – any tourists visiting the Kingdom will have prearranged the majority of their itinerary and will be guided around the country by an official Bhutanese guide (and trekking staff) during the whole stay.

Outside Bhutan there are a couple of adventure travel companies that offer trips to the Kingdom. Search the internet and read advertisements in outdoor magazines.

Inside Bhutan there are many tour operators – new and old, big and small – the number fluctuating from year to year. The Bhutan Department of Tourism (DoT) has a website (**www.tourism. gov.bt**) listing all the (reliable) tour operators' names and contact addresses and many other interesting facts. Also visit the website of the Association of Bhutanese Tour Operators (**www.abto.org.bt**). A tour operator in Bhutan has to follow strict government rules. Any guides used on a trek should be officially qualified.

The former limit on the annual number of tourists visiting Bhutan has

PASSPORTS, VISAS AND PAPERWORK

Bhutan requires a valid passport with at least six months' validity from the date of your departure from the country. Your visa application should have been handled in advance through a tour operator; you cannot get your actual visa in advance. You may be able to get your visa clearance number, which can be helpful. Before checking in on the Druk Air flight to Bhutan the ground staff at the airport from which you are travelling will check if your name is on a list with visa clearance numbers. Your visa will be stamped into your passport at Paro international airport.

In Bhutan the tour operator looks after you from start to finish and does all the necessary paperwork: visa application, visa extension (if needed), Druk Air reconfirmation, obtaining road and trekking permits, permits to visit *dzongs*, for fishing, for filming, and so on.

COST

A trip to Bhutan is not cheap, but remember that about $US70 of the daily cost contributes towards education and health; and that the daily sum is all-inclusive.

AVAILABLE MAPS

Note: Detailed trekking maps of Bhutan are unavailable (2007).

- Bhutan road map (1:500.000) by Berndtson & Berndtson (c$US10): a plastic-laminated road map with lots of information, including the main trekking routes with camps. Also includes a city map of Thimphu and Paro.
- Bhutan country map with Jhomolhari trekking map (1:450.000) by Shangri-La Maps in Nepal. Some trekking information is included.
- Bhutan Himalaya (1:500.000) by the Swiss Foundation for Alpine Research (1996). Limited information.
- 'Northwestern Bhutan' by Michael Ward, *The Geographical Journal*, December 1966. Also published in Michael Ward's book *In This Short Span* (London, 1972). Good details and interesting for the Jhomolhari–Laya–Lunana trek.
- Sketch map of Lunana by Augusto Gansser. Published in *The Mountain World* by the Swiss Foundation for Alpine Research (1968/69). Well detailed.
- Bhutan guidebooks (see Bibliography).

CONTACT DETAILS – TOUR OPERATORS

www.tourism.gov.bt provides addresses of Bhutanese companies.
Outside Bhutan: listed below are a selection of companies offering cultural and trekking holidays in Bhutan.
Himalayan Kingdoms **www.himalayankingdoms.com** UK
KE Adventure Travel **www.keadventure.com** UK + USA
Dav Berg-und-Skischule **www.dav-summit-club.de** Germany
Hauser Exkursionen **www.hauser-exkursionen.at** Germany
Horizons Nouveaux **www.horizonsnouveaux.com** Switzerland
Kipling Travel **www.kiplingtravel.dk** Denmark
Snow Leopard Adventures **www.snowleopard.nl** Netherlands
Tirawa Himalaya **www.tirawa.com** France
Above the Clouds **www.aboveclouds.com** USA
Bhutan Travel **www.bhutantravel.com** USA
Geographic Expeditions **www.geoex.com** USA
Mountain Travel Sobek **www.mtsobek.com** USA
Wilderness Travel **www.wildernesstravel.com** USA
World Expeditions **www.worldexpeditions.com.au** Australia

BEFORE YOU GO

Before you visit Bhutan ensure that you have:
- compiled a (fixed) itinerary
- made any necessary payments
- booked flights and obtained visa clearance
- had the appropriate health checks and vaccinations
- checked your trekking equipment
- visited the gym and
- left home not feeling stressed

been lifted, but the high daily charge (check **www.tourism.gov.bt** for daily tariff, discounts and surcharges) and restricted infrastructure and facilities ensure that the Kingdom will never be overrun by visitors. This is in line with the national tourism policy: high income – low impact.

Trekking with a Group or Alone?
It is possible to visit Bhutan as part of a group or as an individual, but in both cases a Bhutanese tour operator is needed and you will always be guided.

Organising your own trek is possible, but the trekking experience is not the same as in Nepal. Staff looking after you will accompany a trek in Bhutan. There are no teahouses and lodges along the treks, as there are in Nepal, where you can obtain meals, drinks and accommodation. Even if you use a Bhutanese tour operator for the paperwork a trek can't be undertaken alone.

GETTING THERE AND GETTING AROUND

Bhutan can be reached by air and by road. Try Google 'carbon calculators' to see the link between travel and global warming.

By air the national carrier Druk Air connects Bhutan (Paro) with Delhi, Kathmandu, Bangkok and Kolkata, and sometimes other destinations are planned in the flight schedule (**www.drukair. com.bt**). Bookings are normally made through your travel agent. There is another airstrip in the far east of Bhutan, but this is impossible to use due to wind. Feasibility studies for new domestic airports are being conducted (2007) for Bumthang, Yonphula, Trashigang and Phuentsholing. Druk Air flies two new Airbuses (2005), and offer scenic flights (see website). Airport departure tax is included in the air fare.

Kira: dress for women

Taksang Lhakhang (or Tiger's Nest) – Paro valley

Helicopter services are rare; any helicopters used come from outside the country.

By road Bhutan is connected with India and can offer some exiting mountain driving. Bhutanese travel agents have their own fleets of buses and small cars to transport visitors, and will pick up and deliver any traveller arriving at/departing from the Indian border.

Taxis are available in the bigger towns, and a city bus operates in the Thimphu valley.

Be aware that travelling in and around by road Bhutan is time-consuming, includes possible delays and involves very winding roads. There are other means of getting around, besides motorised transport: mountain bike, horseback, rafting or on foot.

ENVIRONMENTAL AND CULTURAL AWARENESS

Bhutan is known for its unique environment. It has beautiful flora and wildlife and an unspoiled Buddhist culture. The country's government is trying hard to maintain this situation. Trekkers can support this worthy effort by understanding that the country's isolated villages are surprisingly fragile, and minimising foreign cultural impact and avoiding all forms of pollution.

Bhutanese girl in Paro

- Lakes are often considered holy, with deities living in their depths. Please respect this belief by not disturbing the waters, particularly by not throwing anything into them.
- Always go in a clockwise direction around holy places (*lhakhangs*, *chortens*, *stupas*, *mani* walls). If you are allowed to go inside a temple, always take off your hat. Check with the caretaker to see if you need to remove your shoes (not always necessary on a concrete floor). Have some small change ready and, if it is allowed, put a donation on the altar. Do not take any photos or disturb praying monks. Bring a torch to find your way.
- Sweets: give staff sweets without wrappers, but do not give any to children.
- Toilet and rubbish: on trek toilet holes will be provided at camp. On the more popular treks the toilet holes are starting to spoil the campsites. If no toilet holes are available make sure to bury your waste with sand and/or stones to avoid contamination being spread by flies or animals. If the camp crew has a campfire burning don't throw rubbish onto it, as this is believed to bring bad weather. Collect your personal rubbish and give it to the staff in the morning for burning in a separate fire or to be carried out.
- Campfire: in general, not allowed (but at some camps the residents are allowed to sell firewood).
- Take old batteries home with you.
- Leave campsites cleaner than you found them.

Laya woman at harvest

- Most Bhutanese villages have seen foreigners by now, but some will still be very curious. Please keep displays of Western goods to a minimum and be respectful by not being intrusive with Western ways. Dress modestly, especially in villages and temples.

- Washing: keep a good distance away from any water source when you wash clothes or yourself. Dirty water should be spread so the soil can filter it.
- Water contamination: use toilets wherever possible. If that is not possible then (below the tree line)

25

bury your waste; above the tree line try to cover it with stones. If you're in snow, make sure to dig all the way down to the soil.

- Short cuts cause erosion, so stick to the main trails.
- Photography: in general the Bhutanese are not shy about having their picture taken, but ask for permission first and follow up if you promise to send a picture to someone. Don't take pictures inside temples.
- Begging is not a big deal yet. Try to keep it that way by not handing out inappropriate gifts.

BEGGING AND PRESENTS

In the Bhutan Himalayas you will visit or camp close to remote villages and yak herders' tents. Meeting the very friendly mountain people is one of the best parts of being on trek. All your movements will be observed closely. Interaction with the mountain people is wonderful, but please be respectful. Sharing games, songs and family photographs as well as trying to say some Bhutanese words can be a wonderful experience.

Bhutan has very few beggars. Rarely will somebody put out his/her hand and/or beg for something. Try to keep it that way. Why do trekkers give? Obviously because trekkers like the happy smiles they receive. It is easy to feel generous with little effort. If you feel like handing out something, do it very discreetly. Don't give something away in order to have a person do something for you, like posing for a picture. Give something when you think it could be useful! For example, you may see herders repairing clothes with bad quality needles or thread, or see elderly people with bad eyes (knowing that you have several old pairs of glasses back home in a draw). Being invited in a home or yak herder's tent and presented with some tea is also a good moment for a simple gift.

Below are some examples of presents that are generous and useful gifts.

- School materials, like an inflatable globe, atlas, picture book, puzzle, etc (should be given to the head teacher of a school)
- Prayer flags and incense to offer on mountain passes and in chapels
- Hairclips for the girls
- Safety pins, strong (big) needles (needles are regarded as symbols of life in Bhutan) for sewing, zips, buttons, etc
- Postcards from all over the world
- Old sunglasses and prescription glasses (hand out to locals while crossing high passes to protect from the fierce sun and to elderly people with eye problems)
- Hand or moisturising creams
- Plastic sheets and bags
- Socks

Mountain deities
and Buddhist customs

Lhakhangs (temples) and monasteries (gompas), meditation cells, holy places, chortens, caves, mani walls and prayer flags can be found throughout Bhutan, making the countryside both colourful and interesting (there are more than 2000 temples and monasteries throughout the country). Even more colourful is the mystique and spirituality behind those sites. For instance, the mountain deities, gods, spirits and ghosts cannot be seen but are ever-present on mountaintops, in rivers and streams, in lakes, in caves, in stones and big boulders, in forests and in houses, sometimes having a supernatural existence.

The Bhutanese are devoted to worshiping and making offerings to the deities and gods, the protectors of their religion and nature. It is a religious goal to tame the harsh land, which can require considerable time and money. In return for their offerings, the deities will protect the Bhutanese against all sorts of calamities and enemies: optimising good luck and minimising bad luck. One of the more important ceremonies in many Bhutanese households is the placing of decorative spirit-catchers, which turn bad fortune to good.

Whilst on trek through Bhutan you come across many examples of the relationship between Buddhism and nature (see box).

BUDDHISM IN NATURE

- Seven black crows in the air signify good luck.
- According to some Bhutanese it is a bad sign to see large numbers of snow partridges towards the end of September, because it means excessive snow and rain.
- Yeti are called Migoi in Bhutan (see Merak–Sakteng trek); many mountain people believe in this creature and will be careful not to meet him/her.
- Some Bhutanese affix empty eggshells on the trees near farmhouses to protect them from evil and bad spirits.
- Farmers, before they start ploughing a field, hold a puja (religious ceremony) to please the deity of the ground, who will be disturbed or offended by the ploughing.
- Boulders are not usually removed from fields, because one could house a deity and the removal might upset him/her; improving the fields and developing roads and dams is not always easy because of these beliefs. In addition, stones can carry powers believed to protect their owners; the Bhutanese often keep special stones in their homes.
- It is believed that climbing a mountain near the summit will disturb the abode of the mountain gods.
- Cutting trees in a forest angers the forest god.
- Seeing a white yak in a lake is a sign of good luck. ▸

- Bhutanese houses are well decorated with symbols to protect the inhabitants from evil deities and bad luck. These symbols include wooden phalluses pinned with a wooden sword at each corner of the house or crossed above the entrance, and painted phalluses next to the main door or on the walls. Also, animals believed to convey protection are painted on the houses to keep away evil and bad luck.
- Every house (even a modest yak herder's tent) has an outdoor chapel/altar and a small stone structure for the daily ritual: early in the morning, juniper and small alpine rhododendron leaves are mixed for burnt offerings, producing a very sweet incense.
- Religious and holy places, like a *lhakhang, chorten, stupa, mani* wall or group of prayer flags should all be passed clockwise.
- Hunting or fishing is not tolerated in the Buddhist philosophy (except 'catch and release' fishing, which is gaining acceptance).
- There are auspicious days on which you should or should not do certain things, like travel, start a new business, get married or hold a funeral.
- Moving the cattle between summer and winter grazing involves certain rituals to please the deities and gods of the mountains.
- A dog following a trekking party the whole time is believed to be the soul of a dead trekker.
- There is a belief in flying mountains (mountains that move around!).
- Prayer flags on holy mountains are put up to control the earth and render it submissive, binding the earth and spirit powers. To appease the mountain gods in the Buddhist tradition, you could place your own prayer flag on top of a pass. Buy them in Paro or Thimphu before you start your trek. Count the number of passes you cross and buy accordingly. The flags in the shops are not blessed, but your guide might be able to arrange this.
- Bhutanese can be superstitious about cloud formations. A certain shape can be inauspicious, proclaiming that somebody is unlucky.
- Rain and sunshine at the same time is called *metok-chharp* (blossom rain), and is believed to be very auspicious.
- According to Buddhist beliefs, throwing meat (or bones), used papers or old clothes on a fire will provoke the deities, resulting in bad weather the next day!
- In the old days, when crossing a bridge Bhutanese would remove their caps and loudly recite prayers to please the deities of the river; crossing a bridge was (is) considered auspicious.
- The sound of the cuckoo heralds the onset of the warm season.
- One Bhutanese saying states that a man should eat a female raven, and a woman a male raven: this has medicinal power. So catch a raven!

Section of a mani wall

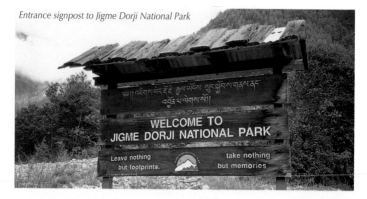

Entrance signpost to Jigme Dorji National Park

Two of the more interesting papers on the subject are 'On local and mountain deities in Bhutan' by Françoise Pommaret and 'Gods and Sacred Mountains' by Christian Schicklgruber (see Bibliography).

PROTECTED AREAS

The protected areas of Bhutan comprise four national parks, four wildlife sanctuaries and one strict nature reserve. The network encompasses 27.8 percent of the country (10,673km²). In 2007, an additional 9.9 percent was demarcated, made up of corridors linking all nine protected areas. The diverse natural flora and fauna includes more than 5400 species of vascular plants, about 620 species of birds and close to 200 mammals. All parks are legally protected. For more information on national parks check out **www.wwfbhutan.org.bt**.

Torsa Strict Nature Reserve (644km²) protects the westernmost temperate forest, from broadleaved forest to alpine meadows within an altitude range of 1400–4800m, and includes the small lakes of Sinchulungpa. Unlike Bhutan's other protected areas, Torsa has no resident human population.

Jigme Dorji National Park (4200km²) is the largest protected area, with an altitude range of 1400–7000m+. The park is a vital watershed covering almost half of northern Bhutan, and an important natural conservatory of glaciers, alpine meadows and scrublands, sub-alpine and temperate coniferous forest, warm and cool temperate broadleaved forest, major rivers and streams, and the flora and fauna that inhabit these ecosystems. Jigme Dorji harbours numerous species of wildlife, many of which are endangered or extinct elsewhere in the world, including the tiger, snow leopard, takin, blue sheep, musk deer, Himalayan black bear, marmot, red panda and several species of pheasant. The park also is famous for its flora; more than 300 species are used in indigenous medicine. Jigme Dorji has a resident human population of more than 1000 households.

National Parks of Bhutan

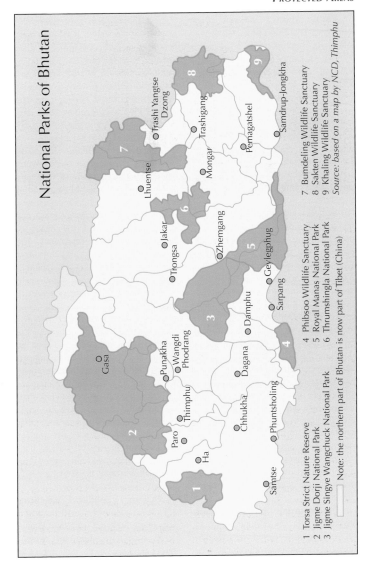

1 Torsa Strict Nature Reserve
2 Jigme Dorji National Park
3 Jigme Singye Wangchuck National Park

4 Phibsoo Wildlife Sanctuary
5 Royal Manas National Park
6 Thrumshingla National Park

7 Bumdeling Wildlife Sanctuary
8 Sakten Wildlife Sanctuary
9 Khaling Wildlife Sanctuary

Source: based on a map by NCD, Thimphu

Note: the northern part of Bhutan is now part of Tibet (China)

Royal Manas National Park (1023km²) The oldest protected area is also Bhutan's conservation showpiece. It is next to Jigme Singye Wangchuck National Park and forms a trans-frontier reserve with Manas National Park in India. Royal Manas is therefore part of a complex of protected areas ranging from 150–2600m altitude, including habitats from lowland tropical forests to permanent ice fields. It is also the only park in Bhutan where the greater one-horned rhinoceros and water buffalo occur. The rare golden langur, pygmy hog and hispid hare also are found there. Royal Manas holds more significant species than any other park, and 365 species of birds, including four species of hornbills (rufous-necked, wreathed, pied and great Indian), have been confirmed. Several plant species are valued as food crops, while a number are of commercial, medicinal and religious significance. Read more on the park in Trek 27.

Jigme Singye Wangchuck National Park (1400km² – formerly called Black Mountains Park) covers a wide range of habitat types, from broadleaved forest at 600m to coniferous forest, alpine pasture and lakes to permanent ice on the peak of Dorshingla at 4925m. The park constitutes the largest and richest temperate forest reserve in the entire Himalayas. More than 449 species of birds, including the endangered black-necked crane, inhabit the combined area of Jigme Singye Wangchuck and Royal Manas National Parks.

Thrumshingla National Park (905km²), with an altitude range of 700–4400m, is the second major temperate park in Bhutan and protects large tracts of old-growth fir forest. Six species of globally threatened birds are found here: rufous-necked hornbill, rufous-throated wren-babbler, satyr tragopan, beautiful nuthatch, Ward's trogon and chestnut-breasted partridge; as well as a recently discovered new species, the wedge-billed wren-babbler. With only 20 households this is one of Bhutan's lesser-populated protected areas.

Bumdeling Wildlife Sanctuary (1300km²), ranging from 1400–6000m, contains a rich diversity of flora and fauna as well as some of Bhutan's most scenic alpine lakes. Bumdeling valley – located within the sanctuary – is also one of two wintering spots in the country for the endangered black-necked crane. The sanctuary contains 190 resident households and several cultural and religious sites of international significance.

Sakten Wildlife Sanctuary (650km²), ranging from 1800–4400m, is designed to protect the easternmost temperate ecosystems of Bhutan where some endemic species are found, including the eastern blue pine and black-rumped magpie, and yeti (migoi), among others.

Khaling Wildlife Sanctuary (273km²), the smallest protected area, with an altitude range of 400–2200m, is important for elephant, gaur and other tropical wildlife, and may also contain the rare pygmy hog and hispid hare. Both are known from the Khaling reserve on the Indian side of the border, with which this forms a trans-border reserve.

Phibsoo Wildlife Sanctuary (278km²), a relatively small protected area ranging from 200–1600m, is known for its especially important biogeographic position. It is the only reserve in

Bhutan to have chital or spotted deer, as well as the only remaining natural sal forest in the country. Like the Manas region, Phibsoo is also home to the elephant, tiger and gaur.

FLORA AND WILDLIFE

The forest is a peculiar organism of unlimited kindness and benevolence that makes no demands for its sustenance, and extends protection to all beings, offering shade even to the axe man who destroys it.

Lord Buddha

Bhutan is the world's most mountainous country, comprised mainly of hills and mountains from 200 to 7000m+. About 18 percent of the total land area is above 4200m and is covered by snow and glaciers. The Bhutan Himalayas make up 340km of the 2400km-long Himalayan range.

Due to the wide range of altitude, climate, and a forest/shrub cover of around 80 percent, Bhutanese flora and fauna are exceptionally diverse, with new species of plants and animals still being discovered. In 1949 the British botanist Frank Ludlow said of Bhutan, 'Nature has run riot there', a sentiment shared by today's visitors. There are 48 species of rhododendron and over 300 species of medicinal plants, many of which can be easily seen, as well as a rich range of wildlife.

Bhutan offers a limited number of flora and fauna tours, and some tour operators have specialist guides. One of the highlights used to be the spectacular Royal Manas National Park, located in the south-central part of the country on the border with India, but now closed due to security concerns. There are also birdwatching trips that seek out the more than 620 species of birds that inhabit or frequent the country.

Bhutan has many parks and protected areas, and some of the parks have visitor centres. A day trip from any hotel in the country will take the visitor into the heart of the natural environment.

Flora

Several vegetation zones are as described in *Flowers of Bhutan* by Nakao and Nishioka:

1   Lower tropical zone (up to 1000m), including giant bamboos and a rich variety of palms and rattans.

2   Shiny-leaved forest zone (1000m–2500m), a rich zone of temperate,

SOME ENVIRONMENTAL ORGANISATIONS

- National Environment Commission
- Royal Society for Protection of Nature, with nature clubs throughout the country
- WWF
- Nature Conservation Division
- Department of Forestry Services
- Bhutan Trust Fund
- UN
- Donor organisations
- Association of Bhutan Tour Operators (organises clean-up trips along the treks).

evergreen, broadleaved forest including oaks, chestnut, cinnamon and *lindera pulcherrima*.

3   Dry valleys.

4   Cultivation zone; including pine trees.

5   Coniferous forest zone; including rhododendrons and daphne.

6   Alpine meadow (up to 4500m), with primroses, blue poppy, iris, asters and edelweiss.

7   Northern border to Tibet .

Cinquefoil

Daphne

Some parts of the lower tropical zone are probably going to be opened up to visitors (see **www.tourism.gov.bt**). A small number of the plants, flowers, shrubs and trees to be seen along the treks are described below, along with some plants used in agriculture (see also the Bibliography).

Arisaeme, the Himalayan cobra lily, a beautiful plant with unusual flower shapes found in the temperate forests of Bhutan (see photo Trek 9, and Trek 3, day 2). Some of the tubers and leaves are eaten.

Blue poppy, Bhutan's national flower, local name *euitgel metog hoem*. It grows above 3500m and flowers from late May to July. There are 13 species in Bhutan and 50 throughout the Himalayas: some taller species (up to 1m) are found in the upper parts of the coniferous forest, with shorter species on the high meadows. Large, blue flowers are characteristic, but red, yellow, and purple are also found. The blue poppy is also called 'Queen of the Himalayan flowers'.

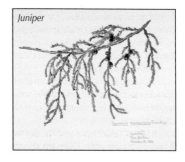

Juniper

34

Daphne is a flowering shrub with whitish fragrant flowers, usually growing in mixed conifer forest and locally important. The bark of this plant is used in making the local paper *day-sho* or *desho* (the bark is leached in water, pounded and boiled). The plant is poisonous when eaten.

Delphinium is a beautiful herbaceous plant with blue/violet flowers, found in the temperate forests.

Eriophyton is a dwarf, woolly little alpine plant with flowers of red, pink or purple. It grows above 4000m.

Euphorbia is a small shrub with a many-branched flat-topped structure of red to yellow flowers. The milky juice in the stem has some medicinal properties: it removes hair, warts and induces vomiting. Cattle will not eat the plant, so it is found in abundance.

Fern, a primitive plant with large delicate leaves and no flowers. The Bhutanese enjoy eating young fronds, collected in spring and summer and called *na-kwe* (spring) and *ran-kwe* (summer).

Gentiana, a lovely alpine flower usually widespread in alpine meadows and hillsides, normally occurs above 3000m. Don't be surprised if you observe one of the Lunaps eating gentiana; it is taken for colds and coughs.

Hydrangea heteromalla is a shrub or small tree of up to 10m tall, growing up to 3300m and flowering late in October. Flowers are greenish-white or pinkish.

Indigofera is a shrub of 2–3m high, with beautiful purple flowers which draw attention to the plant (it would otherwise go unnoticed). The plant is used for making dye.

Irish ('Clarkei') has a dark purple flower on a long stem. There are several

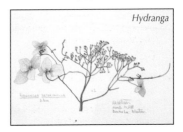

Hydranga

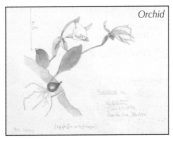

Orchid

species of Irish in Bhutan, and the plant can cover entire hillsides.

Orchids, one of the most spectacular sights in Bhutan's forests, diverse in form, shape and colour. Bhutan is the land of orchids. They flourish in the shiny-leaved forest zone, forming 'hanging gardens' on the trees, occasionally with other epiphytic rhododendrons. There are over 369 species of orchids recorded in Bhutan. Some of the flowers are gathered and eaten as a vegetable.

Piptanthus nepalensis is a shrub that grows up to 4m tall with dark green shining bark. The flowers are bright yellow and about 3cm across. The leaves are split into three leaflets.

Plumbago bushes are found throughout the country near road sites, with common names such as plumbago and leadwort. The name plumbago comes

35

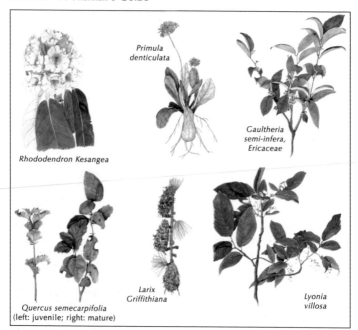

Primula
denticulata

Gaultheria
semi-infera,
Ericaceae

Rhododendron Kesangea

Quercus semecarpifolia
(left: juvenile; right: mature)

Larix
Griffithiana

Lyonia
villosa

from Latin *plumbum* (lead), either from the lead-blue flower colour of some species, or from the plant at one time being a supposed cure for lead poisoning.

Primula, widely known as primrose, is one of the most beautiful flowering herbs that adorn the temperate and alpine hillsides; very few occur in the lowlands. There are 71 species of primula recorded in Bhutan, ranging from white, yellow, blue, purple and violet. The leaves of some species contain grease, used by yak herders as a protection against dry skin in winter. Yaks avoid eating the leaves of primula, so the flowers remain intact and create an impressive display.

Rheum nobile is a giant member of the rhubarb family. It is one of the more spectacular and surprising plants of the high Himalayas, growing on open hillsides and rocky slopes at an altitude above 4000m, preferring the cold summer with rain and sleet. In contrast to most plants at altitude, this grows rather tall, up to 2m and more. It looks like a glowing yellow beacon and can be seen over a long distance. It grows at an amazing rate, developing from a small yellow circle of leaves to a large plant over 2m tall. The seeds ripen through the action of the big transparent leaves. These act as a greenhouse, raising the inside temperature at least 5°C, thus creating comfortable conditions for insects to pollinate.

The young leaves and the central stem (or stalk) are eaten as a vegetable or used in salad. The leaves are also used for wrapping round balls of yak butter. The plant also has a medicinal function: it promotes heat and is used against the retention of body fluids, swelling and fullness of the abdomen (maybe for altitude sickness). It is also used to decorate the Lamanistic deity. It is much sought after and nowadays only can be found on the more inaccessible cliffs at high altitude.

One story goes that in 1888 when the British troops entered Sikkim some mistook these harmless plants for a party of the enemy and fired a volley into them (Douglas W. Freshfield, *Round Kanchenjunga*).

Rhododendron in Greek means 'rose tree' (*rhodon* = rose; *dendron* = tree). Bhutan has 48 species, of which four species are endemic. Rhododendrons are very often picked by travellers and put on top of the pass to please the gods and deities. North of Bumthang, yak herders wrap stones in big rhododendron leaves and put these along the trail to protect their yaks and other stock whilst migrating. Rhododendrons covering whole hillsides can be an overwhelming sight, as the botanist George Sherriff said in April 1937 on visiting the Black Mountains: 'A week or two earlier the deep rich red form of *Rhododendron arboreum* must have inflamed the valley.'

Lichen festoons many trees in the wet forests of Bhutan. The lichen most commonly seen at altitude is also referred to as 'old man's beard', or (wrongly) as 'Spanish moss'. It is the longest-growing lichen in the world. It is a fungus that lives in symbiosis with an alga. This makes lichens very unusual organisms, because they are not actually plants but two different organisms that live in close association: a fungus, which we usually know in the form of mushrooms, and an alga, which usually is found in water, such as a sea-weed.

Trees

Weeping cypress is the national tree of Bhutan (*tsenden*). It is the native tree in the conifer zone (2500m–3000m) of the Himalayas, and can grow as high as 45m. The tree commands much respect and is planted near Lamanistic temples or at other sacred places. The Bhutanese National Anthem analogises the strength and development of the nation as the majestic growth of cypress trees.

Juniper. Three species of juniper are found, called *sup* in Dzongkha, and all species are used as incense. Junipers are sacred all over the Himalayas, and juniper wood is preferred for funeral pyre wood. The tree is also called 'pencil cedar' by some botanists, implying slow-growing trees; some junipers are believed to be more than 200 years old. Thrushes and grosbeaks prefer the juniper berries.

Larix griffithiana, or Himalayan larch, grows to 20m high and has low-hanging yellow-grey branches. It grows up to an altitude of 4000m.

Magnolia is one of the most beautiful flowering trees in the temperate forests. The stunning white fragrant flowers bloom in spring. Just after crossing the Dochu La pass between Thimphu and Punakha you have a good chance to

SACRED JUNIPER

'The oldest pre-Buddhist beliefs claim the juniper tree to be the abode and symbol of the goddess of fertility, second only to the divine goddess of fortune. Juniper twigs are the symbol of life, and to break one is symbolic of death; the incense of juniper is the perfume of the gods, and juniper branches are burnt as incense in all monasteries and houses of the Himalayas. In the water mills juniper wood is pulped against rocks, then collected in cloth sieves and dried to form thin incense sticks that burn night and day in chapels all over the Himalayas. When sacrificing a goat to the goddess of fortune in far western Tibet, the pagan priests hold a twig of juniper in their teeth. If the twig breaks, it is the worst of omens. Juniper is all-important as a symbol and ever-present fragrance all over the Himalayas and Tibet.'

Michel Peissel

see some on the Punakha side. The flowers can be as big as cauliflowers.

Maple There are several species of maple in Bhutan, nearly all growing from 2000m–3500m (they have even been sighted at 3900m). The tree is not that big, and the trunk not very thick. The knobs of the maple tree make the best drinking cups and are used for endless cups of butter tea.

Pine Blue pine, Bhutan pine and chir pine are the common species. Blue pine and Bhutan pine grow at the same alti-

tude range, 1800–3000m. Blue pine grows in the west and Bhutan pine in the east of the country. Pine is mostly used for construction and carving. Cones mature in two years; the nutcracker is the only bird that likes the resinous seed. Chir pines grow at lower altitude in drier valleys. The timber is exported for making railway sleepers.

When the Bhutanese want to show respect to a special visitor, they erect freshly cut pine or other evergreen or coniferous trees, and spread the pine needles on the ground. A tent may be pitched on the leaves. The pine tree, *tomphu-shing*, is believed to prevent the possible incoming of bad fortune.

Oak grows from 12–20m high, between 1300–2500m. Oak leaves are collected in spring and carried to the fields, either mixed with dung and used as fertiliser, or as cattle feed; oak wood is preferred above all others for burning in stoves during the winter.

Sal in the eastern Himalayas makes very valuable and durable timber that lasts for centuries. Sal trees can reach a height of up to 30–45m. The species has special significance to Buddhists, since the Great Teacher passed away beneath a sal tree.

Silver fir is distributed all over Bhutan from west to east, and known as *dungshing* in Bhutanese. This species is specifically used for roofing shingles.

Ethno-botanical interests (plant–human relations)

We use plants, flowers, shrubs and trees for a wide variety of practical purposes. Over the centuries the Bhutanese have developed their own special uses: food (rice, wheat, fruit, vegetables), medicine, drinks (tea, alcohol), practical purposes (building, baskets), oil (lemongrass) and decoration.

Buckwheat is a staple of diets in cold areas. Two types of buckwheat are cultivated: sweet and bitter. Sweet buckwheat has pink flowers and bitter has green flowers.

Bamboos abound in Bhutan; it is not known how many species flourish. Some species will probably remain undiscovered since parts of the country are virtually inaccessible. Bamboo is found all over the Himalayas, from the lowlands up to 4000m. It is an important natural product, used for house construction, ropes, mats, baskets, fencing, instruments, and so on.

Cannabaceae (cannabis or hemp) grows wild everywhere up to 3000m and is fed to the pigs to make them lazy and so maintain fat. It is actually just a weed, and can grow up to 2m high.

Mustard Young mustard leaves make very good curry. Handmade mustard seed oil is pure and tasty; the residue of the seeds is used as animal feed. It has very beautiful yellow flowers in spring and autumn.

Rice is the main staple food in Bhutan, cultivated in wet paddy fields or on terraced fields with irrigation systems. Because the paddies are situated in dry valleys, rice can be cultivated up to 2700m in Bhutan, whereas in other parts of the Himalayas it is only possible up to 1800m. The Bhutanese paddy fields receive more hours of sunshine and higher temperatures then elsewhere. Bhutan is famous for its red rice grown at higher altitude.

Wildlife

Bhutan's fauna is very rich as a result of the altitude range and also a spiritual adversity to hunting. In Buddhist philosophy, no living creature should be killed. Bhutan's many parks encompass a range of different altitudes, enabling animals to migrate through protected areas between the seasons. Many animals in neighbouring China and India flee from hunting and local deforestation into Bhutan.

Bhutan has nearly 200 species of mammal, including: wild pig/boar, Himalayan black bear, red panda, yak, yeti, Tibetan antelope (possibly), blue sheep, musk deer, sambar, barking deer, swamp deer, marmot, takin, grey and golden langur monkey, tiger, civet, clouded leopard, golden cat, snow leopard, wild buffalo, wild elephant, rhino, several species of snake, marten, otter, and so on (see *A field guide to the mammals of Bhutan*, in the bibiography). In addition, Bhutan has many species of butterfly. Even within the cities there is a varied fauna: street dogs sometimes form threatening packs (in 2007, Thimphu had more than 5000 dogs). Bhutan also offers excellent opportunities for birdwatching, with a number of rare species that are difficult to find elsewhere.

Bhutan's wildlife is not a universal attraction. Wild boars are an enormous problem in areas where farmers try to grow crops; in some communities night watchers are hired to chase them away. In the southern belt of Bhutan, wild elephants can destroy a field in minutes. Snow leopards, Bengal tigers and other cats attack cattle. Bears have been known to attack people throughout the country.

Snow leopard (photo by Joe Fox, used by permission of the International Snow Leopard Trust)

Unfortunately many of Bhutan's animals (or parts of them) are traded and sold, especially musk deer tassels, bears, stag beetles and the horns of the blue sheep.

Bengal tiger Bhutan has 115–150 Bengal tigers (local name *taa*), the third-largest population of Bengal tigers in Asia. The tiger is mainly found in the south, but can be spotted as high as 4000m. Often mistreated in India, the tiger seems to fare better in Bhutan.

Snow leopard The local name for the snow leopard is *chen*. Found at over 4000m (even 6000m) in summer, they stay above 1800m in winter. Both sexes look alike, standing 40–50cm at the shoulder, with tails almost 1m in length. The leopard has a very large hunting territory (c10.000km²), mainly as a result of scarcity of prey at high altitude. Its prey consists largely of blue sheep and (baby) yaks. The coat is extremely beautiful and so the animal is hunted. A coat, retrieved from poachers, is on display in the JDNP head office at Damji.

Only the yeti would be more difficult to photograph than the snow leopard. Footprints (pug marks) are often sighted in the Bhutan Himalayas. The JDNP park is the only place in the world where tiger and snow leopard can be found in the same area (recorded by JDNP staff in 2001 at 4100m, just north of Barshong).

Red panda The local name for the red panda is *a(am)chu dongkha;* it is also called a red cat bear. It is a smaller relative to the well-known giant panda, measuring about 60cm tall and with a 40cm-long light-and-dark striped tail. The face has a white, short nose and its fur is a bright, rusty red. It is usually active around dawn and dusk. It is a good climber and spends a lot of time in trees. The diet is mainly vegetarian: bamboo leaves, berries, mushrooms and grasses. Some meat is eaten, along with insects, bird eggs and mice. Good places to spot them include the passes at Pele La and Trumsing La and around Gasa.

Marten There are several species of this small, ferocious animal. Above the treeline the stone marten is found; the yellow-throated marten is found below.

Marmots Marmots are widespread in Lingshi, Laya and east of the Me La pass. They live in areas of summer grazing, near cattle and humans. They live in large colonies, digging into sunny slopes at altitudes from 4200–5200m. They hibernate in winter in their deep holes, so in spring have to work hard to procure food, eating grass, leaves and roots. Their holes not only damage pastures but can also cause yaks to break their legs. The marmot is a member of the squirrel family, growing to a length of about 60cm with a tail around 10cm long. The fur is a pale yellowish-brown, with dark brown spots in the underparts. The pelt is soft and warm and used to be valued by the Bhutanese for caps and gloves. A disturbed marmot will sit up and tweet, then give a loud whistling scream, which will send its companions scurrying back to their holes.

Blue sheep There are two species of blue sheep (bharal): the dwarf blue sheep, only found in China, and the blue sheep, which looks like a sheep and behaves like a goat. Thanks to their impressive horns, the blue sheep (local name *nau*) has become a worthy trophy animal and is now on the endangered list.

Blue sheep stand three feet high at the shoulder and weigh well over 70kg. Both sexes carry a pair of dignified horns measuring about 58–61cm. Their coats undergo seasonal colour changes -slate blue in summer and slate grey during the winter. Rams (male) have a black stripe along their back but ewes (female) lack it.

Herd size and composition varies from 50 to 200 individuals. Generally males separate from the females when the rut is over, when they form their own groups until next rut. A few males, however, remain with the females throughout the year.

Blue sheep are known to consume a broad spectrum of alpine herbs, forbs and shrubs. Their winter food consists of mainly dry grass. Mating occurs between October and January, with the young being born from May to July. Life span: 12–15 years.

Musk deer Local name is *lochuem*. The deer is 80–100cm long and stands 50cm high. Its coat has a somewhat greyish brown colour – the chest features a wide vertical whitish-yellow band, which extends up the throat to the chin. Its body slopes forward, since the forelegs are one third shorter than the hind legs. Both sexes have strong upper canines, reaching a length of 7cm in males, and they sticking out from the mouth in a fang-like manner. The musk deer is mostly active between dusk and dawn, and it lives at an altitude of 2500m–4000m. The deer eat leaves, grasses, moss, lichens, shoots and twigs. Its main predators are the yellow-throated marten, fox, lynx and human beings.

The musk deer's aromatic name comes from its distinct smell. Musk, a brown waxy substance, is produced in a gland of the males. The musk produced is highly prized for its cosmetic and supposed pharmaceutical properties.

Sambar/shou The sambar is found throughout Bhutan. It is nocturnal and feeds on shrubs and foliage. In some parts of Bhutan, they ravage crops such

Yellow-billed Blue Magpie (Carl D'Silva)

Ibisbill (Peter Hayman)

Red-billed Chough (Carl D'Silva)

Lammergeier (Kim Franklin)

Himalayan Griffon (Kim Franklin)

Golden Eagle (Tim Worfolk)

White Wagtail (Clive Byers)

Ruddy Shelduck (Jan Wilczur)

White-capped Water Redstart (Alan Harris)

Common Hoopoe (Jan Wilczur)

Blood pheasant (Daniel Cole)

Common Raven (Carl D'Silva)

Black-necked Crane, (Carl D'Silva)

Grandala (Alan Harris)

as rice, wheat and millet. The sambar in Bhutan is associated with mythology, folk tales and it is even celebrated in mask dances like the shazam (the dance of the four stags).

Takin The national animal of Bhutan, the takin, is a member of the goat/antelope family (see Trek 3, day 8; and photo Trek 6, day 13).

Leeches Bhutan has a range of leeches with all kinds of different local names depending on their size. The most active leech is small and brown, about 3cm in length before feeding, and the thickness of a knitting needle. Others are 'elephant' and 'horse' leeches – these are taller, and usually green or brown. The biggest leeches can be as thick as a little finger. Leeches usually clinging to a leaf or twig, or wait on the ground for their victim. They jump onto you with incredible speed, often alerted by the vibrations of footsteps. Prevent leech attacks by wearing tight gaiters or concentrated lemon oil on your shoes. Cigarette ash, a burning cigarette, tobacco water or salt sprinkled on the leech should remove them.

Monkey Spotting a monkey while travelling is a traditional sign of good luck in Bhutan. Bhutan has six species, including the rhesus monkey and grey langur and, most famous, the **golden langur** (local name *raksha*). The golden langur is unique to Bhutan, and there are over 4000 in the country. Its head and body ranges from 50–75cm in length, with the tail from 70–100cm. The coat is golden creamy-white in the summer and changes to red in the winter and breeding season. They live in the southern part of Bhutan.

Birds: Another highlight for visitors to Bhutan is birdwatching, and the chance to see rare species that are difficult to find elsewhere, such as rufous-necked hornbill and Ward's trogon. With more than 620 species you could spend many months in Bhutan trying to spot them. The biggest attraction for bird lovers is a visit to the Phobijikha valley to see the black-necked cranes during the winter months.

The sketches printed here are only some of the many beautiful sketches in *Birds of Bhutan* by Carol Inskipp, Tim Inskipp, Richard Grimmett and others: an absolute must for every birdwatcher (see Bibliography). Included are some examples of birds that can be seen in the Bhutanese mountains.

Yaks: Read more in Trek 3, days 5 and 6; end of Trek 4; Trek 16, day 8; Trek 18, day 7; and see photo in 'Medical Considerations' in the Introduction.

GEOLOGY: THE FORMATION OF THE MOUTAINS

Before the Swiss Professor Augusto Gansser visited Bhutan on several occasions and published his geological findings, only a handful of geologists had been to the country: Godwin-Austen in 1868, Mallet in 1875, Mallet and Pilgrim in 1906, and H. H. Hayden in 1907. Gansser's book *Geology of the Bhutan Himalaya* is still one of the major reference sources. The Geological Survey of India began regional investigations in the foothill zone after 1960, including some traverses into central Bhutan (less than 30 percent has been geologically mapped).

The formation of the Himalaya was a direct result of the collision between the Indian plate and central Asia about

Masa Gang c7100m (Trek 7)

50 million years ago. The site of this collision roughly follows the course of the Indus–Yarlung Tsangpo suture zone in southern Tibet, north of Bhutan, where remnant oceanic rocks are exposed. The Indian plate was originally attached to southern Africa, Madagascar and Antarctica, but began to drift away approximately 150 million years ago. India travelled northwards until it collided head-on with the southern margin of Asia, which at that time lay roughly in equatorial latitudes.

As India continued to drive northwards, it buckled and pushed under the southern margin of Asia, resulting in thickening and uplift of the Tibetan plateau and the piling up of thrust sheets along the Himalaya. The Bhutan Himalaya is part of the highest chain of mountains in the world, which stretch for over 2500km from Pakistan to Assam.

The Bhutan Himalaya is composed of rocks belonging to the Indian plate. Most of the high mountains comprise deep crystal metamorphic and granite

rocks formed between 5 and 30km deep and thrust up to the surface during the collision process. As sedimentary rock formed near the Earth's surface are under-thrust and buried they undergo mineralogical changes due to the increase in temperature and pressure, converting shales and mudstones to schists and gneisses. New minerals such as micas, white muscovites and dark biotites are formed, as well as common metamorphic minerals such as garnet. At the highest temperatures (around 700°C) the rocks actually begin to partially melt, forming small granitic pods, representing the first liquid phases. These pods gradually coalesce into larger pockets of magma which flow into cracks by forces of vapour pressure and hydraulic pumping. Many of the larger mountains of Bhutan, such as Jhomolhari, Jitchu Drake and Masang Gang, are composed of these granites. The granites contain distinctive crystals of black tourmaline, red garnet and white micas as well as white feldspar and colourless quartz crystals.

The deep-crust metamorphic and granitic rocks of the Bhutan Higher Himalaya were initially formed at depth beneath the southern part of the Tibetan plateau. They were squeezed out by southward expulsion along a large channel, which reaches the Earth's surface along the High Himalaya. The channel is bounded by two large shear zones. At the top lies a low-angle normal fault, termed the South Tibetan detachment, which clips the very summits of the highest peaks along the Bhutan–Tibet border and separates sedimentary rocks above (in south Tibet) from metamorphic and granitic rocks below (in Bhutan). Along the base of the extruding channel another very large-scale shear zone (the main central thrust) was responsible for placing these deep crustal rocks above shallower rocks in the lesser Himalaya, in the far south of Bhutan. The main central thrust is characterised by inverted metamorphism where hotter, deeper rocks have been placed above colder, shallower rocks. Both these shear zones – and the granites along the higher Himalaya – were active around 20 million years ago, when the range probably reached its maximum elevation and erosion rates were drastically increased.

In the last 10 million years tectonic activity has shifted southwards to the southern limit of the Himalaya along the main boundary thrust. This is the major zone along which the Indian plate is presently under-thrusting the Himalaya, and where most of the earthquakes occur today. As the Indian plate dives down to the north beneath the Himalaya, it buckles and flexes producing a foreland basin, rapidly filled with the detritus eroded off the uplifting Himalaya to the north. The Siwalik range (along the southernmost part of Bhutan and across into India) is com-

Tang valley – Bumthang (Trek 20, day 3)

posed of young Tertiary sediments formed by deposition from rivers flowing south from the high mountains. Gentle folding in these sedimentary rocks result in the characteristic whaleback folds seen along the southern margin of the Himalaya.

The uplift of the Tibetan plateau and the Himalaya has been one of the major causes of climate change in Asia and the northern hemisphere. The jet stream, which flows from west to east along the Himalaya, divides two very different climate systems: that operating in the Bay of Bengal from that operating over Tibet. In summer an enormous high-pressure system sits over Tibet, which sucks in warm, moist air from the Indian Ocean and results in the monsoon. The Indian monsoon usually lasts from mid-June to mid-September when the southern slopes of the Himalayas are affected by torrential downpours. The Himalayan peaks act as a major barrier and the relatively dry Tibetan plateau to the north lies in their rain shadow. The highest rainfall recorded anywhere in the world is in the eastern Himalaya from Bhutan to Assam.

Global positioning satellite (GPS) networks across Bhutan and Tibet show that the Indian plate and Asia are still converging at a rate of approximately 5cm/year. As long as India continues to move north relative to stable north Asia, and convergence is taken up along the Himalaya, the mountains of Bhutan will continue to rise. The forces of erosion will continue to try and tear them down, through glacier, wind and water erosion. Tectonic activity continues with lots of earthquakes, mostly along the main boundary thrust in southern Bhutan, along which the Indian plate presently slides northwards beneath the Himalaya and south Tibet (**www.mti.gov.bt/dgm**).

RIVERS AND GLACIERS

Rivers

Many trails in Bhutan parallel rivers, a paradise for whitewater activities, fly fishing and birdwatching. In addition, the rivers are 'white gold' for Bhutan, creating profitable revenue through hydropower. There are five main rivers (*chhu*) running north to south. These rivers fall within discrete drainage basins, namely:

1 Amo Chhu: districts Haa and Samtse
2 Wang Chhu with tributaries Haa Chhu, Pa Chhu and Thim Chhu: districts Paro (Jhomolhari), Haa, Thimphu, and Chhukha
3 Sunkosh Chhu or Puna Tsang Chhu (the longest river in Bhutan c250km) with tributaries Mo Chhu, Pho Chhu and Dang Chhu: districts Punakha (Lunana), Wangdue-Phodrang, Tshiring and Sarpang
4 Manas Chhu with tributaries Mangde Chhu, Chamkar Chhu, Kuri Chhu and Dangme Chhu: districts Zhemgang, Trongsa, Bumthang, Mongar, Lhuntse and Pemagatsel
5 Nyera Ama Chhu: districts Trashigang and Samdrup Jongkha

The rivers and their tributaries flow into the Brahmaputra, one of the world's greatest rivers. Millions of people in India and Bangladesh depend on the Brahmaputra River to sustain them through fishing, aquaculture and irrigation. The overall health of this river is closely influenced by the health of major watersheds in the Himalayan region, including Bhutan.

Glaciers

The snowline in Bhutan is at about 5000m. Many peaks are above the snowline so precipitation is always in the form of snow. Over the course of years fallen snow changes into ice and a downward flowing ice mass or glacier is created. The movement of the glacier erodes its surroundings and the debris (earth and rocks) is deposited; this is called a moraine. Climatic changes cause the size and shape of glaciers to fluctuate.

There are 618 glaciers and 2664 glacial lakes (above 3500m) in Bhutan. The glaciers comprise an estimated 75.5km^3 ice reserve. Except for the Amo Chhu, Nyere Ama Chhu, Haa Chhu and Dang Chhu rivers/basins all the rest have glaciers, the Pho Chhu having the highest number. The Pho Chhu, Mangde Chhu and Chamkhar Chhu consist of more than 500 glacial lakes each.

Bhutan has suffered a couple of glacial lake outburst floods (GLOF). These can be observed in the Lunana area. In 1994 the Lugge Tsho glacial lake partially burst and caused devastation along the Pho Chhu, including part of the Punakha *dzong*. A GLOF warning system has now been set up.

Glacier traverses are not (yet) a part of trekking itineraries in Bhutan.

Chanterelles mushrooms ~ common in Bhutan

Bhutan food item number one: chillis

ACCOMMODATION AND FOOD

Facilities have developed enormously in the last couple of years and there is now a wide choice of very good hotels, guesthouses and restaurants. Some impressive hotel chains have been introduced to Bhutan recently, but you won't find them on trek! Some hotels have

TYPICAL FOOD AND DRINK ON TREK

- **Breakfast:** choice of eggs on order, toast, baked beans, sausages, French fries, French toast, pancakes, porridge, cornflakes, muesli, poori with alu dam, cheese, honey, peanut butter, jam, butter, (powdered) milk, juice, tea, water, coffee
- **Lunch:** fried rice, chicken, bread, chapatti, cheese momo, noodle soup, boiled egg, fruits, juice, tea
- **Tea:** crackers (ask for peanut butter), biscuits, tea, chocolate drink, butter tea
- **Dinner:** various types of soup; chicken and assorted other meat dishes; various styles of vegetables; mushroom dishes; Indian-style food; spring rolls; plain, red or fried rice; dal (lentil soup); Tibetan *momo* (dumpling); *ema datse* (see below); chilli variations; vegetable chow mein; rice pudding; cream caramel; fresh and tinned fruits; tea; chocolate drink; water; coffee.
- There are many drinks to choose from. Tibetan butter tea (*sudja* in Bhutan) can often be found when visiting nomads or farmers in the mountains.

cottages in their grounds. Your Bhutanese tour operator will pre-book your accommodation, so details of hotels and restaurants are not covered here. In general accommodation is built in authentic Bhutanese style, and you will immediately feel at home. The Bhutanese like to serve national dishes (see below); in a bar, try to get hold of 'Panda', the Bhutanese-produced beer, or other stronger liqors manufactured by Gelephu Distillery.

Eating in Bhutanese hotels and restaurants is nearly always 'safe'. Nonetheless, it is not a good idea to touch buffet-style salads unless you are on trek with a kitchen crew trained in sanitary food preparation.

Bhutan is known for spicy food. Its national dish is chilli and cheese – *ema datse* – and cheese is also often mixed with cooked potatoes or vegetables to create other tasty dishes. Another speciality is pe of dumpling based on the Tibetan

dish *momos*, served steamed or fried with cheese, vegetable or meat fillings.

Meat, especially pork, is an important part of the diet for those who can afford it. Yak meat is tasty but only available in late autumn and winter. Beef, chicken and fish are generally available, but at times meat is unavailable because of periodic bans on the slaughter of animals.

In some areas farmers grow buckwheat, used to make pancakes and noodles. Rice – particularly the local red rice – is also a staple of the diet. Like all Himalayan people, the Bhutanese eat *tsampa*, ground barley that is 'popped' like popcorn, making it suitable for eating without any further processing. The *tsampa* is very rich in calories and is either eaten dry as a snack or mixed with tea and formed into little balls as part of a more substantial meal. There is a good choice of vegetables in Bhutan.

Eating well on trek is very important, and a healthy appetite is always a good sign. Bring some snacks to eat during the day. As mentioned earlier, food on trek is well prepared by trained kitchen staff whose repertoire increases every year. In addition the locals along the way might offer tea or a meal. This is a real treat, as much for the chance to get inside a farmhouse or yak herder's tent as for the meal itself.

On a long trek of more than 14 days some meals will probably be repeated several times. The kitchen crew will run low on fresh supplies, so canned food is used more frequently after the first week. Breakfast is served at camp; the cooks also prepare lunch early in the morning and carry with them to be served later in the day. Tea is normally taken around 1700hr, and dinner is served at the night's camp. There is a wide variety of Bhutanese food.

MEDICAL CONSIDERATIONS AND FITNESS

Accidents and medical crises create anxiety and tension. In the mountains you may be far from help with few resources, and basic first-aid knowledge is a must when venturing into remote areas. Helicopter service in Bhutan is limited. There are some hospitals in Bhutan, with the best one in Thimphu; complicated cases have to be transferred to Bangkok.

Before venturing into remote areas you should:
- Work on physical fitness
- Have a dental check up
- Consult a doctor (in good time) about immunisations and medications to take with you; give your doctor details of your itinerary
- Make up your own medical kit – see below
- Read up on first aid in the wilderness (see Bibliography)

Yellow fever immunisation is the only one visitors are required to have before entering Bhutan, in case a visitor is arriving from an infected area of the world. However, immunisation against polio, tetanus, typhoid and hepatitis is recommended.

First aid checklist: make up your kit from the list below, adding personal items
- biodegradable soap
- bandages: elastic, crêpe, triangular, bandage strips (assorted)
- Elastoplast strip
- gauze: sterile plain + non-sticky
- surgical tape
- duck tape
- Steri-strips
- wound dressing
- moleskin (plasters)
- antiseptic swabs
- thermometer
- scissors
- tweezers
- sunscreen
- lip care
- eye bath

Extra items: SAM splint; penlight; oral airway; irrigation syringe; antiseptic concentrate tincture of benzoin; finger dressing; tube gauze; safety pins; first aid handbook.

Described below are a few basic medical problems; for more information see the Bibliography.

Common gut problems

Hygiene Water and food are the most common sources of disease via infected faeces and urine of disease carriers, for example typhoid, shigella, cholera and hepatitis A. Food and drinking water become contaminated directly by faecal bugs, or shit-eating flies. Drink only pure water, eat clean fresh food and dispose of sewage efficiently. Wash your hands more frequently than at home and keep your nails short and clean.

Yak's feet – perhaps the only type of feet that don't get tired and blistered!

LOCAL REMEDY

A kitchen helper cut a finger badly. Standard medical care didn't work, so the Bhutanese applied their own remedy: a big portion of toothpaste on a bandage directly on the wound finally stopped the bleeding!

Water Consider all water, even in hotels and restaurants, unsafe to drink unless boiled; kitchens are probably only as clean as the toilets. Bottled mountain spring water is available (the downside being the resulting empty plastic bottles). On trek the kitchen crew will supply boiled water. If more drinking water is needed carry drinking water purification and neutraliser tablets.

Diarrhoea This causes more trouble than all other medical hazards encountered abroad. Diarrhoea may arise from toxins, waste products of certain bacteria that grow on food (travellers' diarrhoea = food poisoning), or from infection by disease-causing bacteria carried in water and food (bacterial diarrhoea = dysentery). Wise doctors recommend preventive hygiene before treating travellers' diarrhoea with drugs. Use antibiotics with discretion. Keep your fluid balance up.

High-altitude problems

Acclimatisation is the physiological process that allows humans to adapt so they can live and work in the oxygen-thin atmosphere of high altitude. Low oxygen pressure in the atmosphere, and hence in the lungs and blood, increases the rate and depth of breathing. Initially the heart

Looking east towards Jichu
Dramo camp 5060m
(Trek 3, day 20)

beats faster and more strongly, increasing the flow of blood to the lungs, and breathing deepens and quickens; this soon settles back to normal.

Mild AMS Many people who climb high (over c2500m) are fit on arrival but feel ghastly over the next couple of days, with headache, breathlessness, insomnia (sleeplessness), fatigue, poor appetite, nausea and dizziness. As they adapt to the altitude, these symptoms usually pass off.

Mild AMS has vague symptoms but can drift subtly into severe AMS, which can be fatal. Some people never get used to the altitude, their symptoms worsen, and death is possible from HACE (High Altitude Cerebral Edema) or HAPE (or High Altitude Pulmonary Edema).

Acute Mountain Sickness (AMS) Anyone venturing into the high, cold, thin air is wise to study AMS, which can kill the unwary, the bold and the previously healthy. It affects those who ascend too high too fast, and is usually cured by immediate descent.

Predicting AMS

No one can predict who will suffer from AMS, whether it will be mild or severe, or when it will strike. Trekkers who have performed well at altitude will probably do so each time they go high. Those who have suffered AMS before may suffer again and at a similar altitude. Fitness and training guarantee no protection, the sexes succumb equally and no age is exempt. Weight gain during ascent means water retention, which bodes ill.

Signs of mild AMS

These develop 12–48hr after arriving at altitude.

51

PREVENTING AMS

- Allow ample time at various levels to acclimatise. AMS is more likely to occur the higher, the faster, the harder, and the longer the climb. Cold and wind, fear and fatigue, dehydration during rapid ascent and strenuous exercise soon after, and upper respiratory infection, all predispose to AMS.
- Climb without haste: above 3000m gain height slowly and steadily at ideally c1000ft/300m a day; take a rest day every c3300ft/1000m.
- Avoid strenuous exertion soon after arriving at altitude.
- To help the process of acclimatisation hike up high but sleep low.
- Drink sufficient fluid: 4–5 litres daily should balance the heavy losses caused by strenuous breathing in cold, dry, thin air, and allow peeing a clear, colourless, copious urine. Dark yellow urine is concentrated, usually indicating dehydration.
- Avoid alcohol and coffee.
- Eat a high calorie diet, with plenty of carbohydrate before and during ascent. A good appetite suggests good acclimatising.
- Don't take salt or sedatives.

If, despite these precautions, a trekker gets sick and does not improve on rest, descend quickly until he starts to feel better. Even 1000ft/300m will help; 3300ft/1000m may save his life. If the person feels ill and does not improve quickly on descent, insist that he does not reascend on that expedition.

- *Headache* Headache, usually at the back of the head, often develops during the night so is present on waking (the head feels tight, the sufferer may feel giddy and light-headed).
- *Fatigue; appetite loss, nausea and indigestion; sleep disturbance*
- *Shortness of breath on exertion (dyspnoea)* The chest feels uncomfortable and tight, but quiet easy breathing resumes after rest.
- *Shortage of fluid (dehydration)* Urine output is low for 24hr with a back-up of insufficient fluid intake.
- *Swelling* Face puffy; rings on fingers feel tight.

Action

Rest, wait and see. Additional oxygen may fool you into thinking the victim is better. If he has not improved within 24hr consider he has severe AMS, so descend.

Mild AMS may blend unnoticed into severe AMS. HACE or HAPE become manifest depending on whether body water settles in the brain or lungs or both. The entire drama can unfold within hours, and usually does so at night.

Signs of severe AMS
High Altitude Cerebral Edema (HACE) is like an exaggerated form of mild AMS and usually occurs above 3600m. Severe AMS can kill quickly, so act decisively.

Headache Severe and constant. No relief from paracetamol, codeine or a night's sleep.

Inco-ordination (ataxia) The victim staggers as if drunk, and fumbles fine movements such as handling a camera.

Languor Extreme fatigue is not reversed by rest. The victim won't talk, eat or drink; he lies curled up in a sleeping bag, is irritable and confused. If still active, he may show poor judgement and thus make bad mountaineering decisions. Sleep is fitful and punctuated by bad dreams. He may hallucinate. He may be incontinent.

Vomiting Severe vomiting leads to dehydration, which cannot be reversed by drinking. Urine is scanty and dark yellow.

Coma Drifts into coma and may die. Convulsions are rare.

High Altitude Pulmonary Edema (HAPE)

In HAPE the lungs become waterlogged. HAPE is rare below 3000m; it begins 36–72hr after arriving at altitude and is cured by descent. Rest and oxygen may help temporarily. It affects children more than adults, men and women equally. It may be related to severe exertion and rate of climb. It worsens at night.

Shortness of breath (dyspnoea) Occurs on slight exertion and is even present at rest. Breathing is irregular and fast at more than 25 breaths per minute. The victim does not improve with rest, and is hungry for air. The chest feels full and tight.

Cough and sputum Early cough is tickling, hacking and dry – without sputum. Later the sputum is frothy and pink. By contrast sputum in pneumonia or bronchitis is yellow-green.

Chest sounds Crackling, moist sounds (crepitations) can be heard by placing an ear against the back of the victim.

Cyanosis At rest the lips, face and fingernails look blue.

Pulse The pulse will be rapid, more than 110 beats per minute.

Action in the case of severe AMS

Descent usually cures severe AMS miraculously. Do not delay. The victim should descend at least 300m, preferable 1000m. The greater and faster the descent, the swifter the recovery. Once down the victim should stay down.

The forms of treatment listed below play for time but should never take preference over evacuating the victim immediately to a lower altitude.

- **Rest** Prop the victim up and keep him warm and relaxed.
- **Oxygen** Give 100 percent oxygen. A change in the victim's colour from blue to pink shows the effectiveness of oxygen, which may relieve headache and help pulmonary oedema.
- **Fluids** Drink (4–5 litres daily minimum) enough to maintain a copious flow of urine (1 litre daily minimum).
- **Drugs** Acetazolamide (Diamox): 125–250mg once or twice daily, a mild diuretic that appears to help acclimatisation without masking the symptoms of AMS (unlike steroids), and diminishes the incidence and severity of AMS symptoms of headache or nausea. Do not give Diamox to someone with a known allergy to sulpha drugs. Diamox can also be taken in preparation for high altitude: start dosing yourself two or

three days in advance. Dexamethasone (Decadron): 4mg twice daily starting on the day of ascent and for 3–5 days.

- **Gamow bag** A portable, inflatable pressure chamber can lower the

virtual atmospheric pressure while the victim is in the bag.

With good sense AMS and its sinister off-spring, HACE and HAPE, should not occur. But if they do, prevent their deadly

USEFUL MEDICAL/TRAVEL-RELATED ADDRESSES AND WEBSITES

www.thehtd.org UK: Hospital for Tropical Diseases Health-line (tel: 0845 155 5000 or 020 7387 4411)

www.lshtm.ac.uk/contact/medadvice.html London School of Hygiene & Tropical Medicine Health-line (tel: 0891 600350)

www.fco.gov.uk Foreign and Commonwealth Office

www.masta.org Masta: Medical Advisory Services for Travellers Abroad, UK

www.cdc.gov/travel/destinat.htm USA: Centers for Disease Control and Prevention

www.tripprep.com Travel Health Online

www.high-altitude-medicine.com High Altitude Medicine Guide

www.istm.org The International Society of Travel Medicine

www.who.int WHO: World Health Organisation

www.ciwec-clinic.com Travel Medicine Centre in Kathmandu

STRETCHING FOR TREKKING

This is an important part of preparing for a trek. For most of us, a strength work-out (jogging, step machine) of 1hr daily might be followed by a stretching routine of 5min at best. This would be OK if you are in your twenties or thirties, but as we get older the effects of muscles being tight take a greater toll on the body in the form of pain, stiffness and postural distortion.

The ups and downs of trekking place the foot and ankle at a different angle than usual to the foreleg, so the calf/shin muscles get a different workout from normal. This can result in some surprisingly sore muscles. Stretching in the morning is a good start to the day after a night on a mattress you are not used to, and ideal for getting the body warmed up for the day's journey.

Start with a hanging forward bend (hopefully you can touch your toes!), then round back up to standing, and bend over again. Repeat several times, holding the stretch a little longer each time. You might also want to try undulating the spine gently while hanging.

The lunge stretch (also known as 'runner's lunge') should be your best friend. Step one leg forward so that the knee is bent over the ankle at a 90-degree angle, the back leg extended so that the kneecap is resting on the ground. The upper body can rest forward on the bent knee with hands on the ground, or with hands on the bent knee pushing the upper body into an erect position (the latter is more challenging). This stretch should be felt most strongly in the groin crease of the back leg. If the kneecap on the ground hurts, place a small towel or cloth under it.

In order to really change the muscle length and improve the range of motion, hold each stretch for 2–5min. Muscle and its surrounding connective tissue is rather like toffee: like a brick when it's cold but, when warmed up, it will stretch forever.

Five minutes is a long time to hold a stretch, and if you are accustomed to stretching for 20sec graduate the length of hold, adding 15–20sec per week. At that rate, it might take 6–9 months to reach a hold time of 5min. The changes experienced in the body in that period will be profound, both physically and emotionally, as stretching is great way to relieve stress.

Many of us count our breaths to measure time and think we are holding much longer than we actually are. Check with a clock or watch; find out what your time really is.

Stretching is a practice of patience. We need to engage the tissue to the point of mild to medium sensation, but not pain, and hold there. Wait for the sensation level to decrease and then take up the slack, going back to that point of your own 'perfect edge'. Not too much push, but just enough so that the tissue is being challenged to move beyond its normal set point. This process needs to be repeated many times. It's like a rubber band: it will stretch and then return to its starting point. What we want to do is to hold it such that when we release that starting point is just a little bit longer.

Pushing aggressively in typical masculine fashion will not work. This is a feminine style of patience and waiting; there are no timetables, and every day is different. If you push too much and overdo it, you may be sore for days.

Joining a yoga class would be very good in preparation for a trek. Pick a class or teacher where there is approximately an equal degree of strength and length being practised. Some yoga styles are all about strength and not at all appropriate for beginners. Be careful.

consequences by rapid descent to a lower altitude.

EQUIPMENT

- **Backpack** with a **plastic bag** for keeping everything dry, or a **rain-cap** to put around the backpack. The

Gyo Gompa in Lingshi valley (Trek 3, day 5)

backpack should be big enough to carry personal items such as a first aid kit; (two) water bottle(s); snacks; camera; jacket; fleece; warm hat and gloves; sun cream; umbrella; sunhat; lip balm; whistle; small torch; bird/flower book. Carrying all your kit yourself involves great effort and is satisfying, but hiring porters and/or pack animals creates income – and you might enjoy the holiday more.

- **Kitbag with lock** (duffle bag) for storing personal items, only accessible at camp. Bring some **big plastic bags** to keep spare clothes and other items such as sleeping bag dry.
- **Foot gear**, the most important piece of equipment. These should be all leather, all Gore-Tex, or a combina-

tion of the two. There are many types of hiking boots on the market. Most important is that the model is comfortable and has been broken in before trek. Remember that when you are walking the weight and forces involved are borne by your joints, particularly your hips, knees and ankles. A good pair of boots will alleviate these stresses, support and help protect them. Wear them on the plane to make sure they don't go missing in your hold luggage!

- **Socks** and **inner soles** can make a big difference to how comfortable you are. Make sure you have good socks (and enough to allow for regular changes). Take **spare shoelaces** and **shoe polish (wax)** with you.

Bring **plasters (moleskin)** for blisters. Because many treks in Bhutan begin or end in muddy areas, consider bringing an old pair of hiking boots to use and then leave behind.

- **Light shoes/sandals/trainers** to wear around the campsite.
- **Gaiters** can be very useful for coping with snow at higher elevations and to protect against leeches at lower ones.
- **Underlayer trousers/skirt** It's important that the material is thin and strong, fast-drying and very comfortable. They should not restrict movement in any way. Pants with zip-off bottoms are very handy. Shorts are not considered sufficiently modest in some parts of Bhutan. **Fleece pants** are great if you get cold easily or are on one of the treks in higher elevations; they can also double as sleep pants.
- **Rain jacket and trousers** A good Gore-Tex jacket-and-trousers combination is ideal for rain protection. Make sure the jacket has a hood (but that it's not too big to stop you from seeing where you're going!). A nylon poncho or umbrella is useful.
- **Down jacket** You will only need this if you go on the Lunana trek in late autumn, or if you get cold easily.
- **Sleeping bag** If you bring your own bag, make sure the temperature it's specified for will be appropriate. On a colder trek a **fleece material inner liner** would be smart.
- **Mattress** Most companies offer the possibility of renting one. Bring along a repair kit to fix holes.

- **Fleece pullovers/shirts** Cotton shirts are inexpensive but you stay wet in them and they get smelly. On trek it is always good to bring a thinner one along in your daypack. Merino wool products are now being used for outdoor clothing and are not itchy like earlier wool products. At camp you need a thicker fleece pullover. In Bhutan you can buy fleece products, mainly pullovers and blankets, in the bigger cities.
- **Gloves/hats** Make sure to bring spare gloves and hats. Put them in your pack: you never know when cold weather will show up. Wearing a hat can reduce your body's heat loss by up to 35 percent. Be sure to have a hat for protection against the sun (and a spare one).
- **Sunglasses** Important to have good UV protection. Bring along old (sun- and prescription) glasses to give away to Bhutanese along the route.
- **Walking pole** One or two poles? Two can take time to get used to. One pole is very useful for balance – crossing a stream or river, boulder hopping, helping yourself up – as well as pushing stray dogs and pack animals away; even as a spare tent pole or camera tripod. Two poles are useful on descent: they take an enormous pressure off the knees.
- **Flashlight or torch** A small led headtorch in your pack is very handy; at camp you may find a bigger one useful.
- **Personal medical kit** (see page 49) – ask your doctor.
- **Pocket knife** with scissors and can opener.

- **Whistle**
- **Towel**
- **Sun cream and lip protection**
- **Soap, biodegradable washing liquid/powder**
- **Cash** for tipping according to recommendations from your guide or company.
- Your own **cup** (or marker to identify one).
- **Trekking clothes** you don't use any more and you want to give away at the end of the trek.
- **Swimming costume** for hot springs.

OTHER ACTIVITIES

Outdoor activities

Besides trekking other outdoor activities are available in Bhutan:

- **Fly fishing**
- **Golfing in Thimphu**
- **Flower, Butterfly and Wildlife Tours**
- **Mountaineering** in Bhutan used to be possible (peaks located on the border with Tibet/China will probably all be climbed in the near future from the Tibetan side).
- **Whitewater sports** are becoming popular on Bhutan's fast-flowing and powerful rivers. Sonam Tobgay from Lotus Adventures (**www.bhutanlotus.com**) is the Bhutanese expert dealing with rafting and kayaking.
- Bhutan is a fantastic place for **mountain biking**. In 2002 Rinzin Ongdra Wangchuk, assisted by Piet van de Poel, established the Bhutan Mountain Biking Club. The club has information on a number of trails and the East–West highway, including slope gradients, distances, and altitudes. Mountain biking trips are almost entirely along the National Highways.

Rinzin Wangchuk runs a well-equipped repair workshop in Thimphu and there are a couple of bikes for hire. For more information contact him at Yu-Druk Tours & Treks (**Rinzin@yudruk. com**) and/or visit the website **www.bhutanmtb.com**. Etho Metho Tours & Treks also deals with mountain biking trips.

- In 1997 **rock climbing** became popular at Thimphu's most outstanding rock formation 'The Nose', which has been bolted to provide 13 routes of varying difficulty, with ample opportunities for both beginner and expert (**www.verticalbhutan.com**). Visitors are always welcome to join

INTERESTING WEBSITES

www.rrcap.unep.org/ glofbhutan/start.htm explaining the glacier lake burst
www.rspn-bhutan.org Royal Society for the Protection of Nature
www.bhutan-trails.org
www.bhutan.at
www.bootan.com
www.kuenselonline.com Bhutan's national newspaper
www.library.gov.bt
www.tourism.gov.bt
www.bhutantrustfund.org
www.bhutanstudies.org.bt
www.abto.org.bt
www.bhutan.gov.bt

Rivers suitable for water sports

Location	River	Section	km	Difficulty, class	Sport
Paro	Paa Chhu	Mistsi Zamfoot Freezer gorge section	10	III and IV	kayaking recommended only
Paro	Paa Chhu	lower Paa Chhu	7	III with one class V	kayaking only
Punakha	Pho Chhu	upper Pho Chhu	7	III and IV	rafting & kayaking
Punakha	Pho Chhu	lower Pho Chhu	7	III with one IV	rafting & kayaking
Punakha	Mo Chhu	upper Mo Chhu	3	IV and V	kayaking
Wangdi Phodrang	Dang Chhu	middle Dang Chhu	5	IV with III	rafting
Wangdi Phodrang	Dang Chhu	lower Dang Chhu	5	III	rafting & kayaking
Trongsa	Mangde Chhu	Ema Datsi Canyon	7	III and IV	kayaking, but rafting possible with medium flow & strong team
Bumthang	Chamkhar Chhu	Thankbi	5	II and III	rafting & kayaking

a climb. Contact Dilu Giri in Thimphu, email **verticalbhutan@druknet.bt.**

- The booklet *Mild and Mad Day Hikes Around Thimphu* by Piet van der Poel and Rogier Gruys is an excellent souce of information on more than 25 **day hikes** around Thimphu (2006) (**www.bhutan-trails.org**).

Festivals

Bhutan is well known for colourful, traditional religious **festivals** (*tsechu*). If possible, time your visit to coincide with one of these. For dates (which change every year) visit the Department of Tourism website (**www.tourism.gov.bt**).

LIST OF APPROVED TREKS

These treks are currently open.

Note: New trekking routes are always being explored. For any developments on the approval of new routes please double check with the Department of Tourism or a tour operator.

1   Haa – Nub Tshona Patta Tsho – Rigona
2   Paro – Jhomolhari – Lingshi – Laya
3   Paro – Jhomolhari – Lingshi – Laya – Lunana – Nikka Chhu
4   Paro – Jhomolhari – Lingshi – Laya – Lunana – Bumthang
5   Paro – Jhomolhari – Bonte La – Drugyel Dzong circuit
6   Paro – Jhomolhari – Lingshi – Thimphu

Note: Trek 17 is not described in this book.

ABOUT THIS GUIDE

The following section of the guide describes the itineraries of 27 treks. At the start of each trek is a box which gives general information on the whole trek, such as a difficulty grade, days needed to complete the trek, total distance covered, total altitude gain and loss, and a note on the status of the trek – open, closed or requiring double-checking. Some of the treks in the guide are not open at present, but all are existing routes. Nearly every trek is accompanied by a map, or you may be referred to a map used in another trek.

Each trek is described in day sections, but these divisions are suggestions only – you can split the days up as you choose and stay at different places for the night halt, if the infrastructure permits. Each day section starts with a box giving information (if available) on walking time, walking distance and altitude gain and loss. The day's route description follows, with

> **Note:** Some of the treks mentioned in this guide are not possible at present – hopefully they will open up at some stage in the future. The status of each one will be found in the information box at the start of the route description.

details on what to expect along the way and on points of interest to be seen during the day. Some days offer suggestions for side trips or alternative routes, and Trek 2 has a summary of a rafting/kayaking trip.

The treks can be combined, and suggestions for this are offered in the text (or you may wish to devise your own variations).

Treks 1–12 are located in the western part of Bhutan. **Trek 3** is the main trek for the western area, and finishes in central Bhutan. **Treks 4, 5, 6, 7, 11 and 16** are related to Trek 3. **Treks 13–23** are located in the middle part of the Kingdom. The Bumthang area is the location for **Treks 16–22**. Trek 21 carries on to the east of Bhutan, where **Treks 24, 25 and 26** are also located. **Trek 23** leads from central Bhutan to the south, where **Trek 27** can be found.

Jitchu Drake 6850m

TREK 1

HAA VALLEY–SAGA LA–DRUGYEL DZONG

Grade	easy
Time	2–3 days
Distance	14.3 miles/23km
Altitude gain	3306ft/1008m
Altitude loss	3739ft/1140m
Status	double check if open

Haa valley is worth a visit and could be combined with one night in a hotel.

This 2- to 3-day trek is also called 'the Haa Planters' Trail', harking back to the time when it was used by rice planters from Haa on their way to help people in Paro who relied heavily on their labour during the planting season (mainly May–June). In return, the people of Haa received red rice after the autumn harvest.

This trek is easy, passing through villages in the Haa valley and dense forest on the Paro side. The ascent is on good trails through forest and meadows. The descent is on a steeper trail with loose boulders, so be careful. The trek ends at the road near Drugyel Dzong. You could travel from Paro, crossing the Jilay La (12,400ft/3780m) down into the Haa valley, and start the trek the same day.

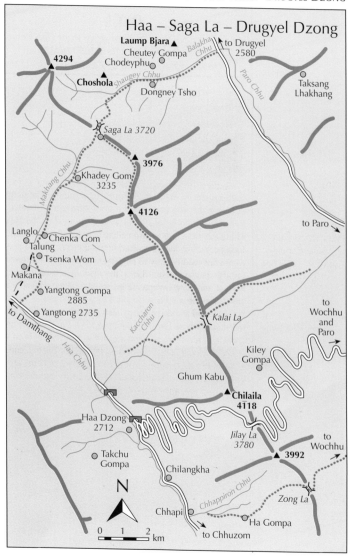

Haa – Saga La – Drugyel Dzong

Laump Bjara ▲
Cheutey Gompa
Chodeyphu
Choshola ▲
Dongney Tsho
to Drugyel
2580
Taksang
Lhakhang
Balakha Chhu
Shaugey Chhu
Paro Chhu

4294 ▲

Saga La 3720

3976 ▲

Khadey Gom
3235

Makhang Chhu

4126 ▲

Langlo
Chenka Gom
Talung
Tsenka Wom

to Paro →

Makana
Yangtong Gompa
2885
Yangtong 2735

Kaccharon Chhu

Kalai La

to Damthang

Haa Chhu

to
Wochhu
and
Paro

Kiley
Gompa

Ghum Kabu
▲ **Chilaila**
4118

Haa Dzong
2712

*Jilay La
3780*

to
Wochhu

▲ 3992

Takchu
Gompa

Chilangkha

Chhappiron Chhu

N

Chhapi
Zong La
Ha Gompa

to Chhuzom

0 1 2 km

DAY 1

Haa valley (8895ft/2712m) drive from Haa town (20min) to beyond Yangtong (8971ft/2735m); trek to Khadey Gom (10,611ft/3235m)

Time	4–5hr
Distance	5 miles/8km
Altitude gain	1640ft/500m
Altitude loss	0ft/0m

If you prefer to make this a three-night outing, **Yangtong** could be the first campsite if a hotel stay is not planned. Yangtong camp is located in a meadow next to the Haa Chhu; there is a *chorten* with a flag hoisted in honour of the local protecting deity, 'the Powerful Chhundu'.

A dirt road bypasses Yangtong Gompa and goes direct towards Talung village. From Yangtong a steep climb (150m) leads to **Yangtong Gompa** village, set on a hilltop right above camp. The big temple, surrounded by a few houses, is about 300 years old and dedicated to Guru Rinpochey and his eight manifestations.

Haa valley, Khadey Gom camp

A more-or-less level trail through pines brings you back to the main trail to the valley below Saga La. Here the Makhang Chhu flows through the area called **Talung**. Talung has three beautiful villages – Chenka Gom, Tsenka Wom and Langlo – about 80 households in all.

The trail winds around farmlands fenced with piles of stones to protect the fields from deer and wild boar. Climb to a wooden bridge, Chagdo Zam ('iron bridge'), so-named because locals claim that the 14th-century saint Thangthong Gyelpo (the iron-bridge builder in Bhutan) constructed the original one. Cross more meadows and some forest until you reach a rock with twin eyes and a distorted mouth. This is the Nyela Doem or Nyela Demon, who was subdued by the saint Thangthong Gyelpo using the Sword of Ignorance (*raydee*) to slash the demon's mouth and turn it into a rock. Ever since then travellers using this ancient trail have walked in peace without fearing this ferocious demon. This holy rock is located in the **Khadey Gom** (the upper Khadey) meadow, where tonight's camp is situated.

DAY 2

*Khadey Gom (10,611ft/3235m) to
Dongney Tsho (10,496ft/3200m)
via Saga La (12,200ft/3720m)*

Time	5hr
Distance	5 miles/8km
Altitude gain	1591ft/485m
Altitude loss	1706ft/520m

Today the climb to Saga La is on the programme. A gradual hike for about 1hr through meadows and coniferous forest is followed by the 2hr climb to the pass. It is customary to take a gift for the pass; either pick up a rock or break off a twig/flower to pile it on the mini *stupa* (*chorten*) built by thousands of former travellers. Once on top of **Saga La**, shout

'Lhagyelo' ('May God always win over evil') and you will be blessed. On a clear day there is a fantastic view on both sides of the pass. The view towards Paro (east) includes sacred Mount Jhomolhari (23,993ft/7315m), Chaterake (18,270ft/5570m), and below in the valley the Drugyel Dzong and the sacred Taktsang monastery. Looking to the west the peaks of Haa forming the border with Tibet can be seen.

From the pass it is all downhill. Beware of loose gravel and boulders on the trail. A good 2hr downhill hike through mixed conifer forests and rhododendrons will bring you to the camp in an open meadow at **Dongney Tsho**, surrounded with tall firs. To the left is the black Choshola mountain: a holy place from which a lake escaped.

DAY 3

Dongney Tsho (10,496ft/3200m)
to Drugyel Dzong (8460ft/2580m)

Time	3hr
Distance	4.3 miles/7km
Altitude gain	0ft/0m
Altitude loss	2034ft/620m

The first part of today's hike is steeply downhill for about 1.5hr until you reach the Genchu Zam (bridge). The hike is through thick vegetation, and laughing thrushes, magpies, nutcrackers and pheasants are often seen. There is a beautiful small village comprised of eight households and a temple on the left side of the trail: Chodeyphu, set picturesquely at the base of the mountain Laump Bjara ('Foggy Mountain', inhabited by mountain goats). Another 1hr from this village will take you to **Balakha Chhu** where the ancient Haa Planters' Trail ends.

TREK 2

HAA VALLEY – NUB TSHONA PATTA TSHO – RIGONA TREK

Grade	moderate–demanding
Time	6–7 days (including a rest day)
Distance	not available
Altitude gain	8443ft/2574m
Altitude loss	8567ft/2612m
Status	open

Haa valley, located in western Bhutan at an average altitude of 9000ft/2740m, is opening up slowly to trekkers. Haa and the surrounding areas offer a number of trekking routes.

This trek starts not far north of Haa town and takes an easterly direction for three days, followed by a three-day return journey that ends at Lukha village near Haa. There are seven passes to be crossed, ranging from 12,800ft/3900m to 13,960ft/4256m. Nub Tshona Patta Tsho (lake) is the point of return, where a rest day is recommended. Several routes lead to this lake.

At the end of the 18th century this area belonged to Sikkim. Haa valley is the ancestral home of the Dorji family, from which Bhutan's Queen Mother descends. The whole region is connected to the legend of Terton Sherab Mebar, his conflicts with the deities of the lakes, and the revealing of treasures from the lakes.

Haa valley has many villages, sturdy-looking farmhouses, monasteries, seven schools, a military training centre, a military hospital, three basic health units, a rather big army centre, a Bank of Bhutan, a petrol station, a couple of shops, bars and hotels. Many buildings in Haa town are built by – and used by – the Indian Military Training Team and the Bhutanese army, as is the golf course. The major cash income is generated from apples, potatoes, oranges and cardamom grown in the south, and other vegetables such as broccoli. Haa produces a famous cheese called *chukho*. The yaks of Haa provide the best-tasting meat in the west of the country; Haa yaks graze for a longer time than others at altitude, and they also eat more medicinal plants, giving the meat a special flavour. In winter, many people migrate south to warmer districts.

Haa valley has a couple of interesting places to visit: the Wangchulo (or Haa) Dzong; Yangthang Gomba, the most secret place in the valley; Kargye Nang Monastery; Trana Monastery; Tenchen Monastery; and, if allowed, the golf course.

Haa valley, along with Paro, celebrates New Year on a different date than the rest of Bhutan, on the 29th of the 10th month of the Bhutanese calendar. It is the same day as celebrated in Sikkim. This festival is worth the visit (check with travel agencies when these dates are).

DAY 1

*Haa valley/Kajenang village (c9020ft/2750m)
to Tsokam (11,600ft/3536m)*

Time	4–6hr
Distance	not available
Altitude gain	2580ft/786m
Altitude loss	0ft/0m

From **Haa town/valley** (8895ft/2712m) drive/walk to the starting point near the village of **Kajenang** (c9020ft/2750m) and start climbing (1575ft/480m) to Dragnag Dhingkha lhakhang (or Bjanadingkha; 10,595ft/3230m). Continue climbing to **Tsokam** (11,600ft/3536m), where tonight's camp is located.

DAY 2

*Tsokam (11,600ft/3536m) to
Wanjithang (12,100ft/3688m) via
Chozu La (12,800ft/3900m), Yulo meadow
(12,600ft/3840m) and Tsabjo La
(13,475ft/4107m)*

Time	5–7 hr
Distance	not available
Altitude gain	1194ft/346m + 876ft/267m = 2070ft/631m
Altitude loss	197ft/60m + 1374ft/419m = 1571ft/479m

A gradual ascent on a good trail leads to the passes of **Chozu La** and Tsabjo La. The route passes near a huge meadow called **Yulo** (12,600ft/3840m); this is the last camp on the way back to Haa. At Yulo meadow several trails come together: from the north a trail descends from another pass, called Tsabjo La-north (the route taken on the way back; 13,500ft/4115m). To the west lies the pass for today, **Tsabjo La-west** (13,475ft/4107m), which leads to the second camp, **Wanjithang** (12,100ft/3688m), in a huge pasture area.

DAY 3

*Wanjithang (12,100ft/3688m) to Nob Tshona
Patta (13,369ft/4076m) via Gongche La
(13,880ft/4231m), Chhosho Lumpa
(12,700ft/3871m) and Tsejey La
(c13,897ft/4237m)*

Time	6–8hr
Distance	not available
Altitude gain	1781ft/543m + 1200ft/366 = 2982ft/909m
Altitude loss	1181ft/360m + 528ft/161m = 1709ft/521m

Cross more high pasturelands with yaks to reach **Gongche La** (or Ganche La), the first pass, then follow a steep descent to the meadow of **Chhosho Lumpa**. Ascend again via Ghoom Maru to **Tsejey La** (or Tshejo La, c13,897ft/4237m), the second pass for today with rewarding views to Kanchenjunga (28,160ft/8586m; the third highest mountain in the world on the border of Sikkim/Nepal), Gankar Punsum (24,735ft/7541m; the highest unclimbed mountain massif in the world, located in Bhutan), Jitchu Drake (c22,470ft/6850m) and, nearer by, Mount Chundu Gang (protector of the Haa Valley).

Descend to a swampy area called Tshew (13,087ft/3990m), then follow another ascent to Dangka Bjido ridge (13,514ft/4120m). The final descent is to Lura camp, located above the holy **Nob Tshona Patta Tsho** (lake).

DAY 4

A rest/exploring day at Lura camp above Nob Tshona Patta Tsho (13,369ft/4076m).

DAY 5

*Nob Tshona Patta (13,369ft/4076m) to camp
(13,420ft/4090m) near Rigona Tsho via
Dong Kacheydo La (13,638ft/4158m)*

Time	5–6hr
Distance	not available
Altitude gain	269ft/82m
Altitude loss	223ft/68m

In northern direction on a very nice trail crossing **Dong Kacheydo La**, with views to Kanchenjunga, an descending to camp (13,420ft/4090m) near **Rigona Tsho**.

DAY 6

*Camp (13,420ft/4090m) near Rigona Tsho to
Yulo meadow (12,600ft/3840m) via Bjara La
(13,960ft/4256m) and Tsabjo La-north
(13,500ft/4115m)*

Time	6–7hr
Distance	Not available
Altitude gain	545ft/166m
Altitude loss	1365ft/416m

The route now takes an easterly direction. There is a hard start to the day, climbing on rocks to the pass **Bjara La** (1–1½hr), the highest pass of the trek, and descending on rocks (½hr); after that the trail is fine. From the pass Jhomolhari (23,995ft/7315m) and Jitchu Drake (c22,470ft/6850m) to the north should be visible. After some hours the day's second pass is reached, **Tsabjo La-north** (13,500ft/

4115m). **Yulo meadow** is the same place you passed nearby on day 2 of the trek.

DAY 7

Yulo meadow (12,600ft/3840m) to Lukha/Haa village/town (8895ft/2712m)

Time	7–8hr
Distance	Not available
Altitude gain	0ft/0m
Altitude loss	3700ft/1128m

A long, long day of descent through silver fir and pine forests, finally reaching the village of **Lukha**, near Haa town.

HAA VALLEY–AMO CHHU–PHUENTSHOLING TREK

The trekking/rafting route from the first edition has been replaced with the newly opened route in Haa. However, there is a brief description of the original route given below, and the full trek is available on the author's website.

It is a 9–10 day trip combining moderate trekking with a class III+ run rafting, suitable for intermediate kayakers and novice rafters (double check with authorities if area is open).

Day 1 Drive from Haa to Bjenkana and trek to Chhutak Loompa meadow (9250ft/ 2820m); **day 2** to Tshochhu meadow (9000ft/2745m) via Tego La (12,000ft/ 3660m) with views to Jhomolhari; **day 3** to Dorithasa (3936ft/1200m) via Puli La (10,500ft/3200m); **day 4** to Rangtse village (3608ft/1100m); **day 5** to Throlo Dumtey (5248ft/1600m); **day 6** to Denchhuka Zam (1446ft/441m) where rafting/ kayaking starts; **day 9** final day of river travel exchanged after some hours by bus travel to Phuentsholing.

TREK 3

Lunana Trek – the Queen of Himalayan Trekking

PARO–JHOMOLHARI–LINGSHI–LAYA–LUNANA–NIKKA CHHU

Grade	strenuous
Time	24 days
Distance	216.7 miles/349.5km
Altitude gain	31,429ft/9582m
Altitude loss	23,770ft/7247m
Status	open

The Kingdom of Bhutan hosts one of the most difficult and beautiful treks of the whole Himalayas: a 24- (or more) day trek over high alpine country, from Paro to Jhomolhari camp and through the first high pass onwards to Lingshi and Laya. After Laya, the route crosses the Karakucha La into the wonderful Lunana district. After several days travelling eastwards, the last tough section begins: six days in a southerly direction over several high passes and overnight stays at high campsites to reach Nikka Chhu and the lateral, or main, road of Bhutan.

Lunana Trek, Snowman Trek, Jhomolhari Trek, Laya Trek … the trek (or parts of it) has various different names. There are also several variations. The longest version is from Paro to Lingshi, Laya, and Lunana, exiting at Bumthang. There are six or seven different exits/entrances, most of which are described here.

The main districts (*gewogs*) traversed are Lingshi, Laya and Lunana, a total area of c336,000ha. Snow and glacier cover account for 11 percent, 30 percent and 31 percent respectively; forests, including scrub, for 14 percent, 35 per-

More people have reached the summit of Everest then have successfully completed the Lunana trek!

Beginning of Jhomolhari trek

cent and 24 percent; and natural pasture for 39 percent, 12 percent and 3 percent. Arable land is insignificant. The topography is characterised by rugged mountains with snow-clad peaks, steep slopes, narrow gorges and flat, narrow valley bottoms. The permanent snowline varies between 15,416ft/4700m on the shady faces to over 18,040ft/5500m on the sunny eastern and southern faces.

Very few people have visited Lunana. Bhutan has been reluctant to allow access because of natural hazards such as snowfall blocking the passes, and flood damage to trails and bridges. In addition, emergency rescue is difficult. If an accident occurs a helicopter has to come from India (20–25 minutes' flight from Punakha to Lunana), and even then it might be difficult to find those in trouble. On trek, satellite phone is almost the only reliable means of communication. There is radio/telephone connection with Thimphu at a few places (Lingshi, Laya BHU, an army camp below Laya, and at Lhedi and Thanza in Lunana), but it's unreliable. A telephone is planned for the Lunana district in 2005.

So why is the Lunana trek one of the most difficult in the world, with only a 50 percent success rate? It comes down to a combination of factors: weather and snow conditions; having to cross several high passes; camping at high altitude; long days with very great distances to cover; the remoteness of the area; physical demands of altitude and duration; the need to start with a demanding section.

Lunana can be accessed by six or seven routes, and a new route is planned from Punakha, following the Pho Chhu. Except for the latter, they all involve going above 16,400ft/5000m. The route from the west (Laya/Gaza) crosses Karakachu La (16,465ft/5020m). From the south there are three passes: Gonju La (16,400ft/5000m) from the Punakha–Ramena trail; Sintia La in combination with Rinchen Zoe La (Nikka Chhu); and Gophu La (Bumthang). From the north there are two passes, Gonto La or Gangto La (16,990ft/5180m into Tibet) and probably Oke La, which is located on the west side of Table Mountain (Gangchen Singye).

The Lunana district is drained by the western and eastern branches of the Po Chhu, which meet below the village of Woche. The long eastern branch has its source in the enormous glaciers below the Gonto La, an immense stretch of the most outstanding and least-known ranges of the Himalaya. From Woche the river starts its journey south via Punakha, where it joins the Mo Chhu from the west and changes its name to Puna Tsang Chhu. The river is known as the Sankosh for the final stretch through India before it flows into the Brahmaputra.

The Lunana area has 10 villages, Thanza (13,450ft/4100m) being the highest permanently inhabited village in Bhutan. Approaching from the west, these are Wochey, Tega, Shanza, Lhedi ▶ , Tasho, Rilo, Chozo, Dyotta, Thanza and Tajilancho (see Lunana overview map, days 14 and 16).

A documentary film has been made about the school in the village of Lhedi, located in the heart of Lunana area – 'School among Glaciers' by Dorji Wangchuk 2005.

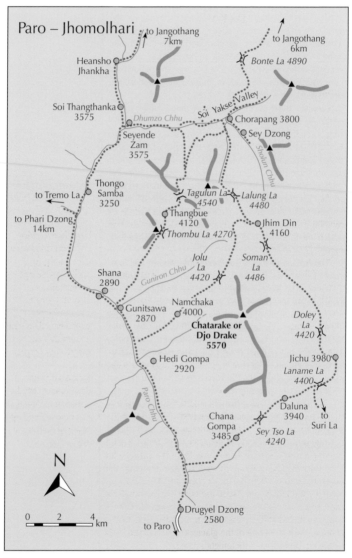

Paro – Jhomolhari

to Jangothang 7km

to Jangothang 6km

Bonte La 4890

Heansho Jhankha

Soi Thangthanka 3575

Dhumzo Chhu

Soi Yakse Valley

Chorapang 3800

Sey Dzong

Seyende Zam 3575

Sholun Chhu

Thongo Samba 3250

to Tremo La

Tagulun La 4540

Lalung La 4480

to Phari Dzong 14km

Thangbue 4120

Thombu La 4270

Jhim Din 4160

Jolu La 4420

Soman La 4486

Guniron Chhu

Shana 2890

Gunitsawa 2870

Namchaka 4000

Chatarake or Djo Drake 5570

Doley La 4420

Jichu 3980

Laname La 4400

Hedi Gompa 2920

Paro Chhu

Chana Gompa 3485

Daluna 3940

to Suri La

Sey Tso La 4240

N

0   2   4 km

Drugyel Dzong 2580

to Paro

DAY 1

Bus to Drugyel Dzong (8460ft/2580m),
trek to Shana (9480ft/2890m)

Time	5hr
Distance	9.3 miles/15km
Altitude gain	1020ft/310m
Altitude loss	260ft/80m

At the end of the road north from Paro lie the ruins of Drugyel Dzong with Mount Jhomolhari (23,995ft/7315m) behind – a wonderful vista for the start of this trek. Bhutanese trekking staff and the first group of pack animals are met here. Walk along a dirt road for 1hr through a wide, rich, culivated valley, beneath forest-covered mountains, following the Paro Chhu. Beware of the sun, which can be very fierce at this altitude.

At Tshento (Chang Zampa) – the first small settlement encountered – there is a small shop and a Basic Health Unit (BHU), which cares for people who live far away from hospitals. High up to the right on cliffs is a hermit building, the **Chona Gompa** (11,430ft/3485m). Throughout the valley there are big, magnificent, traditional Bhutanese farmhouses with bright red chillies drying on their roofs in season. Farmers in the upper Paro valley grow red rice, potatoes and wheat. ▸ At the end of the dirt road a Swiss-built suspension bridge (8150ft/2485m) is crossed.

The trek continues on the east side of the river. The trail climbs gently and will probably be muddy. Not far from the suspension bridge you pass a traditional stone bath, then a *chorten*; walk around its left side. After 2–2.5hr, just before entering a forest below a farmhouse, there is a spring with holy water that originates from **Hedi Gompa** further up the valley. In the forest there is another *chorten* (8,450ft/2577m), normally the lunch spot. There are two streams round the *chorten*: the smaller one, on the left, is holy water. The larger one, which has to be crossed by the bridge next to the *chorten*, starts from one of the glaciers on Chatarake. This mountain can be seen from tonight's camp.

It is strongly recommended to stay a day or two in the Paro valley in order to have time to enjoy its beauty and, more importantly, to acclimatise before starting this trek.

Note: Carry a sweater/fleece in your daypack in case you reach Shana before your luggage.

Farmers measure their land in *langdo,* a section of land that can be ploughed by a pair of bulls in one day.

Cross the main bridge and continue on a pleasant trail with no steep climbs through forest next to the Paro Chhu; look for the famous **Hedi Gompa**, located 200m higher. This is a very important monastery with some large old statues. At the hamlet of Chobiso (9120ft/2780m) there is an arch *chorten* (*khonying*) with prayer wheels; you gain merit if you walk through. Just before the *chorten* you will see the sign-board for the Jigme Dorji National Park (JDNP) (see photo in section 'Protected Areas' in the Introduction), indicating the entrance to the park. The valley widens, and after 2–2.5hr the big military camp is reached, with 'Welcome to Gunitsawa – the Phurba Battalion' painted on a boulder. The camp has a big school and some shops, and your trekking permit will be checked at the camp entrance. Next to the entrance is a house with a tall, water-powered prayer wheel and a Bhutanese-style house/chapel with Buddha statues and an enormous phallus fixed to its outside wall.

From the military camp you can see a ridge coming down from the northeast. This is the route for descending from the Jhomolhari circuit trek, which starts and finishes in Drugyel Dzong/Paro (see Trek 4, day 8). The trail bypasses the camp and crosses Paro Chhu on a footbridge. After the bridge, turn straight to the north-northwest following a trail next to the river, which climbs for 10min. After another 10min through forest, you suddenly see the camp in a big open field at **Shana** (Sharna Sampa; 9480ft/2890m). Be aware of burglary at this camp! A big area of this campsite has recently been fenced to keep out mules and horses. A cooking building and some camping structures have been erected. Looking back from camp you can see a big snowy peak, Chatarake (Djo Drake, Jo Darkey: 18,270ft/5570m or 21,320ft/6500m), was first climbed in 1993 by two Dutch climbers.

DAY 2

*Shana (9480ft/2890m)
to Soi Thangthanka (11,730ft/3575m)*

Time	6–8hr (add 1hr if trail is muddy)
Distance	13.6 miles/22km
Altitude gain	2250ft/685m
Altitude loss	0ft/0m

Sun reaches camp at about 0700hr. This is a hard day, with a lot of distance to cover. The altitude gain is above the limit, and after lunch the trail is rough and stony with many rises and drops. Count on a late arrival at camp and carry an extra sweater.

Follow the river upstream on its right side on a muddy trail. After 10min a new and an old ruined bridge (Penji Zam or Shana Zampa, 9440ft/2878m) are reached. The old bridge was destroyed by major floods caused by glacial lake outbursts in 1950 and 1960. The bridge, named for a Bhutanese official called Sharna Dungpa, was used in the old days by travellers coming from or going to the north, to Phari in Tibet. It was the first bridge reached en route from Tibet to Bhutan, and was administered by the Shana Dungpa (Dungpa = a chief of a sub-district). Traders returning from Tibet paid tax here in the form of salt; traders from Bhutan had to pay in different goods. There is also a *lhakhang* on the other side of the old bridge. In 2005 a new cantilever bridge was built here next to the original bridge.

The trail climbs steadily through a beautiful thick forest of oak, rhododendron, bamboo and ferns. Look out for birds: there are many species here. After crossing a couple of small streams and trekking for 2–2.5hr, a clearing with two houses, Shing Karap (10,170ft/3100m), is reached. Home-brewed beer is sold, and the house is plastered with empty bottles. Not far after Shing Karap, the trail forks, marked by a big cairn heavily decorated with flowers and prayer flags. Turn right – 'Way to Soe' is written on a stone, with an arrow pointing right.

It might be better to split this day into two, especially if anyone shows signs of developing altitude sickness (though the effects of altitude are more likely to kick in at the next two camps).

Follow the main river upstream (named Seyende, Sey, Soe, Pa or Jangkhochang Chhu according to various

THE WAY TO TIBET

The left trail, which is clearer and has a stone-paved surface, leads up the easy, forbidden pass Tremo La (15,090ft/4600m or 16,200ft/4940m) and onwards to the city of Phari Dzong (14,130ft/4308m) in Tibet (8.5 miles/14 km). Within 1hr the trail splits into three possible passes, all crossing into Tibet. From the top of Tremo La you can see Phari town. This used to be the old trading route, and traders still 'illegally' cross this and other passes further on in the valleys by night. Let's hope that one day cross-border trekking will be permitted again.

In 1774, when George Bogle had been in the capital of Bhutan (then called Tassisudon) for three months, his party crossed from Bhutan to Tibet over a high pass, most probably Tremo La. The surrounding peaks were covered with snow, and Bogle's Bengali servants, unfamiliar with snow, asked the local porters for an explanation: 'God in his mercy had dropped white cloths on the mountains to keep them warm!'

sources). The trail makes a short steep climb and descent, followed by a big bridge at 10,660ft/3250m, crossing to the east side of the main river. Five minutes later comes a big clearing in the forest, **Thongo Samba**, a possible lunch spot or campsite.

FLORA EN ROUTE

Watch out for the beautiful little medicinal plant *Arisaema*. It looks like the head of a small, standing cobra and can grow about 30cm tall. There is also plenty of daphne to be spotted, as well as the red flowers of euphorbia ('gopher bane'). In spring look out for *Piptanthus nepalensis*, a shrub growing up to 4m tall with bright yellow flowers. Climbing higher and higher, different coloured rhododendrons engulf the trail in spring. The trees are festooned with lichen (old man's beard), which the Bhutanese use for filling pillows and mattresses.

The trek to Soi Thangthanka continues for 3–4hr through beautiful forest consisting mainly of birch, fir, larch, maple, blue pine and rhododendron. This 300m+ climb could easily amount to 500m or more due to all small rises and drops.

After about three hours cross a big bridge (11,675ft/ 3560m). Be careful: yaks may be encoutered from now on – always give way for yaks, and make sure you move onto the upper side of the track, not the lower, as they pass. A short climb follows and a big *chorten* and a second bridge appear ahead, at the confluence of the two rivers Paro Chhu (Sey Chhu) from the north and Ronse Ghon Chhu from the west. This is Seyende Zumb or Seyende Zam. From the bridge leading to the *chorten* you might see Jhomolhari to the north. A big valley, called Soi Yakse, opens up to the west with several big snowy peaks between 16,400ft/5000m and 18,530ft/ 5650m at its end. Further up the Soi Yakse valley is the camp that is used on day six or seven of the Jhomolhari Trek, which starts and ends at Drugyel Dzong/Paro. (See Trek 4.)

To reach Soi Thangthanka camp don't cross the second bridge but continue for 20–30min on a good trail along the west side of the river. **Soi Thangthanka** or Tshajeu Din Kha camp is in a big meadow. The camp is deteriorating because of the many old toilet holes (2006). The Department of Tourism once built a tourist bungalow here, but it has collapsed and is beyond use.

DAY 3

Soi Thangthanka (11,730ft/ 3575m)
to Jangothang (Jhomolhari camp)
(13,260ft/4044m)

Time	4–6hr
Distance	10.5 miles/17km
Altitude gain	1530ft/469m
Altitude loss	0ft/0m

After enjoying the view to Jhomolhari and a good breakfast, walk for 1hr through forest. Gradually the view is lost, but the mountain will be seen again in its full glory from Jangothang (Jhomolhari camp). Somewhere between Soi Thangthanka camp and the military camp the border

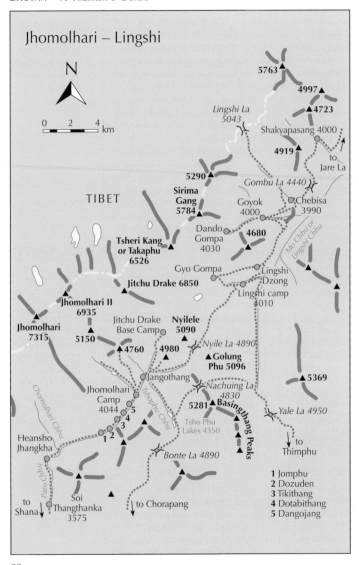

Jhomolhari – Lingshi

N

0   2   4 km

TIBET

5763
4997
4723
Lingshi La 5043
Shakyapasang 4000
4919
to Jare La
5290
Gombu La 4440
Sirima Gang 5784
Goyok 4000
Chebisa 3990
Dando Gompa 4030
4680
Tsheri Kang or Takaphu 6526
Gyo Gompa
Lingshi Dzong
Mo Chhu or Lingshi Chhu
Jitchu Drake 6850
Lingshi camp 4010
Jhomolhari II 6935
Jitchu Drake Base Camp
Nyilele 5090
Jhomolhari 7315
5150
4760
4980
Nyile La 4890
Golung Phu 5096
5369
Jangothang
Nachuing La 4830
Jhomolhari Camp 4044
5
4
3
1 2
5281
Basingthang Peaks
Yale La 4950
Tsho Phu Lakes 4350
Chomolhari Chhu
to Thimphu
Heansho Jhangkha
Bonte La 4890
Tshophu Chhu
Paro Chhu
to Shana
Soi Thangthanka 3575
to Chorapang

1 Jomphu
2 Dozuden
3 Tikithang
4 Dotabithang
5 Dangojang

between the Paro Dzongkhag and Thimphu Dzongkhag is crossed. A *dzongkhag* (district) is divided into smaller *gewogs*. We now enter the Soe (Soe Yutey) *gewog*.

The greatest part of today's climb comes within the first hour or so. The trek over the second part of the day leads to several small villages.

Today's trail again follows the river and changes direction several times. Late in spring, towards the treeline, the blue poppy (Bhutan's national flower) has been spotted. At 12,235ft/3730m a military camp with Bhutanese and Indian army personnel is reached. The camp (Soe Makhang, **Heansho Jhangkha**) has a helipad, and guards another pass into Tibet, 11km away from Phari.

About 1hr beyond the camp, the trail turns right at a *mani* wall. Climbing a ridge, we reach a big open meadow with a *chorten* in the middle, a beautiful campsite: Geza (or Genza or Heysi Thangka). Yaks are kept here in winter. In the bushes near the river is a ruin, supposedly a small *dzong* built to 'stop' invasions from Tibet. Take it easy now since the altitude is approaching 13,120ft/4000m.

JHOMOLHARI LHAKHANG

The *Lhakhang* is located on the west side of the valley 2–3hr north from the village Jomphu. The small Jhomolhari Lhakhang is located at the base of the huge glacier, partly hidden in the rocks, and is worth a visit. Lam Gyalwa Lorapa established the monastery in the 18th century. The temple is covered with the warm colours of *thankas* and frescoes. Three beautiful golden Buddha statues are placed on the altar. In the centre is the Buddha Amitabha, the Buddha of infinite life with the blue begging bowl, with a statue of the founder of the monastery on one side. Other statues are of Avalokiteshvara, Guru Padmasambhava and Vajradhara. There are three permanent monks and a couple more who often meditate for a period of three years, three months, three weeks and three days. The monastery is totally silent except for the sound of the wind and avalanches, and the caretaker who prays and meditates. In 1996 some treasures were stolen, and since then people stopped performing their annual *choku* here.

There are a few small villages ahead. Soe Yutey has six villages: (from south to north) Jomphu, Dozuden, Tikithang, Dotabithang, Dangojang and Jangothang. The population of the area was about 220 in 2001, down from about 460 in 1966, when the area was heavily populated by Tibetan refugees, who returned home because of high taxes. Soe Yutey has suffered various problems over the years: natural disasters like flooding by a glacial lake burst, heavy snowfall, and erosion that affected houses, land and cattle; temporary overpopulation; and the effects of tourism. Fear of fast population growth may soon put pressure on the limited resources. Development in the area has included a mule track along the Paro Chhu; vaccination programmes for children and cattle; the supplying of yaks for breeding; breeding sheep; supplying vegetable seeds; cultivation of medicinal plants; an Out Reach Clinic; and a school at Lingshi.

Note: If you decide to visit Jomphu, make sure you find the split in the trail, and tell someone in your group where you are going.

The first village, Jomphu, is above the actual trail. ◄ There is a split here and the higher track leads through the village, which has five households. (Watch out for dogs!) You might be invited into one of the houses for a cup of the famous butter tea. It is considered impolite to refuse. Don't drink the tea in one gulp because it is customary to refill the cup as soon as even a little has been taken. Think of butter tea as soup, which might make it easier to accept the taste (or call it 'gorgonzola tea' – butter tea is sometimes rancid due to the oxidisation of the fatty acids; rancid butter doesn't get contaminated with bacteria).

At Dangojang, 30min before Jhomolhari camp, there is a JDNP and a BHU building. Nearby a trail nursery was established in 2002 to grow trees like juniper and willow to (possibly) satisfy demand for firewood. There are also plans for a school (2003).

By now there should be a view towards the summits of the spiky peak Jitchu Drake (about 22,470ft/6850m) and Tsheri Kang to the right (21,405ft/6526m). Slowly the ruin of a *dzong*, located on a rock near camp and decorated with prayer flags, appears to get closer. Cross a bridge and suddenly the overwhelming snow- and ice- covered east face of Jhomolhari (23,995ft/7315m) appears, with its massive 3200m-high wall of granite, marble, and quartzite. We have reached **Jhomolhari camp**!

Strangely this place has not been used as base camp by any expeditions that have climbed Jhomolhari, but is probably called so because it is located at the base of the mountain. Jangothang, located 15min further on, means 'the land of deserters' because the local yak herders, aggravated with heavy taxes levied by the local authorities (*dzongpons*), decided to run away and leave their stone houses. (See below for an alternative version of the story.)

Chorten at cremation ground before Jangothang

A small stream runs through the camp, and there is a smoky tourist bungalow. A caretaker comes around, sometimes selling firewood, and collects payment for using the campsite from your guide. Sun leaves camp around 15.30–16.00hr.

Jhomolhari camp is where mules and horses are changed for yaks, the first of several pack animal 'swaps' on the Lunana trek. The trek is divided into stages, and for each stretch a village that owns pack animals is responsible for transporting luggage, not only for tourists, but also for officials travelling though the area.

KING OF JANGOTHANG

There is a story about a king who took care of Jangothang at one time. This king lived in the *dzong*, the ruins of which still remain near the tourist camp at Jhomolhari camp. He did not like the location of the *dzong* and decided to pick a different site, further to the south, where there should be more sunshine. However, this site wasn't any better since a huge mountain (Bolula) blocked the sun's rays. So he ordered the people to cut down the mountain peak before building the new *dzong*.

The people were unwilling because their task was impossible, and they met to try and find a solution. During the meeting an old woman stood up and suggested that they kill the king rather than obey his command. The people agreed; the king was killed, but the people feared that they might be in danger, and fled to Tibet. This is Soe Yutey's population dropped. Tibetans eventually destroyed the *dzong* near Jhomolhari camp.

DAY 4

Rest day at Jhomolhari Camp (13,260ft/4044m)

Rest/exploration/
recovery/washing
day.

Sun reaches camp at 0800hr in fall. Most people will feel the effects of ascending 1800m in three days, so a rest day at Jhomolhari camp will help with acclimatisation. There are some good day hikes from Jhomolhari camp, and it is important to hike today so that you will acclimatise. Follow the standard rule: trek high, sleep low.

The area is rich in livestock, which has always been very valuable at these high altitudes since cultivation is so difficult. Yaks are by far the most important animals here (see details on yaks in Trek 3, day 6; Trek 7, day 3; Trek 16, day 8). Horses are kept for carrying loads and sometimes for riding. Only a few people try to keep sheep. Cattle have suffered from diseases such as gout, and in a couple of hard winters (1985 and 1995) some households lost half their yaks. Dogs and snow leopards kill baby yaks and sheep, and occasionally sheep die from eating poisonous plants.

Some agricultural development has taken place recently, mainly because of encouragement from Thimphu in the form of education and supply of suitable seed. Cabbage, potato, radish, carrot, onion, and green sage are grown. Mustard plants, wheat for animal feed, and medicinal plants are also new products. The latter have always been collected in the area, but now are cultivated to generate extra income. In summer, Tibetan poachers try to steal these plants. Park guards attempt to catch them, confiscate what they have collected, and send them back to Tibet. Incense collection – four different species grow here – is also important. Incense and chillies had equal barter value in the old days: one *drey* of incense equalled one *drey* of green chilli.

Jhomolhari camp, ruin and Jhomolhari 7315m

Side trips for the rest day

1   An easy day hike up the valley towards the foot of
    Jhomolhari; there are several yak trails. After nearly 1hr
    there is an open sandy space, once probably a big lake.
    Follow a trail that climbs the moraine on the right and
    go as far as possible on this towards Jhomolhari. The
    moraine-ridge walk gives a good view down to the
    glacier. Ahead, the east face of Jhomolhari gets closer
    and closer. Watch out for a herd of Himalayan blue
    sheep in this valley.

2   One of the more beautiful hikes goes eastwards up to
    the twin lakes Tsho Phu (14,270ft/4350m), which are
    full of trout (2hr to the lakes; 1.5hr back to camp). From
    the lakes there is a spectacular view back to Jhomolhari
    and Jitchu Drake. Watch out for the yak herders' dogs:
    they are sometimes kept half-starved and are trained to
    drive unwelcome visitors away. Start by going up the
    valley from camp. At Jangothang, just at the first house,
    a bridge crosses the river at the start of an obvious steep
    trail. For more information about the area and a note
    on fishing, see Trek 4, day 5.

3   The most challenging day hike is up the steep, grassy
    ridge located next to camp to the north. It takes 3–4hr
    to reach the final rocky summit (15,974ft/4870m). The
    views get better and better, first of Jitchu Drake (about
    22,470ft/6850m) and, at one point, when crossing over
    a ridge, Jhomolhari (23,995ft/7315m) is just opposite.
    The last part of the rocky summit can be tricky due to
    loose rocks and wind; bring a windproof jacket, gloves
    and hat.

4   A very pleasant hike (2–2.5hr up, 1–1.5hr down) goes
    in the direction of Jitchu Drake. Walk northeast from
    camp, following the same trail used to cross Nyile La to
    Lingshi (see day 5). Pass the last house in Jangothang
    and find a bridge to cross the river (the second bridge at
    Jangothang). Immediately after crossing the bridge, turn
    left and follow a less steep trail into the valley that
    leads to the foot of Jitchu Drake. You could turn around
    once you reach a major side valley. A little bit higher
    up there is a big, flat meadow that used to have a
    memorial plaque for two Italians who were killed on
    Jitchu Drake in 1984; unfortunately, the plaque was

CLIMBING JHOMOLHARI

Jhomolhari (Jomolhari, Chhomolhari, Lho Cho Lari) (23,995ft/7315m) means 'Goddess of the Holy Mountain' or 'Goddess of the Mountain Pass'. On a map produced in England in 1773 it has the name Chimalari, and on the list of peaks by the Survey of India produced in 1861 it is called Peak I. There is a great variation between official and actual heights of peaks in Bhutan; however, there is apparently little confusion surrounding the name or the height of Jhomolhari (apart from some varied spellings).

The summit of Jhomolhari is considered to be the abode of the goddess Jomo Lhari (Jhomol). It is the perfect mountain – more or less symmetrical – a real throne for a goddess.

Jhomolhari was climbed first by Frank Spencer Chapman (UK) and Sherpa Pasang on 21 May 1937. At that time the mountain was one of the highest climbed peaks in the world. Kamet (25,447ft/7761m) had been climbed in 1931 and Nanda Devi (25,645ft/7822m) in 1936. Although many Everest climbers had considered an ascent of Jhomolhari, Chapman, Charles Crawford and three Sherpas were the first to take up the challenge. Mr Odell, from the 1924 Everest expedition, had made a reconnaissance of the mountain.

On the western border of Bhutan with Tibet, the west side of Jhomolhari drops down dramatically to the Chumbi valley. Until the occupation of Tibet by the Chinese in the 1950s, Chumbi valley was part of the traditional route from India to Lhasa. Many travellers, missionaries, traders, surveyors, military person-nel, climbing expeditions and finally the Dalai Lama on his escape from Lhasa have passed through the valley, beneath the spectacular 3000m snow, ice and rock cliffs of Jhomolhari, rising from the dusty Tibetan plateau. According to Chapman it was thought by many to be the most beautiful mountain in the whole length of the Himalaya.

In the eyes of Tibetans and Bhutanese Jhomolhari is a very sacred mountain; more sacred than Everest to the Tibetans, according to Chapman. Several reli-gious processions make their way up to its foothills every year to win the favour of the goddess, and there are some important monasteries on its lower slopes on the Tibetan side. In 1950 a glacial lake dam burst, causing havoc lower down in Bhutan; locals believed this was due to the 1937 climb. After the 1970 climbing tragedy (when two Indian mountaineers died on descent) – and because of pres-sure from the local villagers, concerned that their cattle were suffering as a result of the climb, and the local deity being displeased – a complete ban was imposed on climbing the mountain.

However, in 1996, 2004 and 2006 Jhomolhari was climbed again from the Tibetan side. Whether the Tibetan and Bhutanese Buddhists are happy with these ascents is not known.

A climber approaching the summit of Jitchu Drake (photo: Doug Scott)

removed in autumn 2003. This hike gives you a nice view towards Jitchu Drake, Jhomolhari and the glaciers. Above the big meadow a trail starts leading to a pass, Bake La, and onwards to Lingshi valley.

5   Another viewing point is the steep, grassy hill (16,334ft/4980m) that starts from the second bridge at Jangothang. There is no real trail, just endless switch-backs uphill. It's about a 3hr climb to reach a prayer flag (clearly visible from camp) from where you get a superb view back to the Jhomolhari/Jitchu Drake group and camp. If it is wet, be careful on the descent.

6   Try to climb up the rock on which the ruined *dzong* is situated. Be prepared to climb Grade V Difficult and higher.

Having visited the area more than 15 times, I prefer no 3 for a hard trip and no 4 for an easy hike. Both have nice views. Number 5 is a good middle choice. You can also put your rest day to good use and enjoy have a decent foot massage!

From Jhomolhari Camp to Bonte La and onwards to Paro see Trek 4.

CLIMBING JITCHU DRAKE

The estimated height of Jitchu Drake varies from 22,020ft/6714m–22,925ft/6989m, and it has a variety of names: Kungphu, Ts(h)erim Kang (*khang* = house), Shumkang, Jichi Dak Keth ('sparrow rock sound'), Tseringegang, Tsheringme Gang ('snows of the goddess of long life'). Some other intrepretations are 'angry bird' or 'angry swallow'.

The final summit is a double peak, which has its origin – according a local story – when a young girl, Tshering Kang, was weaving and Jitchu Drake teased her. She got upset and hit Jitchu Drake on the head with the 'sword' (*tham* = the hard piece of wood used to beat a new line of weft) resulting in the double peak of Jitchu Drake (not visible from Jhomolhari camp).

In 1983 the Bhutanese decided to systematically open up their mountains for climbing, and Jitchu Drake was the first peak out for tender. Before the summit was finally reached there were two Japanese, an Austrian and two Italian expeditions. The first Italian group lost two of their climbers when a crest of the ridge broke away as they were breaking camp. They fell down the east face 750m and their bodies were never found.

In May 1988 Jitchu Drake was finally climbed by Sharu Prabhu, Doug Scott and Victor Saunders, via a new route on the south face. During the last part of the climb their ice axes occasionally poked through the cornice and they could look right down the east face for 1200m toward Chung Kang and the Tibetan plateau. The summit is inside Bhutan.

DAY 5

*Jangothang (13,260ft/4044m)
to Lingshi camp (13,150ft/4010m)
via Nyile La (16,040ft/4890m)*

Time	5–6hr
Distance	13 miles/21km
Altitude gain	2780ft/845m
Altitude loss	2890ft/880m

Do not howl on the high mountains and passes or you will be rewarded by a hailstorm. The Bhutanese mountain people believe this is because the deities are upset; from the scientific point of view, the charged atmosphere is disturbed.

Leave camp and walk north to the houses of Jangothang. At the first house there is a good view of Jitchu Drake (22,925ft/6989m). Continue hiking to the last of the three houses and find a log bridge crossing the river. (This is the second log bridge; the first leads to Tsho Phu lakes.) A steep switchback trail starts climbing out of the valley into another that leads to the final climb and pass.

One year a dead yak – slaughtered or accidentally killed – lay in the river, near the first house. The people of this area only cut meat from a carcass on a date advised by the astrologer, which can be up to a week after death. They believe that cutting fresh meat may lead to more cattle dying. The corpse is kept in the stream to keep the meat from rotting. One man from Jangothang is known to be a good astrologer, the only one in the area and well respected by the people. People seek his advice about illness in both humans and livestock.

It is a long climb – 3–3.5hr – to reach the first high and very windy pass of this trek, the **Nyile La** (16,040ft/4890m; Nglele La, Ngile La, Nheri La; 'sleepy pass'). A yak ride up to the pass is an option (although you need luck to find one calm enough to ride!). Today's trek will test your level of

acclimatisation. If you're having problems this is the time to turn back; once you've crossed over to Lingshi you can only get out by crossing high passes.

From Nyile La you can see far towards the east-northeast into the trekking area covered over the next couple of days. The mountain Tsheri Kang (or Takaphu, 21,405ft/6526m) dominates the view towards the north. Tiger Mountain is the main mountain to be seen looking east. ▸

From the pass, descend a short, steep section with some loose stones. Be careful if the yaks are on their way down at the same time; if they start running they are difficult to stop. Less than 30min down is a flat, more sheltered area – a good lunch spot.

Continuing to descend and passing a narrow gorge with a small river crossing, you can spot Masa Gang peak in the far distance. The trail is now easy, flat and good, leading to a viewing point from which Lingshi Dzong can be seen in its full glory; a powerful, solitary structure in the middle of an enormous wilderness.

Lingshi Dzong gets closer during the steep 900m drop, and camp is located next to a tourist bungalow.

View east from Nyile La 4890m – in distance Mount Gangcheta or Great Tiger Mountain 6840m

Those who are fit can ascend two hills from the pass, both fihr one way: Golung Phu (16,715ft/ 5096m) on the right side (southeast) or Nyilele Peak (16,700ft/5090m) to the left (west). Both give a nice view.

Exploring from Linsghi

Stay an extra day here to explore the surroundings. Looking towards the east from camp are views of Takaphu (21,405ft/6526m) and its glacier. At the end of this valley (1hr walk) are two big old yak herder houses at Guilpho (Jukhuje) and a little *gompa* called **Gyo Gompa** (see photo in 'Equipment' section in Introduction). Gyo Gompa was built on a rockface at the beginning of the last century, and can be reached by climbing some stairs. Its setting is dramatic, with Jitchu Drake in the background. Another day hike could be to visit the lake Chhokam Tso (14,225ft/4337m) near the base of Jitchu Drake. From here a pass called Bake La – as difficult as Nyile La – leads to Jitchu Drake base camp on the Jangothang side.

From Lingshi, the capital Thimphu can be reached in 3–4 days by a route that goes south, crossing the Yale(y) La (about 16,070ft/4900m). For details see Trek 5.

The Lingshi tourist bungalow (totally out of order – 2006) is another big shelter with a shingled roof, built by the former government-run tourism company, BTCL. There are only three tourist bungalows in Bhutan (2002), but there are plans to build new ones and to renovate the three existing ones. There is a separate room for cooking, and a big room where the group can sit, trying to survive the smoke of a welcome fire. The bungalows normally have a caretaker who keeps the campsite in shape, sells firewood, some vegetables and other products. One night in 2001 the bungalow at Lingshi was attacked twice by a Himalayan bear. The bear tried to get in through the roof, but the caretaker scared him away. His wife had died the previous year, and he believed she had taken all the good luck with her!

Lingshi Dzong and Kang Bum c6500m in distance

LINGSHI DZONG (YUGYEL DZONG, JAGOE DZONG)

Cross the Jaje Chhu next to the campsite and make the steep climb to the *dzong*. Take a torch with you.

The *dzong* was originally constructed in 1222, and in 1668 the third Deb Raja Minjur Tenpa (or third Druk Desi) started some work on it. It used to be an important lookout for checking people crossing the Lingshi (Phyen) La (16,540ft/5043m), which can be reached without too much difficulty from Chebisa village, our next campsite. This was one of the three trading routes used by the Indians/Bhutanese and Chinese/Tibetans. En route from Tibet to Bhutan, Shabdrung Namgyal is said to have meditated in a cave near the *dzong*.

The earthquake of 1897 destroyed part of the interior, which now has been renovated. On the second floor of the central building, the *Utse*, there is a temple, to which entry is forbidden; according to some Bhutanese, you will die if you do so. The temple has some fine statues of Buddha Sakiamunis, the local god Pajo, another local god She Kinga Tong, Guru Rinpoche, and Shabdrung Nawang Namgyal. The Kajur Tanjur books are stored on some shelves. The *Utse* has an entrance hall on the ground floor and a storeroom on the left

Being on one of the main trading routes, Lingshi Dzong has undergone many sieges. After many attempts to take the *dzong*, the Tibetans used to bypass it. The thick circular walls have many small holes through which the defenders used to shoot at their assailants. Water was collected from the river at its foot by means of a secret passage. There are some dark cells deep underground, which were used as to imprison murderers and temple robbers.

In the 1950s the building was reconstructed, and since then has been used as an administration residence for the Drungkhag of Lingshi. However, the administration rooms are used irregularly. The monastic community did not return to the *dzong*; a caretaker and a monk live there now, and religious ceremonies are held a few times a year. Since 2003 the Je Khenpo (the spiritual leader in Bhutan) has planned to have all remote *dzongs*/lhakangs populated by monks (a head lama, a consoler, and a couple of students) to benefit the locals. In autumn 2003 Lingshi Dzong already had a couple of novices.

When leaving the *dzong*, please donate some money, which will be used for necessary renovation. **Update on the renovations:** 2006 *utse* finished; 2007 surrounding buildings; 2008 surrounding wall.

Below the *dzong* is a village with a boarding school, and a BHU. The school has seven teachers and more than 50 students. The Lingshi area has 118 households and about 300–400 people, some of whom live a great distance from Lingshi. There also used to be some Tibetan refugees. The language of the people of Lingshi is a slight variation of the national language Dzongkhag. Some Lingshi people tend herds belonging to people in the central valleys of Bhutan. Below the village is a military camp and a small hydro power plant. The Hospital for Traditional Medicine in Thimphu has a plant nursery here, and several kinds of medicinal plants have been grown successfully.

Lingshi has a nine-month winter and a brief summer. There has been a telephone connection since 1999, installed on the occasion of the Royal Coronation Jubilee. It operates by solar power, so the best chance of being able to use it is in the morning when the sun is out and the panels may have recharged. Even international calls are possible. Sun leaves the camp at 1600hr in autumn.

DAY 6

Lingshi camp (13,150ft/4010m)
to Chebisa (13,090ft/3990m)

Time	3–4hr
Distance	10 miles/16km
Altitude gain/loss	No major elevation gain or loss

Chebisa is a cold and windy place, so carry warm clothes with you today in case the yaks with the luggage arrive late.

Sun reaches camp at 0800hr in autumn. Leaving Lingshi village behind, the most pleasant walk of the whole trek starts on a wide trail located high above the valley floor. The hillsides are partly covered with medicinal plants. In the far distance Jhari La, the pass crossed in two days' time, can be seen. The river Mo Chhu (Lingshi Chhu), which meets the Po Chhu at Punakha, flows in the bottom of the valley. Looking south, some lofty peaks at an average height of 4500m make a beautiful vista. After 1hr a small cairn with some prayer flags is reached on the ridge called Talela (13,450ft/4100m). Looking back from here, Nyile La and Jitchu Drake (22,470ft/6850m) are visible.

The track descends into a side valley to a village called **Goyok** (Gangyu[e]l; 13,120ft/4000m) (*gang* = hill; *yul* =

Trail between Lingshi and Chebisa, looking northeast

village). Another translation of 'Gangyul' is based on the spelling 'Ganyul': *gan* = egg and *yul* = turquoise. Shabdrung visited the place and an egg was offered to him. When he opened the egg, it appeared to be turquoise.

There are 25 households and about 100 inhabitants, and a new BHU building higher up the hill. There is Ja Goed Dzong, one of four built by Phajo Drugom Zhigpo. Goyok is next to some impressive rockfaces, and in one of these there used to be a ruin (the Bja-Ghi Dzong). In the summer of 2003 the community renovated it on their own initiative over a couple of months. Building materials, carried by yaks, came from the distant forest between Shana and Soi Thangthanka; one day down, and two days back up. This *dzong* is one of the oldest and most sacred in Bhutan, believed to have been built in the 16th century by Phajo Drukgom Zhipo. There is a *lhakhang* in the *dzong* with several statues, and a caretaker and lay monk. You might be able to visit the inside; bring some incense and a small donation.

DANDO GOMPA

Up the valley from Goyok village (1–1½hr) is Dando, Tongo, or Tandro Gompa (*ta* = horse; *dro* = to go) (13,220ft/4030m) and the mountain Takaphu (21,405ft/6526m) or Jangyonpe Gang. The trail is easy, passing the second part of the village and a big ruin that looks like a *dzong*. Blue sheep wander round the houses, licking salt from nearby rocks. There are a couple of beautiful *mani* walls on the way, and the whole valley walk is photogenic. The monastery is located in a rockface, and around the *gompa* there are some hermitages. There are two main buildings, one for the caretaker and some monks and the other containing the main chapel, in which there are some beautiful old wall paintings and impressive *thankas*. Opposite the *gompa* (which looks ancient both inside and out) is a big rockface leading up to a peak called Sirima Gang (18,970ft/5784m). Below the monastery is an area where corpses are put on top of a huge rock next to a *mani* wall. The body is exposed on that rock for a sky burial and the lamas observe whether vultures appear – a good omen – since it indicates the rebirth of the deceased.

Close to Chebisa, looking west to Jitchu Drake 6850m and Tsheri Kang 6526m

Leaving Goyok village, we stay high above the valley and after 1–1.5hr reach a little pass from which Chebisa village and our campsite (13,090ft/3990m) can be seen. **Chebisa** village contains 15 houses. 'Che' means tongue; Shabdrung, while visiting this place en route from Tibet, was offered a special dish made of yak's tongue.

At the end of this valley a waterfall – which freezes in winter – emerges from of a gorge. Next to this waterfall a trail leads to a pass into Tibet (another of the three main routes). This pass is given different names and altitudes in different sources: Lingshi (Phyen) La (Jam La, Chiw La; 16,540ft/5043m). It is 12 miles/19.5km to the border, 8hr of hard trekking. The military controls the border and during the night smugglers try their luck. Near the pass the rare medicinal plant *Delphinium brunonianum* 'Royle' can be found. It is a beautiful, light purple, delicate-looking flower, which blooms in the summer and has a musky fragrance. During summer, the seeds are collected.

YAK CARE

Take time to study the yak handlers when they take the luggage and saddles off their animals. Food bags, saddles, and extra luggage are all piled up and covered with blankets woven from yak hair. The yaks are then chased up the hill so that they graze their way down to camp during the night, saving time tracing them in the early morning. The yak herders help the kitchen crew by collecting water, and in return the kitchen crew prepares their food and tea. In the morning, take a moment to watch the whole routine of getting the yaks started (see more about yaks in Trek 3, day 5; end of Trek 4; Trek 7, day 3; Trek 16, day 8; Trek 18, day 7).

DAY 7

Chebisa (13,090ft/3990m)
to Shakyapasang (13,120ft/4000m)
via Gombu La (14,560ft/4440m)

Time	5hr
Distance	9 miles/14.5km
Altitude gain	1470ft/450m
Altitude loss	1440ft/440m (plus few small ups and downs of less than 30m)

Note: There might be a river crossing at the end of the day, so bring a pair of sandals if you want to save your boots.

In autumn, sun reaches camp at 0700hr. Beware of dogs while crossing the village. After the village a stiff, steep climb of about 450m up a grassy slope leads to a peak called Inela (15,373ft/4687m). During the climb you might see herds of Himalayan blue sheep, and possibly the bearded vulture, perhaps in connection with a sky burial. The trail levels out and traverses a pass – Gombu La (Gobu La, Gogu La, Gokhu La; 14,560ft/4440m; 2–2.5hr) – over a ridge. Some prayer flags on poles indicate the pass (if they haven't been blown over by the fierce wind). Just before the pass the trail is a little tricky, with a steep drop down into the valley.

From the pass the side valley Dhulung Ghang opens up, covered with rhododendron forest. On a sometimes steep and slippery trail descend 250m, cross a stream, to reach an attractive lunch spot (Chumiten). Except for the presence of some yak herders, the valley feels totally abandoned. According to the *Geological Map of the Bhutan Himalaya* by Augusto Gansser (1977), an old pass called Chung La crosses into Tibet either from this valley or the next (where we camp).

It is 1hr more to today's campsite. The trail passes some rock cliffs containing salt minerals. Animals lick the salt from the rocks: white marks indicate fresh licks, yellow marks old ones.

If the group is fit enough you could carry on for 1hr into the side valley, which leads to tomorrow's pass, to find two other possible campsites.

The last part of today's hike descends though a forest on a wet trail (look for tomorrow's pass) to finally reach the Jholethang Chhu (or Zasey Pasa Chhu). The river appears to be a distant headwater of the Same Chhu, which joins the Mo Chhu near Gasa Dzong. This is Shashepasa or **Shakyapasang** or Sabzi Passum (13,120ft/4000m), and the valley is one of the more beautiful ones on the trek. Camping is possible on both sides of the river, and there is a helipad nearby. The sun leaves camp early (1500hr in autumn). ◄

DAY 8

Shakyapasang (13,120ft/4000m)
to Robluthang (13,645ft/4160m)
via Jare La (15,695ft/4785m)

Time	7–8hr
Distance	10 miles/16km
Altitude gain	2575ft/785m + 525ft/160m at the end
Altitude loss	2575ft/785m

Sun reaches camp just after 0800hr. The day starts with a climb of about 200m, after which the trail levels and changes from a southerly to an easterly direction. The area is full of yak herder huts.

Crossing the Yarila Chhu twice, following a good trail most of the time, the valley is gradually left behind. Watch for herds of Himalayan blue sheep; snow leopard footprints have been spotted here. Finally a steep 30min climb, with several switchbacks on a chalky white trail, leads to **Jare La** (15,695ft/4785m), a pass with several cairns and prayer flags (Jhare La, J[Y]ari La, Zari La). It normally takes 3hr from camp to reach this pass, which marks the border between Lingshi and Laya for grazing yaks.

From Jare La there is a good view to the east and northeast almost to the next pass to be crossed, Sinche La (16,400ft/5000m). Gangchhenta or Tiger Mountain (22,435ft/6840m) is the big snowy peak to the north-northeast. Looking back Jitchu Drake (22,925ft/6850m) is visible in the distance on the left, with a tiny glimpse of the summit of Jhomolhari I or II in between and Takaphu mountain (21,405ft/6526m) to the right. A couple of minutes up from the pass, Kang Bum (21,320ft/6500m) can be seen to the southeast near Gasa.

Side trips from Jare La

From the pass there are three possible outings.

* The easy one is to walk 20–30min to the west. There is

Note: There might be a river crossing at the end of the day, so bring sandals if you prefer. There are three possible campsites; see also day 9.

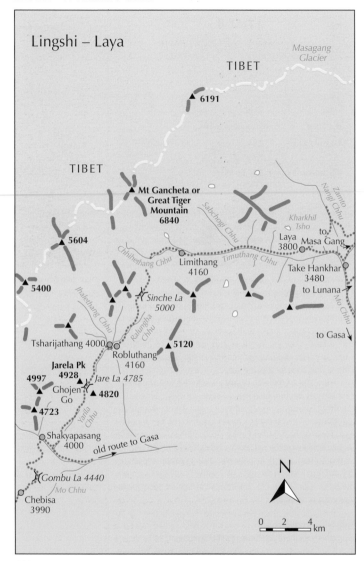

Lingshi – Laya

no trail, but just stay at the same altitude through an area called **Ghojen Go**, leading to a col. From here a panorama of wild valleys and border peaks opens up.

- The same view – but better and higher (to the north) – is gained from the top of Jarela Peak (16,165ft/4928m), over the mountains Tsheri Kang and Jitchu Drake in the west, Kang Bum in the south, and Tiger Mountain. Some peaks of Lunana are even visible.
- The third option is to climb a small peak (15,810ft/4820m) on the southeast of the pass.

The descent starts steeply on a zigzag trail through an eroded area, then rhododendron bushes and a flat stretch. A second steep descent leads all the way down. Just before reaching the forest a good view opens up of a beautiful big valley to the northwest with the river Jhalethang Chhu or Thangkapu Chhu. The hills are covered with spruce, larch, silver fir, oak, various pines and rhododendrons intermingled with grassy slopes. At the bottom of the valley a log bridge has to be crossed. Turn right after the bridge. Following the Thangkapu Chhu upstream leads to some yak herders and finally to a pass called Chung La (Sham La) into Tibet. Watch the yaks here; they are everywhere and have been known to

View west from Jarela Peak (above Jare La): Jitchu Drake 6850m and Tsheri Kang 6526m

The photo above shows a prayer flag with printed inscription/prayers: a lucky horse or wind horse in the middle carries a wish-fulfilling gemstone, and there are protective animals at the corner of each section.

HOT SPRINGS

This area used to have over 100 small salt lakes or hot springs (*tsachus*). The story is that when high officials visited the springs, they expected porter service from the locals. If they refused, the locals would be whipped. In revenge, the villagers dumped corpses into the hot springs until they dried up. This made the powerful local deity so angry that he put a curse on the village, and not long afterwards everybody was killed (look out for ruins in the area).

chase trekkers. Walk next to the river through forest, which opens up after about 20min into a meadow and a swampy area **Tsharijathang** (Tharizaj-Thang, Tsaye Gyatang, Chhijethang, Tree Hong).

Several valleys join here, their rivers combining to form a large river – the Tsharijathang Chhu (Zami Chhu, Lingshi Chhu, Chhijethang Chhu) – which runs first southwards around the mountain Kang Bum, and later east to join the Mo Chhu at Zameyzam, south of Gasa. There used to be a route following the river, which nowadays is only used by migrating takins.

In the trekking season, yak herders from Laya graze their yaks here, camping in beautiful black tents made from yak wool. Watch out for the big Tibetan mastiffs guarding the tents. Try to visit one of the tents; you might be invited in for

On one of our treks to Laya, some of the staff – and the yaks carrying the group's luggage – didn't arrive until 23.00hr. We had to call upon the yak herders' hospitality to sell us some rice, and let us prepare food in their tents. After the sober but rich meal in this down-to-earth atmosphere, we were given yak wool blankets and all huddled up in one yak herder's tent.

a cup of butter tea, and be offered *tsampa*, a roasted barley flour which is mixed with salt and tea and then squeezed into a ball. This dish is originally from Tibet. To please the herders, you should consume at least three cups of butter tea.

Herds of Himalayan blue sheep can be spotted in the valley on their way to find salt. There is some good camping on the valley floor, but it is better to carry on for 45min to make next day shorter.

TAKIN

The Tsheri Jathang valley is a breeding area for Bhutan's national animal, the takin *(Budorcas taxiclor whitei)* – sometimes spelt tarkin – a member of the goat/antelope family (see photo in Trek 6, day 13). The region counts between 400 and 700 animals. They leave the hot area south of Gasa to escape mosquitoes, flies and leeches. To avoid disturbing the takin in their summer breeding period, the area is forbidden to tourists, herders and their livestock. Takins have been spotted in Lunana. If you want to see takin, visit the Thimphu Zoo, which has about 10 animals.

The local name is 'rougimsee' or 'drong gimtse', and some people describe it as a form of wild yak. They look like bison with powerful, thick legs and a massive head with horizontal horns that curl towards the end, like the African gnu. The tail is short and goat-like and the coat long and thick, a mixture of brown and black with odd streaks of golden-yellow curly hair. An adult can weigh up to 270–320kg and grow to 1–1.5m tall.

Takin are good climbers and swimmers, and powerful enough to force their way through the dense bamboo jungle where they feed. Willows, herbs and several species of grasses are also part of their diet. Hunting takin is forbidden (like nearly all animals in Bhutan). Takin travel alone (usually the males) or in large groups; the adult makes a very high grunt to deter intruders and to warn other takin. They are sacred in Tibet (like buffalos are to Native Americans), and the animal is sometimes called 'sacred food of the gods'.

Many legends and beliefs are related to takin:
- The horns and hoofs have a special medicinal quality.
- In Tibet, the horns and flesh are used as an effective medicine against infertility.
- The flesh is believed to be a cure for many diseases and a magic medicine for childbirth.
- The skin is stretched and dried for clothing, or used as carpets.
- The Bhutanese believe that if you drink the fresh blood of a takin it will keep you warm for three weeks.

Crossing the swampy area there is a big river, Tsharijathang Chhu (Tsheri Jathang Chhu), where the 'bridge' will hopefully be found in place. The herders have to rebuild the bridge almost every year, so be prepared to wade the river, which can be cold and powerful depending on the time of year. A steep 40min climb leads to a nice campsite in a meadow called **Robluthang** (13,645ft/4160m; Tshering Yango, Simzo Pang). There is a big boulder next to the camp.

DAY 9

*Robluthang (13,645ft/4160m)
to Limithang (13,645ft/4160m)
via Sinche La (16,400ft/5000m)*

Time	6–7hr
Distance	8.5 miles/14km
Altitude gain	2755ft/840m
Altitude loss	2755ft/840m

Another high pass, Sinche La (over 5000m), is on the programme for today, a 4–5hr climb.

Start early so as to enjoy the best possible view from the pass. Leaving camp, the trail crosses some small streams and after 20min a steep zigzag trail starts leading to a platform with some prayer flags at 4400m. From here a large glacial valley opens up leading to the east and finally to today's pass.

The trail follows several old, some grassy, moraines and crosses a stream (Ralungha Chhu) on a sometimes slippery log bridge, which can be bypassed by continuing up the valley for 30min before crossing the stream at an easier place. (Halfway along the valley the stream can be crossed to a flat area marked by a big boulder, a possible campsite). The shrill noises to be heard are from marmots, whose holes can be seen everywhere. On the right side of this valley, about 150m higher up, are some yak pastures (Gangserry). The trail goes through a boulder-strewn area (watch for blue sheep who could knock down stones), climbs around a moraine and enters a side valley that gives a view almost to Sinche La. At the end of the valley, on a steep ridge, the trail zigzags its way up, leading to the lowest point in the horizon. The pass is just another 20min beyond that point.

The hillsides here are covered with the medicinal plant *Rheum nobile*, about 1m high consisting of a big stem with big, soft leaves that are white in season (see 'Flora' in the Introduction). Crossing the stream by hopping from stone to stone, the trail leads to the near end of the reasonably flat valley with a beautiful snowy peak in the distance (part of Mount Gangcheta). The end of the valley is called Dupchu-na, meaning 'sacred water'. There used to be a painting on the rocks here of Guru Rinpoche, but the painting has been buried by falling stones, and now two trickles of water emerge from rocks near the site: drinking water for yak people.

A final tough climb of about 300m to 16,400ft/5000m will keep legs and lungs busy for the next hour or so. A false pass with a cairn indicates that the real pass is near. After another 10min on a more level trail **Sinche La** (Shinje La, Shingke La, Shee-Thee La) (16,400ft/5000m) is visible in the near distance, with lots of cairns and prayer flags marking the border of the Laya district. To the northeast Mount Gangcheta or Great Tiger Mountain (Gangchhenta, Jakiengephu, meaning 'the proof of a great glaciated mountain') fills up the whole vista. It is a massive holy snow and ice mountain rising to 22,435ft/6840m. Other mountains seen are Masa Gang (23,600ft/7194m) and the Black Mountains range (up to 15,145ft/4617m) in an east–south direction. Straight ahead the mountains of Lunana are visible. Looking back you can still see Jitchu Drake and Takaphu in the west. Tiger Mountain is one of the main sources of the

Gangcheta or Great Tiger Mountain 6840m from Limithang camp

Mo Chhu (Mother River), which flows down to Punakha. Those who want to place a prayer flag higher than the pass, or get a better view of the surroundings, can climb a small peak covered with loose stones on the south side of the pass.

Another 45min down is a sheltered lunch spot. The trail down from the pass is rocky and sometimes steep. Far below an enormous moraine and glacial lake comes into view below Great Tiger Mountain. Cross a side river – Chhihethang Chhu – on a log bridge, with some boulder hopping, and pass a nice, open, grassy field next to a big boulder, Phoudingi (14,600ft/ 4450m).

Continue next to the Ralungha Chhu to a place with some huts, from which there is a good view down to the glacier from Tiger Mountain. From here a short, steep descent leads to a sandy place next to the moraine. Cross a bridge over the Chhihethang Chhu to the right side. Today's campsite is another 20min through a beautiful cedar forest, and is called **Limithang** (13,645ft/4160m), with Great Tiger Mountain looming over camp. Sun leaves camp at 1600hr in autumn.

DAY 10

*Limithang (13,645ft/4160m)
to Laya (12,465ft/3800m)*

Time	4hr
Distance	5.5 miles/9km
Altitude gain	Few small climbs
Altitude loss	1180ft/360m

An easy day's trekking to Laya.

Sun reaches camp at 06.30hr in autumn. Follow the valley down parallel to the Timuchang Chhu through a cedar and then fir forest. Yak people from Laya might overtake with their yaks carrying loads of smuggled goods from Tibet, such as solar panels, rubber boats, down jackets, Chinese cigarettes, thermos flasks, blankets and rugs, and transistor radios. Mules and donkeys are also smuggled: they are stronger then the Bhutanese breed and easily fetch double the price in Bhutan. If caught, the smugglers lose everything!

After 1hr a landslide area is reached, dropping steeply down to the river; watch your footing. Not far from this the Layaps had to build a new bridge (1999) because the old one was destroyed. The river to be crossed is Sabchogi Chhu. Crossing the bridge and looking upstream, you may catch the stunning view of Great Tiger Mountain. Where the two rivers meet the name changes to Mochhu Kango Chhu.

About 30min before reaching Laya, there is a clear split in the trail. The left fork is better, leading to Upper Laya. After some small ups and downs and crossing a ridge you reach a *chorten*, and prosperous **Laya** village ▶ appears before you with Tsenda Gang Peak (22,960ft/7000m or 23,160ft/7200m) in the distance to the northeast. The administrative name for the area is Laya *geog* and the main villages are Toko, Pashi, Neilo, Lubcha, Tongra and Lungo. Laya *geog* is part of the Jigme Dorji National Park.

It is always exciting to see the yaks and luggage arrive at any campsite – and especially at Laya, since the yaks have a tendency to get lost in the forest on their way to the village!

The richest people in Laya own herds of over 300 yaks. With an average price of $500 per animal, each herd represents assets of some $150,000.

DAY 11

Rest day in Laya

Supplies will be checked, and may be topped up with those brought up from Punakha from the south. Yaks and herders that started from Jangothang will return there, and a new group of yaks will be picked up; final arrangements will be made between the guide and the local contractor. Yaks will be exchanged for horses and mules if the trek is continuing down to Punakha, three days away.

Laya village is worth a visit. There is one *lhakhang* in the village, and another above, which can be seen from camp. The people of Laya – children in particular – might visit the camp and stare at you, or try to sell souvenirs. In 2002 the school had 110 students; the next school catering for children in the area is in Gasa, two long days' walk away. Above the school is an old temple where Shabdrung stayed,

A chance for trekkers and staff to clean all their gear, with Tiger Mountain as a backdrop.

THE WOMEN OF LAYA

In contrast to women in the rest of the country, Layap women wear their hair long (although this is changing: in the bigger towns women are starting to do the same). Layap women wear a distinctive dress made of yak hair and sheep's wool: a black skirt with brown vertical stripes, a black jacket (*khenja*), a special conical bamboo hat balanced on top of the head, with much decoration hanging from the back of the hat. This hat is associated with fertility and the fact that women are normally the yak herders here (the same clothes are worn by the powerful local deity for the yak, Aum Chomo Nosey Gayem). This ensures that the herds remain healthy. In a traditional gesture of respect for visitors, Layap women, at the end of an evening's entertainment, will remove their hats and throw them down in a heap.

and some of his belongings are there: a precious stone and a big brass jar, full of water.

You might see a group of men practising archery, probably with traditional bows. The bow is a 2m length of bamboo (sometimes made of two sections) and the string is made of nettle fibres. The target, a wooden board, is placed about 150m away. The archers use a leather arm pad and finger covers to protect finger tips and forearms.

Since 2004 a new tourist attraction has been offered here: yak riding! Apparently there are more than 20 yaks that are safe enough. The provision of a stone bath is another new attraction under discussion. These are wooden boxes,

Laya village 3800m after a heavy snowstorm

Layap women's head decoration

partly buried in the ground, filled with water; herbs are sometimes added. Stones are heated on the fire and dropped into the water to heat it.

Laya's human population – as well as the number of yaks and horses – is growing fast. Unfortunately, the amount of cultivable land and pasture is not increasing, and the latter – especially the communal fields – are getting overgrazed. Yak owners with insufficient grazing will use the pasture of others in return for labour or other favours. Although they claim that one horse eats the equivalent of 20 yaks, the Laya people like to use horses for portering.

Outings from Laya

- Above Laya (14,596ft/4450m) are holy lakes – Kharkhil Tsho, Paro Tsho and Oneme Tsho – in an area called Chhuton Chhagari. Do not upset the deities of the lakes by swimming or throwing anything into them. The Laya people have been known to become angry with tourists for not respecting the local customs.
- In a valley around the corner there are a few more villages. This will take a full day depending on how many villages you want to visit. A very long trek goes into the valley leading to Masang Gang base camp. This is a trek in itself (see Trek 7), and is often combined with the Laya trek.

SOME FACTS ABOUT THE LAYA DISTRICT

- In the 17th century Shabdrung arrived from Tibet and stayed one night in the village of Tongra.
- In 1944, there was a major flood in Laya.
- In 1959–60 Tibetan refugees arrived with their livestock and the Layaps bought yaks from them for only Nu 3 or Nu 4 per head. Around 7000 sheep were given to the Layaps by the government, but they all died within two months, probably from eating poisoned grass.
- The first tourists arrived in 1987.
- In 1993 a bad winter and heavy snowfall caused the death of yaks and affected crops.
- In 1995 a community school opened with 80 students.
- In 1996 solar lighting was installed.
- In 1998 bears attacked yak calves, killing 10–20. In 1999 wild dogs killed three yaks. There are also stories of cats of all sizes attacking cattle.

Laya school children

DAY 12

Laya (12,465ft/3800m)
to Rodophu (13,825ft/4215m)

Time	7–8hr (including 1hr 40min descent)
Distance	9 miles/14.5km
Altitude gain	3200ft/975m
Altitude loss	1840ft/560m

Note: For the trek descriptions south from Laya to Punakha, and for going to Masa Gang base camp, see Treks 6 and 7.

You've regained your strength, shaved and washed, enjoyed village life and a dancing show by Laya ladies, updated your diary and checked your e-mails. A new group of yaks and handlers have arrived with fresh supplies, ready for the next leg of the journey.

Carry extra clothes today since the first day with a new group of yaks always takes extra time, and the luggage might arrive late at camp.

After a rest day the legs have to get used to working again: it's going to be tough. We say goodbye to Laya (12,465ft/3800m), the last village for the next four days, and find the start of the trail through fields and clusters of houses. Descend through the village entry porch or arch *chorten*, decorated with protecting deities, through some beautiful forest and cross two big rivers, Zamto Nangi Chhu and Togtserkhagi Chhu, fed by Masang Gang glacier (among others). Looking up the valley from the second bridge – where the trek to Masang Gang base camp starts – you might catch a glimpse of Masang Gang Mountain (23,600ft/7194m). The track leads through a military camp where there is a checkpoint.

Another 790ft/240m down (30min), at 10,625ft/3240m, we hit the important fork where the trail goes to the left next to a big tree. **Take care not to miss this fork.**

Enjoy the warmth and the 'thick' air; it will be more than 10 days before you will be at this altitude again. Climb

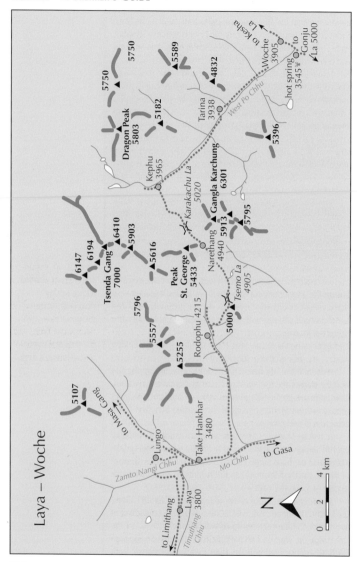

Laya – Woche

steeply through the forest on a muddy trail, which has been widened and improved recently for Layaps to carry supplies up to Lunana, where a Bhutanese/Austrian project is working on controlling the glacial lakes.

Leave the Mo Chhu valley behind and move into a narrow valley to the east. A 40min climb reaches a viewpoint from where the Mo Chhu and a major tributary, the Rodophu Chhu, are visible. Passing several herder huts, the route follows an intermittently exposed and undulating trail that skirts some very steep slopes, accentuated by lack of vegetation. Much of the forest cover in this region has been burned, probably as a result of lightning strikes, or by yak herders trying to create new pasture. After 3hr the lunch spot, on a projecting spur, is reached.

The trail continues through forest with several steep climbs; the going is rough due to big stones and mud. After 1hr the river tumbles over a waterfall with a large landslide on the opposite bank, and the valley opens up briefly. The vegetation is rhododendron and mixed conifers, some of which are covered with lichens. ▸

Just before reaching camp there is one more steep climb through a bouldery area, after which the valley opens up again. There is a bridge (which will be crossed first thing tomorrow), and straight afterwards two stone huts mark the campsite. It takes more than 7hr and 975m of ascent to reach **Rodophu** campsite (13,825ft/4215m; Rodufu). There are two more campsites on the other side of the river.

As usual, the yak herders will send their yaks up the hill as high as possible so that they can graze their way back down during the night. This usually works, but the yaks sometimes wander off, keeping the herders busy for some extra hours next morning.

If you have any energy left, you can climb up some of the hills around campsite to enjoy a view towards the peaks at the end of the valley. The slopes are covered with blue gentians and edelweiss. In the summer some Laya yak herders occupy the valley.

From camp a big snowy peak, Tsenda Gang (22,960ft/7000m or 23,615ft/7200m), is visible on the left at the end of the large hanging valley. The rocky peak on the right side at the end of the valley is Peak St George (17,820ft/5433m), climbed in 1964 by Michael Ward, with

One group, experiencing bad weather day after day, changed the name of this trek from 'Snowman Trek' – its commercial name – into 'Mudman Trek'!

the pass Karakachu La on its east side (not visible). From the campsite looking to the east the beginning of tomorrow's steep climb can be seen.

Some itineraries carry on beyond Rodufu for about 1hr to a camp below Tsemo La. The next day, the Karakachu La is passed, skipping high camp at Narethang and camping at the bottom of the enormous descent into Tarina valley at Cephu (Kephu).

DAY 13

*Rodophu (13,825ft/4215m)
to Narethang (16,200ft/4940m)
via Tsemo La (16,090ft/4905m)*

Time	7
Distance	10 miles/16km
Altitude gain	2375ft/725m
Altitude loss	a little after the pass

Sun reaches camp at 0800hr, by which time today's trek should have started. Crossing the Rodophu Chhu on a bridge – sometimes icy – walk upstream through a wet area (including some slippery boulder-hopping) before crossing a tributary; turn right (east) and go steeply uphill for about 45min (200m) through rhododendron shrubs towards a saddle. Climb steadily parallel to a stream until a high, open valley (15,090ft/4600m) is reached. Vegetation here is mainly alpine herbs, grasses, moss and lichen, a dry, flat, creeping plant, often grey or yellow, growing on rocks. The trail climbs gently through a wet area and then starts to climb steeply to today's pass, the Tsemo La. ◄ In spring look for the unique yellow-coloured cone- or tower-shaped plants called 'chogo metho' (*Rheum nobile*; see 'Flora' in the Introduction). These would look more at home in a science fiction landscape than on a Himalayan mountainside. Most plants at this high, cold altitude are covered with thick 'hair', with some wrapped in silk-like threads.

In 1994 our party had to turn around just after Tsemo La because a glacial lake in Lunana had burst and devastated part of the trekking area. We explored the area around Masang Gang base camp instead.

Looking north between Tsemo La (16,090ft/4905m) and Karakachu La (16,456ft/5020m)

After a steep climb through some boulders another smaller high valley opens up, and the pass can be seen at the end. It takes 3hr from camp to the **Tsemo La** (Tsumi La; 16,090ft/4905m), marked by cairns and prayer flags. On the other side is a small lake, and the mountain Gangla Karchung is visible. Just above the pass to the west is a small hill from which there is a superb view towards Lunana and across to Jhomolhari and Jitchu Drake.

The trail continues for 3–4hr between 4900m and 5000m along a big, generally flat, barren plateau with a few ups and downs. If the day is clear look for the spectacular snowy peak with some big glaciers, Gangla Karchung (20,667ft/6301m, climbed from the other side in 1992 by a French expedition), on the right, and in the distance to the left a rocky ridge with the Rodophu needles, including Peak St George. ▶ Herds of Himalayan blue sheep graze on the plateau, and in the summer it is crowded with yaks from Laya and horses from Gaza: an important area for the economy of north Bhutan. Tomorrow's pass is the border for summer grazing for yaks from Laya. There are many yak trails, so make sure you're with somebody who knows the area well: it's easy to get lost, especially in the mist.

There are two campsites at the end of the day, both equally good. **Narethang** camp (16,200ft/4940m) is also known as Thangnam or Pechu Wom. Camping next to spectacular Gangla Karchung at this altitude feels almost like an alpine bivouac. Settle in for the first really high camp, and remember to drink endless amounts of fluid. From a rocky hump just behind camp there is a view towards Jhomolhari and even Kanchenjunga – the third highest mountain in the world – on the border between Sikkim and Nepal.

In 1964 and 1965 Dr Michael Ward and Dr Frederic Jackson were visiting Bhutan to carry out a medical consultation on King Jigme Dorji Wangchuk. Being keen climbers and explorers they visited the Lunana area and climbed several peaks of between 18,040ft/5500m and 19,025ft/5800m, naming one of them Peak St George (17,825ft/5434m).

DAY 14

Narethang (16,200ft/4940m)
to Tarina (12,915ft/3938m)
via Karakachu La (16,465ft/5020m)

Time	5hr to Kephu at the bottom of the valley; another 2.5–3hr easy going to camp
Distance	10 miles/16km
Altitude gain	265ft/80m
Altitude loss	3550ft/1082m

One of the longer days, so it is sensible to start early.

After a cold night, hopefully with copious 'comfort breaks' (and probably a lot of dreaming and disturbed sleep), you will be served a nice cup of hot tea in your tent. Packing up everyone's gear is a cold job for the crew: keep warm by giving a hand.

A TYPICAL DAY FOR THE KITCHEN CREW

The most junior member has to get up first to start the campfire and boil the water, a couple of hours before the trekkers wake up. The yak people – who also have to get up early to find their charges – might help him. Junior starts breakfast preparations, and the rest of the kitchen staff get up after they are served a cup of tea. The staff sleep in the kitchen tent (always the warmest place). The crew should have mattresses and sleeping bags and warm gear like gloves, hats, and so on.

Tea is served to the trekkers in their tents, followed 15min later with a bowl of warm washing water. Between tea and breakfast, trekkers should pack up their personal belongings and get dressed and ready for the day. If the sun hasn't yet reached camp, breakfast is taken inside the mess tent. Breakfast on trek in Bhutan is good. While the trekkers eat breakfast, the staff prepares lunch. After breakfast, trekkers set off and the staff have their breakfast, pack up camp and try to over-take the trekkers to be ready for lunch. It's important to keep an eye on the staff: if they are not happy service can be affected. Interact, share some goodies, and maybe even some spare clothes.

Lunch in Bhutan is mostly a warm meal packed in insulated containers and carried by the staff. A thermos flask with boiling water will provide a hot drink. After lunch, the crew tries to go ahead again to build up the campsite and prepare afternoon tea. Once they have erected camp, including toilet tent(s), they normally have a short break, drinking tea and possibly their lunch. Then they start preparing dinner, first for the trekkers and then for themselves and the other staff, such as horsemen. In between, they do some laundry. While the trekkers have dinner, the kitchen crew fills up the empty water bottles, which the trekkers can take in their sleeping bags during the night. They eat, wash the dishes, and finally go to bed. On top of this, they cover the same distance as we trekkers do!

The 1–1.5hr climb to pass at **Karakachu La** (Kangla Karchung La, Kang La Ka Chu La; 16,465ft/5020m) is not too hard – about 80m, with a steep section at the end. Crossing the pass leads into the Lunana area. This pass can be closed for four months or more during the winter, and even for some weeks in the monsoon period. An overwhelming view rewards all the hard labour of the last two days. In front and far below three beautiful, dark blue-green lakes are visible, and above the mountain Teri Kang (about 23,945ft/7300m) with some side peaks. In 1955 one of the lakes burst its banks with devastating results downstream beyond Punakha and further into central Bhutan. From the pass it is possible to see the Keshe La, which we will cross in two days' time. ▸

A long and sometimes steep descent (1055m, 3.5hr) follows on a good trail, starting after a moraine beside the north side of a glacier (few rises and drops), and then a long, very steep route down to the bottom of the valley to an area called **Kephu** (Cephu; 13,005ft/3965m). Some Lunana descriptions say that a rope is needed for some sections – ropes for the yaks! It is difficult to concentrate on the trail – which can be extremely muddy towards the end – because of the beauty of the surroundings. At Kephu, six glacial streams join at the end of the valley and it's possible to camp here.

From here, a leisurely 2–3hr walk follows the flat bottom of the valley parallel to the Tarina Chhu, or west arm of the Po Chhu. Several waterfalls cascade down the sides of the valley. Just before camp, cross the Tarina Chhu on a big bridge (which might be washed away, meaning the end of

Carry out the Buddhist tradition of putting up a prayer flag and adding a stone to the cairns at the pass as a thank you for the past journey and a blessing for the one ahead.

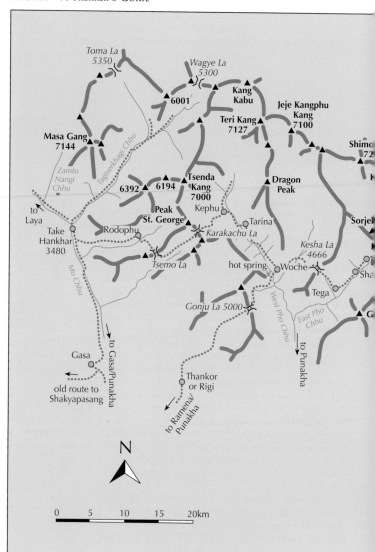

Bhutan – Lunana: overview of the area

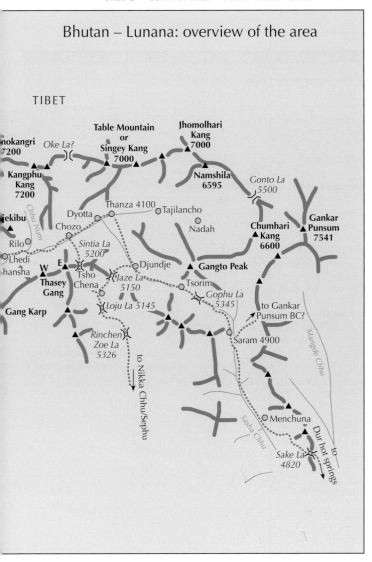

TIBET

nokangri
7200

Oke La?

Table Mountain
or
Singey Kang
7000

Jhomolhari
Kang
7000

Kangphu
Kang
7200

Namshila
6595

*Gonto La
5500*

Chhu Num

iekibu

Dyotta

Thanza 4100

Tajilancho

Chumhari
Kang
6600

Gankar
Punsum
7541

Rilo

Chozo

Nadah

Lhedi

*Sintia La
5200*

Djundje

Gangto Peak

hansha

W   E

Tsho
Chena

*Jaze La
5150*

Tsorim

*Gophu La
5345*

Thasey
Gang

to Gankar
Punsum BC?

Gang Karp

Loju La 5145

Mangde Chhu

*Rinchen
Zoe La
5326*

Saram 4900

to Nikka Chhu/Sephu

Menchuna

Sasha Chhu

to
Dur hot
springs

*Sake La
4820*

the trek!). The campsite is a nice open, flat spot in the forest and is called **Tarina** (Tarizam; 12,915ft/3938m).

LUNANA: 'THE DARK INNER REGION' OR 'BLACK SHEEP'

The Lunana area has seven wicked demons. The story goes that long, long ago, these demons, having been expelled from Tibet, wandered south across the wild frontier ranges into the remote valleys of Lunana. (Some consider them the spirits of seven Tibetan brothers who got defeated in a battle in Tibet and came to Bhutan.) The most powerful are the two brothers Parep (Parip) and Nidupgelzen (Chumna). Parep's home is in a cave by one the many lakes of Lunana; Nidupgelzen lives in the sparse forests of today's Chozo Dzong.

The spirits of Upper Lunana are thought to be especially strong. Yaks (or sheep) are offered to Nidupgelzen. The demons love the highest hill forests, and woe is he who fells trees in them! Due to this superstitious belief there is still some juniper forest around Lunana, and wood for building is carried up from afar. All the same, from time to time, those wicked demons create havoc, and the Lunana people say that it is they who start floods. To avoid disturbing them, people in Chozo still keep their *pujas* as quiet as possible. They also believe that you shouldn't make noise passing the Chozo Dzong in case you could disturb any demon living there. They will stop a herd of animals carrying bells before reaching the *dzong*, and remove their bells.

The evil spirits of Lunana (one in Punakha) are: in Thanza, Parip; in Tyonchho (next to Thanza), Chhuzap; in Chozo, Chumna; in Lhedi, Thasip; in Thega, Gume Bup; in Wachhey, Yangop; in Punakha, Chanyo Gandum. (See also the box on Lunaps in Trek 3, day 18.)

based on information from:
Augusto Gansser and Michael Ward

DAY 15

Tarina (12,915ft/3938m) to Woche +
1.5hr further for camp (13,655ft/4163m)

Time	3–4hr to Woche (12,810ft/3905m) + 1.5hr to camp just below the base of the Kesha La (if you choose not to camp in the village Woche)
Distance	8.7 miles/14km
Altitude gain	740ft/225m
Altitude loss	0ft/0m

Walk for 1hr parallel to the Tarina Chhu, surrounded by some beautiful waterfalls cascading down each side of the valley. The trail becomes muddy through the forest, and after 30min starts climbing steeply, crossing landslide areas, called Dumichusa. Take care.

An easy day at lower altitude.

Setso Lake, southwest of Gonju La on the Ramena trail (Lunana – Punakha)

From here 2–3 days of tough trekking lead across Gonju La (16,400ft/5000m) and Seto La (14,365ft/4380m) to Punakha on a route known as the Ramena trail. This is the fastest route for Lunaps out of or into Lunana if snow doesn't block the passes.

It is said that from now on the Laya yak herders have to guard their animals carefully because the Lunana residents like to take their yaks high up in the mountains and slaughter them.

Woche village might be reached rather early, perhaps too early for lunch and camp. In addition, the people at Woche are not too happy to host yaks because their grazing is already poor. A good campsite can be found 1–1.5hr further on.

Woche (Wachey; 12,810ft/3905m) is the first settlement reached after Laya (or Gasa). Woche forms the boundary between Laya and Lunana, and yaks were exchanged here in the old days. Nowadays the Laya yaks carry on to Thanza, apparently because the Layaps have more yak resources then the Lunana people. Wheat is the primary crop; vegetation is mainly juniper and rhododendron. Woche and Lhedi are part of lower Lunana, also known as Phumey. Below Woche village, next to the Tarina Chhu (western Po Chhu), is a nice hot spring (1hr descent; 11,628ft/3545m). ◀

The path to camp climbs steeply up the Woche valley or Domche Tang valley in a northerly direction, then gradually descends towards two streams. After crossing the second one, the **Woche Chhu** (Lamtachang Chhu; 13,655ft/4163m), there is good campsite.

From camp, climb the little hill (50m higher) to the north to get a good view of the Domche Tang valley, leading up to the glaciers and mountains Teri Kang (23,945ft/7300m) and Jejekangphu Kang (c23,288ft/7100m). ◀

DAY 16

Woche (1.5hr further: 13,655ft/4163m)
to Lhedi (12,790ft/3900m)
via Kesha La (15,305ft/4666m)

Time	from camp to pass, 2hr; after lunch, 2.5hr to camp at Lhedi or 30min beyond Lhedi camp at Shuksa (12,790ft/3900m)
Distance	8 miles/13km
Altitude gain	1650ft/503m
Altitude loss	2510ft/765m

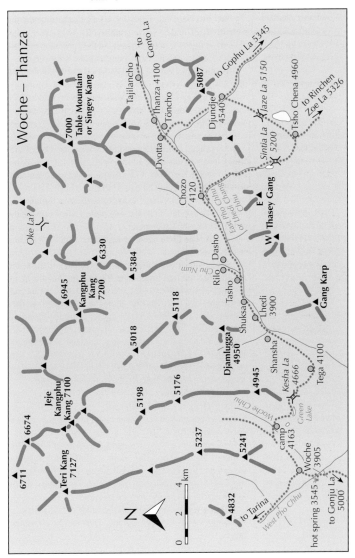

Woche – Thanza

Another pleasant day's hiking, starting with a steady climb up to the pass.

The sun reaches camp at 0800hr; it's a cold place before the sun arrives. The path is wide and sandy, with many small flowers and herbs, and excellent views of the source of the Woche Chhu. Just before reaching the pass, the trail passes a long, narrow lake (**Green Lake**) and a smaller circular one. It takes 2–2.5hr from camp to the pass **Kesha La** (Keche La, Chesha La; 15,305ft/4666m), with some good views of the surrounding mountains from the hills on each side of the pass. Straight ahead is the mountain called Gong Karp. ◀

Wake up early; climb the hill behind camp to get a good view towards the big peaks at the end of the valley. For a special view, start early and climb up the Kesha La pass and mountain on the left side of the pass as you approach.

Some sources say that crossing Kesha La brings you into Lunana proper. A steep descent leads into a side valley of the Pho Chhu (Lhedi Chang Chhu). Towards the end are two small villages: Goptsoe, half a dozen scattered houses, and further down **Tega** (Thayga, Thega; 13,450ft/4100m), a prosperous village where buckwheat, potatoes, turnips and radish are grown. There are two more settlements below Tega: Danlu and Yusana.

From Tega there are excellent views up the Pho Chhu valley towards Lhedi, Table Mountain and the surrounding hillsides, with many different alpine flowers. Below and parallel to the Pho Chhu – after the tiny settlements Wulu and Shansa, and after crossing a powerful waterfall – the trail follows a 'new' route through a boulder area in the riverbed formed after the 1994 GLOF (Glacier Outburst Flood). A moraine dam beyond Thanza collapsed, releasing water from a lake and causing severe damage downstream. Evidence of devastation is visible; parts of the trail disappeared, people and livestock were killed, and houses, infrastructure and the Punakha Dzong were damaged.

An interesting documentary film on the school in Lhedi was made in Bhutan in 2005 by Dorji Wangchuk, called 'School among Glaciers'.

A 20–30min short, steep climb leads to **Lhedi** (12,790ft/3900m). Lhedi is a small, well-established village (no shops) with a school built in the sixties, open for only five months each year. ◀ It has a BHU and a radio wireless station (if it works), and a recently completed park office for JDNP. The children leave school after class 4, after which they are expected to join the family in daily work. The idea was once mooted to start 'mobile schools', which would have meant following the yak herds up to the pastures.

Strong winds often blow up the valley in late afternoon; it is bitterly cold in autumn/winter. Theft can be a problem here.

DAY 17

*Lhedi (12,790ft/3900m)
to Thanza (13,450ft/4100m)*

Time	3–4hr
Distance	10.5 miles/17km
Altitude gain	720ft/220m
Altitude loss	0ft/0m

Today's trek starts through the last forest encountered for the next couple of days (fir and juniper). After some time, a big, unusually deep U-shaped valley comes in from the north. Find the bridge that crosses the Chu Num river, fed by the Rilo glacier on the enormous Kangphu Kang mountain (22,960ft/ 7000m or 23,615ft/7200m) at the end of this valley. ▸ Looking higher up into the valley you can see the settlement **Rilo** on the left side, and **Dasho** on the opposite side. Below, at the entrance of the valley, is another settlement, **Tasho**.

The trail continues following the left (west) bank of the Pho Chhu, crossing glacial drainages, with excellent views of Table Mountain (Gangchen Singye). One of the largest side

Kangphu Kang or Shimokangri was climbed in 2002 by a Korean expedition from the Tibet side.

Chozo village 4000m below Table Mountain (Gangchen Singye) 7000m

glaciers of the eastern Lunana, the Tsonglu glacier, ends before Chozo village. Since 1994 the trail has followed the newly created riverbed; walking over the rubble one can imagine the power of the water. After a 30–45min climb back onto the moraine **Chozo** (Chojo), with an old *dzong*, appears. Chozo is located at the foot of a big grass-covered moraine ridge, with the impressive Table Mountain (22,960ft/7000m) behind. Looking southeast to the snowy peak Thasey Gang East most of the route leading to the Sintia La – one of the passes that exit Lunana – can be seen.

CHOZO

A walk through the village is worthwhile. Hopefully the caretaker of Chozo Dzong (Tshozhong Dzong) – which is in a poor state – will be around, and can open it up. This is Lunana's only monastery fortress, and is built round a courtyard. Despite its condition it is still in use and contains a number of fine statues. The *dzong* dates back to the time of the second or third Head Lama of Bhutan, which makes it several hundred years old (more than 600 according to one source). A *dzongpon* used to reside here seasonally and collect taxes from the Lunaps; according to older residents, the last one was assassinated by locals. See also box at end of Trek 3, day 14.

Camp at Chozo or Thanza (1.5hr further; same altitude). Most itineraries plan a camp at Thanza since it is the starting point of the two most popular exits from Lunana. (See alternative day 19, Trek 3, for an exit from Chozo.)

It is an easy walk to **Thanza** on a good clear trail with little climbing, crossing a big, sandy plain – once a lake – big enough for aeroplanes to use as an emergency landing strip. The Tsonglu glacier (just before Chozo) is surrounded by the biggest moraines in Lunana and dams the water in the main valley, culminating in the 1.5km-long plain between Chozo and Tenchey/Thanza. Some say that the sandy plain results from the debris from the Lugge Tsho outburst flood in 1994, or even an old glacial lake.

Along the way there is a big house, now empty, but previously used by some monks and the caretaker of the holy cave that lies above and next to the house. This was a place of meditation for Guru Rinpoche and his two consorts, Kandrum Hichi Chogyel and Kandrum Mindra Roaw, when they travelled from Tibet to Bhutan in the 8th or 9th century.

Thanza area consist of several settlements: **Dyotta**, **Töncho** (or Tenchey), **Thanza**, and further east, **Tajilancho** and Nadah. Many of the 70 or so households in the Thanza/Töncho region are abandoned during the harsh winter months, with only some elderly people left behind to look after the cattle and houses.

DAY 18

Rest day in Thanza (13,450ft/4100m)

The sun reaches camp at 0700hr. A new group of pack animals will be arranged, and the yaks from Laya will start their return journey. Obtaining yaks in Lunana is not always easy. Even if they have been pre-arranged, they may not turn up. If the system works, the yak people combine carrying trekkers' luggage with their own load of small yak products (and also some yaks to sell). They shop and resupply for the forthcoming winter, visit the hospital and bank, do administration work at the *dzong*, and take children down away from Lunana for the winter.

A day for washing, relaxing, hiking, taking pictures, reading, diary writing or visiting Thanza.

The yak people can't stay down too long in case fresh snow closes the passes, preventing their return. They also fear that their yaks will contract various diseases at lower altitude. The Lunana area is normally cut off during the winter months of November, December, and January (and sometimes February). When trekking south to Nikka Chhu, you can end up with a whole group of villagers and many

For local festivals see Trek 16, day 8.

THE LUNAPS

Where are the Lunaps from originally? One story is that when Zhabdrung had Punakha Dzong built, not everybody wanted to work on it. Those who didn't escaped, and ended up in Lunana.

At camp, the Thanza people will watch trekkers closely. The people of Lunana, the Lunaps, are remarkably tall by Bhutanese standards. They (mainly women) wear a big fur hat, made from lambskin. To keep warm, and to protect against snow and rain, they wear handwoven wool ponchos, with beautiful colours and patterns. In Thanza you may see people weaving, or watch a traditional archery game.

Jejekangphu Kang c7100m (photo taken from camp on Day 15, located between Woche and Kesha La)

more yaks than needed for the actual trek. It is a real privilege to walk with those beautiful people from Lunana and to share their excitement at their visit to the 'big city'.

Hiking options from Thanza

- Carry on along the river in an easterly direction, passing the settlements of Tajilancho and Nadah, to reach the bottom of the glaciers of the Gonto La (Gangto La; 18,040ft/5500m), a difficult glacier pass whose rocky frontier ridge consists of a 30m-high rock cliff (which can only be climbed with ropes). On the other side are the villages of Sumtoshi and Lhodak in Tibet. Before the occupation of Tibet, this was probably the only way between Lunana and the area to the north. (One other pass shown on one map is Oke La, directly north of Chozo). Thanza to Lhodak used to take three days with fully loaded yaks, and only the richer families from Lunana traded with Tibet as trade with Punakha was better. Nobody uses this pass now, and apparently a thick hemp rope lies coiled under a rock on the southern glacier waiting for the day when, perhaps, trekking will be permitted across border passes. In the 1980s a Japanese expedition climbing Kula Kangri from the Tibet side used this pass and pitched Camp 1 here, finding a prayer flag and the skeleton of a yak.
- In the same direction, 1.5hr from Thanza, the path

climbs over a moraine dam which holds back the lake Taksha Tsho. The lake is 500m in diameter and 110m at its deepest point. In 1997 the RGOB, concerned that the dam might collapse catastrophically (as did Lugi Tsho – slightly to the northeast – in 1994), started the

Table Mountain (Gangchen Singye) 7000m

131

process of lowering the level of the lake by cutting a channel through the dam with technical assistance from India. Between 200 and 300 workers were engaged in the project for three months of the year. In 1957, 1969 and 1994 the Lunana glacial lakes had some outbursts with floods running down the Pho Chhu towards Punakha. Bhutan has over 2500 glacial lakes, and the basin of the Pho Chhu River contains over 500 lakes and 100 glaciers. Some lakes in the Bhutan Himalaya could burst and cause a damaging flood, and have to be constantly monitored.

- Hike around the different villages of Thanza.

TABLE MOUNTAIN (OR GANGCHEN SINGYE)

Chomolhari Kangri, Tjojokang or Zongophu Gang: these are all names, found in old reports, for Table Mountain (22,960ft/7000m). In 2002 when Her Majesty the Queen Ashi Dorji Wangchuk visited Lunana, Table Mountain was named Gangchen Singye in honour of His Majesty, Singey, 'who is like a mighty mountain for his people, always there to shoulder their burdens' (*A Portrait of Bhutan*, 2006).

Exits from Lunana

1   From Woche to Punakha via Gonju La (16,400ft/5000m) – the Ramena trail: 2–3 days (see Trek 3, day 15)

2   From Chozo to Nikka Chhu via Sintia La (17,055ft/5200m) and Rinchen Zoe La (17,470ft/5326m): 6 days (see Trek 3, day 19)

3   From Thanza to Nikka Chhu via Jaze La (16,890ft/5150m) and Rinchen Zoe La (17,470ft/5326m): 6–7 days (see Trek 3, day 19 A+B)

4   From Thanza to Bumthang via Gophu La (17,532ft/5345m): 8 days (see Trek 16, in reverse)

5   From Thanza to Laya/Gaza via Karakachu La (16,465ft/5020m) (read Trek 3 from here in reverse)

6   From Thanza to Tibet via Gonto La (c18,040ft/5500m) (see Trek 3, day 18)

7   From Lunana to Punakha following the Pho Chhu (a trek being studied and planned according to the Five Year Plan 2002–2007).

There are other barely explored possibilities.

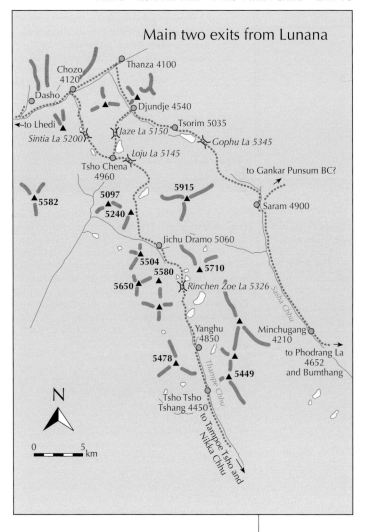

DAY 19A

**(see also alternative day 19, Trek 3 –
route from Chozo to Tsho Chena)**

*Thanza (13,450ft/4100m)
to Djundje (14,890ft/4540m)*

Time	4hr
Distance	4.3 miles/7km
Altitude gain	1640ft/500m
Altitude loss	0ft/0m

Days 19a and 19b
could be combined.

Climb from Thanza/Toencha on a good trail up a rounded and sparsely vegetated hill to the east, to a large square-looking boulder on a hill south of the village (14,350ft/4375m). There are some excellent views over Thanza valley, Chozo and the Lunana mountains. The path then turns south up a side valley, passing high above a multi-stage waterfall, and is generally gentle and easy. The path and the river eventually meet, and follow each other for 1hr. Camp **Djundje** (Danji, Dangey; 14,890ft/4540m) is before a bridge.

DAY 19B

*Djundje (14,890ft/4540m)
to Tsho Chena (16,272ft/4960m)
via Jaze La (16,890ft/5150m)*

Time	3hr to the pass and 2hr to camp
Distance	5.6 miles/9km
Altitude gain	2001ft/610m
Altitude loss	625ft/190m

Near camp there is a trail junction. One trail goes to Gangkar Puensum and onwards to the Bumthang exit. The trail to Jaze

La turns away from the river, crossing a bridge near camp (bridge could be washed out), and climbs in a generally southwesterly direction into a rocky side valley. The trail leading to the pass is good and relatively gradual, and a number of false horizons have to be crossed before reaching **Jaze La** (16,890ft/5150m). The pass is marked by cairns, with many snowy peaks visible. From Jaze La the path descends between snow-covered peaks and passes a string of small lakes. Camp is at 16,272ft/4960m beside one of the larger blue-green lakes, **Tsho Chena**.

ALTERNATIVE ROUTE

ALTERNATIVE DAY 19

(route starting from Chozo, see day 17, Trek 3)

*Chozo (13,515ft/4120m)
to Tsho Chena (16,272ft/4960m)
via Sintia La (17,055ft/5200m)*

Time	7–8hr (5–6hr to top of pass)
Distance	11 miles/17.5km
Altitude gain	3540ft/1080m
Altitude loss	785ft/240m

The route from Chozo involves another six beautiful days of hard trekking with some high camps. There are 11 yak stages from Chozo to Nikka Chhu.

This is a long day, so an early start is required. The route climbs steadily to the Sintia La pass on a clear trail. In the last 1.5hr, the trail leads through some boulders; be careful when they are covered with snow. The real steep climbing may be finished, but the effects of altitude can be felt. En route look out for a beautiful ▶

Carry warm clothes with you today because it is cold on the pass and beyond.

◀ lake on the right side with a small glacier above it, from where a first glimpse of the pass in the distance is possible.

Sintia La (Chinchu La; 17,055ft/5200m) has some cairns and prayer flags. Looking back north Kangphu Kang is still visible in its full glory, with Table Mountain only partly visible. To the south a very flat and wide valley with a lake opens up. The horizon is full of nameless snowy peaks of over 6000m. The trail continues through this landscape for the next two days.

After the pass the trail is not always clear, so keep close to the yak herders or trekking staff. At a certain point, a trail comes in from the left (one of the trails coming in from the Jaze La from Thanza). In order to reach camp, don't lose too much height. Camp **Tscho Chena** is located just after the trail turns around a moraine side through a landslide area. Take care not to miss this corner.

Sun leaves the camp at 1700hr. ◀

Coming from Thanza, this area is approached from a different valley and another spot near by is used for camp (from pass to camp 1.5–2hr).

DAY 20

*Tsho Chena (16,272ft/4960m)
to Jichu Dramo (16,595ft/5060m)
via Loju La (16,875ft/5145m)*

Time	6hr
Distance	12 miles/19.5km
Altitude gain	605ft/185m
Altitude loss	280ft/85m (three climbs and descents of 450ft/135m)

Days 19, 20 and 21 traverse an area that looks rather like the Tibetan plateau.

It is a real treat when the sun hits camp at 0700hr after a cold night with temperatures around freezing *inside* the tent. Try to leave early again to allow time for coping with altitude, for enjoying the spectacular scenery, and for managing the long day.

Climb up to the first of three passes at about 5100m, a nameless pass with a few cairns. There is a beautiful 360° panorama with many snowy peaks. It is apparently possible to see the communication tower at Dochu La, the pass between Punakha and Thimphu. Watch out for snow partridges.

Several trails lead next to a big lake to the second pass, **Loju La** (16,875ft/5145m). Carpets of blue and violet alpine flowers bloom everywhere. Descend to another small lake, go around it and follow the yak people who will show you the way. The third and last pass is a small one; from here go sharply around the corner to get a view into a wide glacial valley (see photo in 'Medical Considerations' in the Introduction). At the end of this valley is today's campsite, **Jichu Dramo** (16,595ft/5060m), located just below tomorrow's high pass, Rinchen Zoe La (17,470ft/5326m).

The vegetation around the camp includes *yartsa goenbu* or catapilliar fungus, which grows only at extreme altitudes and, according to a Bhutanese herder, is used to treat sexually transmitted diseases.

There is sun in camp until about 1600hr, after which the temperature drops sharply. Using binoculars, tomorrow's

In between Tsho Chena and Loju La 5145m

Yak herders preparing dinner at Jichu Dramo camp 5060m

pass can be seen from camp: look for some prayer flags and cairns. At yesterday's and tonight's camp there is always the risk of yaks running home to Thanza or Chozo!

DAY 21

Jichu Dramo (16,595ft/5060m)
to Yanghu, or down to camp at
Tsho Tsho Tshang (14,596ft/4450m)
via Rinchen Zoe La (17,470ft/5326m)

Time	8hr (including 1hr at top of pass and 30min for lunch)
Distance	12 miles/19.5km
Altitude gain	870ft/265m
Altitude loss	2870ft/875m

The sun reaches camp at 0700hr, most welcome after a night with freezing temperatures!

After crossing some moraines and a small stream, the final climb to **Rinchen Zoe La** (17,470ft/5326m) starts on a good path, a gentle climb along two lakes. The pass is clearly indicated by prayer flags and cairns (1–1.5hr). Nearby a big well-decorated boulder gives an excellent view in all directions, including a last sight of the Lunana mountains. To the east part of Gankar Punsum (24,800ft/7561m) may be visible (uncertain due to lack of good maps). To the east of the pass a 395m climb leads to Rinchen Zoe Kang (18,762ft/5720m). ▸

A long descent starts into the broad, sometimes marshy, U-shaped Thampe Chhu valley. Passing several lakes, with a final big beautiful blue-green one at Changay Thang, the valley narrows and the trail goes steeply down the face of a moraine. The trail flattens again and there are several camps along the way. Depending on yaks, trekkers, and the weather, keep going as far as possible to reach the treeline (rhododendron). The first possible camp is just after the steep descent at 15,910ft/4850m, with pasture and stone wall enclosures.

There are various names for the campsites, according to the yak people and other sources: Yanghu, Chhu Karpo, Tsho Tsho Tshang (Thsongsa Thang). Yanghu is a reasonably big, open, flat area, the limit to which the Chozo people are allowed to graze their yaks in the summer. Next is Chhu Karpo at 15,090ft/4600m, but a better choice lies 1hr further on at Tsho Tsho Tshang (14,430ft/4400m; 5hr from the pass).

Today we reach the highest pass of the trek, followed by a long day down the valley.

Rinchen Zoe La is the watershed for the areas drained by the Pho Chhu and Mangde Chhu. The Mangde Chhu leads to Tongsa, the Pho Chhu to Punakha. The drainage from the valley to the south, Thampe Chhu (or Methe Dutha), forms a major tributary of the Mangde Chhu.

HIMALAYAN TREE LINE

The tree line in the Himalayas is high because of the region's combination of low geographic latitude and high precipitation. Latitude influences temperature (increasing latitude means colder temperatures – compare, for example, the tropics and sub-arctic) and precipitation is high because of the monsoon. However, there are also regional variations. As you go west in the Himalayas precipitation gets lower – and so does the timberline. Areas further north are more likely to be in the rain shadow, which means they have less rain. The timberline in Lunana is therefore markedly lower than, for example, in the Black Mountains.

DAY 22

*Tsho Tsho Tshang (14,596ft/4450m)
to Tampoe Tsho (14,285ft/4355m)
(final camp is 2.5hr above
River Gorge camp [13,285ft/4050m])*

Time	3.5 + 2.5hr
Distance	9.5 miles/15km
Altitude gain	1000ft/305m
Altitude loss	1310ft/400m

People from Lunana and Sephu use Tsho Tsho Tshang as a trading place.

The sun reaches camp around 0800hr. There are many small streams to cross by hopping from stone to stone. The trail is very slippery and muddy at first, and later is covered with many boulders. Don't cross the bridges along the trail over the main stream; stay on the west side of the river. Watch for Himalayan partridges. Slowly the trail passes the treeline again. Pass a yak gate, and after 3.5hr reach the **River Gorge** (Gala Pang Chhu; 13,285ft/4050m), which some itineraries use as a campsite.

Shortly afterwards a steep climb through a forest of juniper and silver fir leaves the valley floor behind. A very steep final climb next to a waterfall, and a short walk into a side valley, leads to a beautiful lake, **Tampoe Tsho** (Tempe Tsho), behind a small knoll. The turquoise-coloured lake is situated in a circle of steep mountain slopes, and the atmosphere can become eerie, especially when clouds are coming in. Next to the lake is camp, the last one above the treeline.

DAY 23

Tampoe Tsho (14,285ft/4355m)
to Maurothang (12,130ft/3698m)
via Tempe La (15,300ft/4665m)

Time	1hr to pass + 4hr
Distance	13 miles/21km to Maurothang
Altitude gain	1015ft/310m
Altitude loss	3165ft/965m

Sun reaches camp at 0800hr. It is a reasonably steep climb on a good trail to the pass **Tempe La** (15,300ft/4665m), marked with the usual prayer flags. Bid farewell to the high altitude with its fresh, crisp air. Start with a steep descent, sometimes on ice- or snow-covered stones. The route could be busy, with Lunana people on their way back home with winter supplies, carried by large groups of yaks. Two hours further down they camp at Zezey Thang, from where they will go down lower to attend to their business. Imagine travelling for several days, crossing high passes, just to go shopping!

A little climb through a small gap leads suddenly to a big lake, Om Tsho (Om-Toe Tsho, Omta Tsho), believed to be sacred after Pema Lingpa found *terma* (cymbals, text and artefacts hidden by Guru Rinpoche) in it. Follow the trail around the lake to its outlet, where boulder-hopping is on the programme. Try to stop and balance on a rock to enjoy the view towards the mountains, the lake, and prayer flags. The descent is steep now (150m), passing a waterfall, cascading down c100m to the second, smaller lake (13,610ft/4150m).

A very steep and dramatic descent (150m) follows, to reach Zezey Thang (12,790ft/3900m), probably buzzing with activity. The yaks have a very difficult time descending. Look for a variety of beautiful wildflowers. The second lake also produces a waterfall, spotted after the descent is nearly completed.

The last pass is crossed today.

141

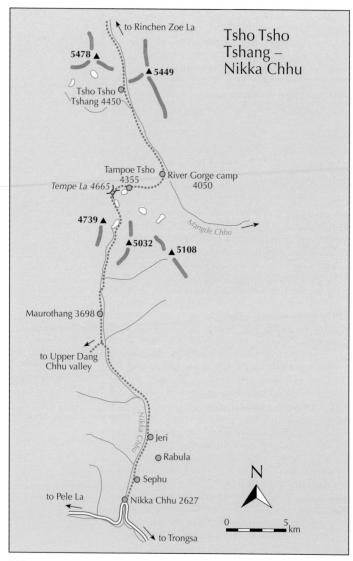

Tsho Tsho
Tshang –
Nikka Chhu

to Rinchen Zoe La

5478 ▲

▲5449

Tsho Tsho
Tshang 4450

Tampoe Tsho
4355

Tempe La 4665

River Gorge camp
4050

4739 ▲

Mangde Chhu

▲5032

▲5108

Maurothang 3698

to Upper Dang
Chhu valley

Nikka Chhu

Jeri

Rabula

Sephu

Nikka Chhu 2627

to Pele La

to Trongsa

N

0   5
km

We are now at the headwaters of the Nikka Chhu (Rinchen Chhu, Maru Chhu), the river we will follow until the end of the trek at Sephu. A good, clear path, rather flat, follows the left (east) bank of the river through forest and meadows. Rerethang is a possible campsite, 45min before **Maurothang**. If everything goes to plan, this should be the last night of camping. The yaks don't go much further down due to the low altitude, warmer temperature, and problems with mixing with cattle.

DAY 24

*Maurothang (12,130ft/3698m)
to Nikka Chhu (8617ft/2627m)*

Time	5hr
Distance	14.5 miles/23.5km
Altitude gain	0ft/0m (some small climbs)
Altitude loss	3510ft/1070m

After a lot of rain today's trek will be extremely muddy, made worse by all the cattle and horses on the trail. Bad conditions can easily add 2hr to the day. Bid farewell to the yak herders; any yaks taken further down are destined for slaughter.

The trail is easy, with only one major split not long after Maurothang. Don't climb up here; the trail going up leads to the Upper Dan Chhu valley and Dang Chhu river, finally reaching the town of Wangdi. Instead, find a bridge that crosses the Nikka Chhu (30min from Maurothang). The flora changes into thick bamboo forest and low bamboo grass.

Several tributaries have to be crossed on various kinds of bridges, as well as a couple of clearings with some huts. Finally, after a long time, the forest/jungle opens up with a view towards the very rich agricultural valley containing Sephu village; the lateral road can be seen. A large suspension bridge crosses the Nikka Chhu, but don't cross it – continue on the big trail, which is a jeep-drivable road here.

The final day of trekking! Hopefully the horses have arrived from Sephu to carry the luggage.

It takes longer than anticipated to get past the village – 1.5–2hr – but suddenly the road is reached.

At **Nikka Chhu** there is a big concrete bridge and a few houses with some shops and a restaurant. Bamboo products are sold here, and hopefully transport will be waiting to take trekkers either east to Bumthang, or west to Wangdi/Thimphu.

TREK DESCRIPTION FROM THE 1940S

After so many days' trekking, cut off from civilisation, you might feel as Guiseppe Tucci described after his long trek in the highlands of Tibet in 1940:

For all my tiredness, the thought that we were at the end of our journey struck me as very painful. In a few days we should wallow in the damp heat of Sikkim. Caravan life would be over; we should be speedily carried around by motor cars and railways, locked up into the engine-driven boxes, which pitilessly subjected man to the whims of machinery and contrivances. We should no more file out slowly against the outside world, reviewing with attentive, inquisitive eyes the landscape as if we were wresting it every minute from strenuously conquered distances. A treacherous prodigy would make the landscape whiz along past our windows, blurring their colours and outlines into a dream-like dimness ... Nowadays we are skimming over the surface of things. Machines had accustomed us to see things from afar and at the surface, thus contributing to that lack of depth lamented by the wise ones in our modern age.

Congratulations! You have completed a very long and challenging trek in one of the more remote corners of the Himalayas.

TREK 4

JHOMOLHARI CAMP–
BONTE LA–TAGULUN LA
OR LALUNG LA–
DRUGYEL DZONG CIRCUIT

Grade	moderate–demanding
Time	9 days
Distance	72.9 miles/117.5km
Altitude gain	10,722ft/3284m
Altitude loss	10,772ft/3284m
Status	open – check for changes

For the first 3 (or 4) days, up till Jhomolhari camp, follow Trek 3. In case the Gunitsawa army camp has to be bypassed two beautiful routes (exits) are described below using Lalung La instead of Tagulun La (see Alternative Routes 1 and 2). Route 2, described at the end of this trek, involves an extra day of trekking: Dhumzo Chhu – Jhim Din – Jichu – Dalanu – Drugyel Dzong.

The Tourism Authority of Bhutan has mapped this circuit. A map has been produced and is available from the Department of Tourism (cUS$6).

Note: If you plan to do this trek in spring, be aware that one or both of the passes could be blocked by snow. If the first pass – the Bonte La – is impassable, retrace your steps back to Soi Thangthanka. Follow the track down from Soi Thangthanka to Seyende Zumb and cross the Paro Chhu on a tall bridge leading to a *chorten* into the Soi Yaksey valley. Camp opposite Lamelakha settlement, located at the beginning of a steep climb leading to an intersection up to Tagulun La or camp at Dhumzo Chhu (Chorapang) for crossing Lalung La. If both passes are blocked by snow, you may have to return to Paro, retracing your steps back to the starting point at Drugyel Dzong.

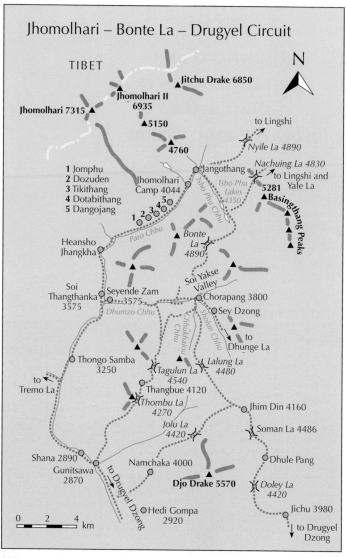

Jhomolhari – Bonte La – Drugyel Circuit

TIBET

N

▲ Jitchu Drake 6850

▲ Jhomolhari II 6935

Jhomolhari 7315 ▲

▲ 5150

▲ 4760

to Lingshi

Nyile La 4890

Nachuing La 4830

Jangothang

to Lingshi and Yale La

1 Jomphu
2 Dozuden
3 Tikithang
4 Dotabithang
5 Dangojang

Jhomolhari Camp 4044

Tsho Phu Chhu

Tsho Phu Lakes 4350

5281
▲ Basingthang Peaks

○ 5 ○
1 ○ 2 ○ 3 ○ 4

▲

▲

Paro Chhu

▲ Bonte La 4890

Heansho Jhangkha ○

▲

▲

Soi Yakse Valley

Soi Thangthanka 3575 ○

Seyende Zam 3575

Chorapang 3800 ○

Dhumzo Chhu

○ Sey Dzong

▲

Chhukhalou Chhu

Sholun Chhu

↓ to Dhunge La

○ Thongo Samba 3250

✕ *Tagulun La 4540*

✕ *Lalung La 4480*

to ← Tremo La

▲ ✕ Thangbue 4120

✕ *Thombu La 4270*

○ Jhim Din 4160

✕ *Jolu La 4420*

✕ Soman La 4486

Shana 2890 ○

to Drugyel Dzong

○ Namchaka 4000

○ Dhule Pang

Gunitsawa 2870

▲ Djo Drake 5570

✕ *Doley La 4420*

○ Hedi Gompa 2920

○ Jichu 3980

↓ to Drugyel Dzong

0 2 4 km

DAY 5

*Jhomolhari Camp (13,250ft/4040m) to
Tso Phu Lakes (14,270ft/4350m)*

Time	2–3hr
Distance	4 miles/6.5km
Altitude gain	1020ft/310m
Altitude loss	0ft/0m

There are two options for today's trek.
- The first option would be to hike to Tso Phu lakes, a relatively short trek that allows for acclimatisation in preparation for crossing the Bonte La; this is the trek described.
- The second option would be to keep going, cross the Bonte La and end up in the Soi Yakse valley.
  Make your decision depending on the conditions of your group, the pass and the weather.

Jhomolhari 7315m taken from Jangothang camp – the first and second ascents climbed from the snow col on the left

Upon leaving camp at Jhomolhari follow the trail to the river, to Jangothang, where there are two bridges. Cross the first bridge and climb the trail that zigzags up the mountainside. ◀

The second bridge leads to the pass Nyile La and on to Lingshi.

The trail climbs steeply after the bridge and ascends about 300m in a very short distance. There are breathtaking (literally!) views of Jhomolhari (23,995ft/7315m), Jhomolhari II (22,770ft/6942m), Jitchu Drake (22,925ft/6989m) and down the valley to Jhomolhari camp site.

A flower-carpeted meadow with several yak herders' tents (in spring) indicates the end of the climb; be wary of mastiffs, often tethered nearby. The rest of today's walk is flat and easy. Yaks can be seen all over the hillsides during the spring months. In the evening they are herded back to the camps for milking but also for protection against snow leopards (when we camped there in spring 2002 one baby yak was eaten, and another earlier that month). Snow leopards aim for calves and youngsters up to about four years old. About six or seven yaks are lost each year in this *geog*. There is normally a flock of Himalayan blue sheep here, high up on the rocky scree slopes.

Jangothang hamlet and Jitchu Drake 6850m

Watch your footing: the ground is uneven and full of marmot burrows. Cross the meadow to find a very clear trail again along the **Tsho Phu Chhu** (sometimes dry in spring). As the hike continues further into this beautiful valley, with towering rocky peaks of 5000m, there are spectacular views back towards Jhomolhari and Jitchu Drake, which slowly

disappear. At the head of the valley is a rockface beneath a snowy ridge. Part of tomorrow's trail can just be seen, switchbacking towards the Bonte La.

Just past several huge boulders the first lake, and first possible campsite for tonight, come into view. Further on – between the two lakes – is another, less flat, camp. There is a problem at the first camp with falling rocks, while this is less of a threat at the second camp. Sun leaves the first camp at about 1600hr. A third camp is located at the end of the second lake, well protected from wind and falling stones.

Once camp is set up, try a cup of *ngad-ja* (black tea with milk and a lot of sugar) served with many biscuits. You might also be offered *zow*, rice that has been boiled and then fried, making it puffed and crunchy. There is a mass of wildlife hereabouts: different species of duck (including the rust-coloured ruddy shelduck, a passage migrant from Tibet), partridge, blue sheep and – although you are unlikely to catch sight of one – the rare snow leopard.

THE TSHO PHU LAKES

There are various stories about the lakes. One of them tells of a pig living there, guarding the area against misfortune and respected by locals.

Warning notices prohibit fishing; in the sixties H.R.H. Prince Namgyal Wangchuk had the lakes stocked with brown trout. The possibility of allowing camping near the lakes is being discussed.

DAY 6

Tsho Phu Lakes (14,270ft/4350m) to Dhumzo Chhu or Chorapang (12,460ft/3800m) via Bonte La (16,040ft/4890m)

Time	3hr to Bonte La + 2–2.5hr down to camp
Distance	9 miles/14.5km
Altitude gain	1770ft/540m
Altitude loss	3600ft/1100m

The highest pass on this trek is crossed today, so it is vital to get an early start. The weather in the mountains tends to be most settled in the early morning, increasing the chance of spectacular views en route.

Sun reaches the first camp at 0800hr. Leaving from camp 1 the trail is level along the shore of the first lake, then begins to climb quite steeply above the second. It is quite exposed, and there are some long drops down the scree slope to the second lake. Sufferers of vertigo need to take special care. This steep part gains the top of the impressive rockface, with superb views of Jitchu Drake reflected in the lakes below (see cover picture). When crossing a mountain stream a vague trail is going left to a pass called Nachuing La (15,842ft/ 4830m), leading to Yale La/Thimphu or Lingshi. The trail to the right winds up and into an upper valley, with snow-capped peaks in the distance, leading to the Bonte La (the pass is first visible at the last 30min). This flat upper valley can be impassable in early spring due to snow.

Bonte La (16,040ft/4890m) is the highest pass of this trek. There are several cairns and prayer flags. Take time to enjoy the scenery, have a snack or put up some prayer flags. There are views of the Basingthang Peaks (around 18,000ft/ 5500m), and a big snowy peak to the south called Chatarake (Djo Drake, Jo Darkey; 18,270ft/5570m). Kanchenjunga (28,160ft/8586m), the third highest mountain in the world, is visible if you climb up the higher peak east from the pass

From Tsho Phu lakes looking northwest to Jitchu Drake (right)

Bonte La pass 4890m

(also seen from Tagulun La – see below). Tracks of snow leopards have been sighted at Bonte La.

The trail drops through a steep, narrow gully with gravel and loose rocks. Watch your step. After the initial steep descent, and passing a small grassy hill topped with a cairn (see photo page 17), the trail drops quickly to a large, grass-covered area tucked beneath an enormous rock cliff and waterfall. The trail braids into many faint trails and it is easy to lose your way. Many stone circles mark the base of former yak herders' encampments. Leave this meadow and descend very steeply through a narrow gully, below the treeline. You may catch a glimpse of the campsite at Dhumzo in the valley below.

The **Soi Yaksey valley** (Dhumzo Chhu valley, Ronse Ghon Chhu valley) is a beautiful site with impressive rock cliffs, waterfalls, deep side valleys, and snow-covered peaks. In the bottom of the canyon are some large farmhouses. According to an elderly local, 200 years ago there were 360 households in this valley. In one of the side valleys is a ruin, **Sey Dzong**, with another stone structure (tower) below it, next to the river. (Read more on Sey Dzong in Day 7.)

Continuing downstream the Soi Yaksey valley leads to two bridges, with a *chorten*, just short of camp 2 on the Jhomolhari–Lunana trek (see Trek 3).

DAY 7

*Dhumzo Chhu (12,460ft/3800m)
to Thangbue (Thombu Shong)
(13,510ft/4120m) via Tagulun La
(Takhung La) (14,880ft/4540m)*

Time	3–3.5hr up to the pass + 1hr down to camp
Distance	7 miles/11km
Altitude gain	2420ft/740m
Altitude loss	1370ft/420m

TWO ALTERNATIVE ROUTES TO DRUGYEL DZONG

From Dhumzo Chhu there are two possible alternatives to the main route to Drugyel Dzong (Days 7–9, see below): Alternative Routes 1 and 2 (see below, following Day 9). Alternative Route 1 (3 days: day 7, 8 and 9) goes to Drugyel Dzong by Jhim Din and Namchaka; Alternative Route 2 (4 days: days 7, 8, 9 and 10) goes by Jhim Din, Jichu and Daluna.

Sun reaches camp at 0700hr in spring and 0730hr in autumn.

A 100m climb from camp through rhododendron/birch/oak forest draped in moss brings you to a meadow with a huge juniper tree. Cross the meadow; round a corner to find a *chorten* and a beautiful *mani* wall. Here the trail splits up. Take the trail that *doesn't* go down to the river (don't cross the log bridge – that's for later). About 20min on a good trail above the river leads to a *chorten*. Beyond, an enormous crack gradually appears in a huge cliff, with the Sey Dzong wedged in it. The Sholun Chhu follows this valley and leads to Dhunge La (c15,410ft/4700m).

Returning to the *mani* wall, the main trail descends and crosses a bridge. Begin to climb again and reach a split in the trail: turn right for Tagulun La, and left for Lalung La. Both trails start to climb through forest. Stay close to your guide here as it is easy to take the wrong path.

SEY DZONG

Sometime before the 19th century there was a Tibetan robber, Jhakpa, who would rob the valley people at night (another story tells of many robbers coming from Tibet). In order to keep their treasures safe the community built a *dzong*-like structure in a cliff. As well as treasures the local people stored yak skin and horns here as an emergency ration. The Sey Dzong – not known as a *dzong* to locals – is an incredibly impressive structure, wedged into a huge overhanging crack in a 300m rockface, 60m above ground. The *dzong*, also used by monks, is a three-storey hermitage thought to have been abandoned at the turn of the century, and supported on a single log – it would be fascinating to know how this log, weighing several tons, was lifted up into position. The structure is well preserved, as it is protected from the rain. Inside it looks as if the monks left only recently; even cooking utensils have been left behind. The main building is connected through tunnels to several meditation caves that, from below, look like holes in the vertical wall. There are remnants of a spectacular zigzag pathway/staircase up to the *dzong*, built into the rock, but some of the wooden bridges have rotted, and a rope is needed to access the *dzong*. This is a very dangerous undertaking as the rock is very loose and the structure may collapse at any time. Two bridges get you closer to the building, but the second one has virtually rotted away.

Having turned right for Tagulun La, walk through forest, then a 200m climb follows to a prayer flag where there are some cairns and a beautiful view of the Soe Yaksey valley and surrounding mountains. Several farmhouses can be seen on the other side of the valley. A nice flat trail now skirts around the hillside covered with rhododendron bushes, changing direction slowly to the south. The **Tagulun La** (Takhung La, Taglung La; 14,880ft/4540m) gradually becomes visible on the skyline. It's a steady, steep climb, which takes around 1hr.

The pass has several cairns wrapped in prayer flags. On both sides you can climb up small hills to get a better view: Jhomolhari, Jitchu Drake and Tsheri Kang, and in the distance Kanchenjunga (28,160ft/8586m) and even Makalu (27,760ft/8463m) blocking the view to Mount Everest. Looking back is the pass crossed yesterday; looking down the other side is tonight's campsite. The trail first stays high to the left with some exciting drop offs, then winds gently downhill to camp.

The wide and grassy Thangbue valley – which has several stone huts – is busy in spring and autumn with a number of families and hundreds of yaks, horses, dogs and goats. In autumn the last herders prepare for migration to lower altitude with their yaks. Saddling male yaks is a dangerous job: as the luggage ropes are tied the yaks tend to swing round, and the yak herders have to get out of the way of their pointed horns pretty quickly.

Thangbue camp is the second highest camp for the trek. The sun leaves camp at about 16.30hr.

DAY 8

Thangbue (13,510ft/4120m)
to Shana (9480ft/2890m)
via Thombu La (14,005ft/4270m)

Time	4–5hr
Distance	9 miles/14.5km
Altitude gain	495ft/150m
Altitude loss	4525ft/1380m

The sun reaches camp at 07.00hr. Cross the valley through a swampy area to find a clear trail through rhododendron bushes that climbs steeply to **Thombu La** (14,005ft/4270m). At the pass there are three cairns and a couple of prayer flags.

To the southeast the big snowy peak Chatarake (Djo Drake, Jo Darkey; 18,270ft/5570m) dominates the skyline. From the pass, on the right, climb a little hill of 14,270ft/4350m for a great view to Kanchenjunga (28,160ft/8586m) on the Sikkim–Nepal border, as well as some peaks of more than 6500m in north Sikkim (Sentinel Peak 21,292ft/6490m; Kangchenjau 22,700/6919m; Pauhunri 23,180ft/7065m). Nearer, on the Bhutan–Tibet border, is a dramatic peak of around 17,056ft/5200m, Drake Gang. Like Jitchu Drake, Drake Gang is the residence of a local male deity, while Jhomolhari is the home of Jomo, a female deity.

The ridge walk from the pass is one of the best parts of the trek: very high above the valleys on a good trail with a beautiful view. It takes about 1hr to reach a big descent. Edelweiss grows in profusion along the trail and huge lammergeiers cruise on the warm uplifts from the valley below. The trail descends steeply for 2–3hr: watch your step and your knees!

The trail ends near the military helipad next to the Bhutanese army camp. The final night's camp is on a pleasant site by the Paro Chhu.

DAY 9

Shana (9480ft/2890m)
to Drugyel Dzong (8460ft/2580m)

Time	4hr
Distance	10.5 miles/17km
Altitude gain	260ft/80m
Altitude loss	1020ft/310m

A 4hr hike through the lovely valley, finishing at Drugyel Dzong where transport should be waiting to take you to your hotel or your next trek!

Note: on the following pages are two alternative routes/exits that are designed to bypass Gunitsawa military camp. Which of these routes will be used for trekkers, and when, is unknown at the time of writing. Please check the latest information on the Department of Tourism website **www.tourism.gov.bt**.

In 2007 neither of the alternative routes was used.

ALTERNATIVE ROUTE 1

For the first 6 days, see Trek 3, days 1–3 (or 4), and Trek 4, days 5 + 6.

DAY 7

Dhumzo Chhu (12,460ft/3800m)
to Jhim Din (13,645ft/4160m)
via Lalung La (14,695ft/4480m)

Time	3.5–4hr
Distance	not available
Altitude gain	2235ft/680m
Altitude loss	1050ft/320m

Turn left at the split (where the right fork leads to Tagulun La) above the bridge. After 10min there is another, smaller bridge. Cross this and continue climbing on a good trail to **Lalung La** (14,695ft/4480m, 2.5hr), following the valley with the Chhukhalou river. From the pass Jhim Din Camp (13,645ft/4160m) is about 1hr.

DAY 8

Jhim Din (13,645ft/4160m)
to Namchaka (c13,120ft/4000m)
via Jolu La (14,498ft/4420m)

Time	4–5hr
Distance	not available
Altitude gain	853ft/260m
Altitude loss	1378ft/420m

From Jhim Din camp the trail leads southwest over a pass (probably) called Jolu La (14,498ft/4420m) and onwards on a ridge called Pachheygan. After a while the direction changes to the south and the trail descends to camp, Namchaka (c13,120ft/4000m).

DAY 9

*Namchaka (c13,120ft/4000m)
to Drugyel Dzong (8460ft/2580m)*

Time	6hr
Distance	not available
Altitude gain	c490ft/150m
Altitude loss	c4660ft/1420m

This involves a long, steep descent of 1320m on a ridge from Namchaka camp to the settlement Mill Chhui (8790ft/2680m), from where it is 3–4hr back to Drugyel Dzong and transport.

ALTERNATIVE ROUTE 2

**For the first 6 days, see Trek 3, days 1–3 (or 4),
and Trek 4, days 5 + 6 (see maps pages 76 and 146).**

DAY 7

*Dhumzo Chhu (12,460ft/3800m) to Jhim Din (13,645ft/4160m)
via Lalung La (14,695ft/4480m)*

See Alternative Route 1 day 7. ▶

DAY 8

Jhim Din (13,645ft/4160m)
to Jichu (13,054ft/3980m)
via Soman La (14,714ft/4486m)
and Doley La (14,498ft/4420m)

Time	6–7hr
Distance	7.4 miles/12km
Altitude gain	1069ft/326m + 558ft/170m
Altitude loss	774ft/236m + 1443ft/440m

From Jhim Din the day starts with a steep, sometimes tough climb in a southerly direction to Soman La. After crossing Soman La (14,714ft/4486m) descend in southeast direction to a yak herder's hut located in the area called Dhule Pang (13,940ft/4250m). After a small climb of 164ft/50m the descent continues to an altitude of about 13,776ft/4200m. After crossing a wide valley in a half-cirque full of rhododendrons and reaching the opposite side of the valley the trail climbs up steeply to Doley La ('beautiful stones pass') (14,498ft/4420m). From Doley La descend in a southerly direction passing five small lakes and a yak herder's place called Chocheding. From here the trail turns southeast down to a yak herder's hut and a wide valley called Jichu (13,054ft/3980m).

DAY 9

Jichu (13,054ft/3980m)
to Daluna (12,923ft/3940m)
via Laname La (14,432ft/4400m

Time	3–4hr
Distance	4.3 miles/7km
Altitude gain	1378ft/420m
Altitude loss	1509ft/460m

From Jichu cross the river and follow a small stream in a southerly direction. After about 1km the trail separates from the stream to climb steeply – first in easterly direction then southwards to Laname La (14,432ft/4400m). From the pass a lake called Laname Tsho can be seen. The trail passes the lake on the west bank and leads in a southerly direction to a small stream after only a few hundred metres. Here leave the trail leading towards Suri and join another trail following the stream in a westerly direction down to a few yak herders' huts at a place called Daluna (12,923ft/3940m).

DAY 10

Daluna (12,923ft/3940m)
to Drugyel Dzong (8460ft/2580m)
via Sey Tso La (13,907ft/4240m)

Time	6–7hr
Distance	8.7 miles/14km
Altitude gain	984ft/300m
Altitude loss	5445ft/1660m

Starting from Daluna campsite the trail follows a small stream in southeast direction. The valley becomes flat and at the 'end' of the valley (13,678ft/4170m) the trail climbs steeply in a southerly direction to the Sey Tso La (13,907ft/4240m). After crossing the pass follow a stream in southeast direction (you can already see the Drugyel Dzong) and reach a deserted yak herder's hut at Chhu Rano (12,595ft/3840m). From here a steep descent follows in a more easterly direction to Chana Gompa (11,431ft/3485m); the main deity of this *gompa* is the deity of thieves. The trail leads further down in an easterly direction to a farmhouse (9447ft/2880m) and finally to the Paro Chhu. After crossing the river the trail joins the original Jhomolhari route to the Drugyel Dzong (8460ft/2580m), where the trek ends.

Note: instead of finishing at Drugyel Dzong the trek could also finish at Tiger's Nest in Paro valley (details not published here).

YAK SONG

This song is in traditional *zhung-dra* (*zhung* = main, *dra* = sound) style, considered to be authentic Bhutanese folk music, developed mainly in the 17th century. It describes the feelings of the yak Lhadar, slaughtered in connection with a ritual in Laya, the Gasa district in northwest Bhutan. It is said that later his reincarnation sung the song, the theme of which is 'the soul knows no death'.

Yak legbi Lhadar

Wonderful and handsome yak Lhadar	*So yak legbi lhadar zshel legsa*
wonderful and nice yak Lhadar	*yak legbi lhadar lhachu dhi*
No need to know my birth and dwelling	*so yak kayyul droyul shedming go*
Or, should one know about them?	*yak kayyul droyul shed go na*
High up in the snow-clad mountains	*so thow gangri karpoi zshaylu lay*
Dry fields in the high altitudes	*pang ser shog khajel thosa lu*
Where the flowers are beautiful	*so ya metog baabchu legsa mo*
There, yak my homeland is.	*yak rang gyi phayul dhilay inn*
Grasses, I eat from the mountain fields	*so tsa zawa ganglay zengo za*
Water, I drink from the clean lakes	*chhu thungma ngomchhu tsholay thung*
But, sad it is for me, Lhadar	*so na thruelni lhadar nga thruel way*
Unfortunate and pitiful me, Lhadar.	*Nga laywang che gyi lhadar mo*

This text is taken from a CD produced in Norway in 1998 by Grappa Musikkforlag, with Jigme Drukpa performing different instruments and singing. Jigme Drukpa is one of the best Bhutanese musicians regarding classical Bhutanese music. Keep your ears open and you may hear this song somewhere in the mountains.

For more information on yaks see Trek 3 day 5; Trek 3 day 6; end of Trek 7; Trek 16 day 8; Trek 18 day 7; and the photo in 'Medical Considerations' in the Introduction.

TREK 5

JHOMOLHARI–
LINGSHI–THIMPHU

Grade	moderate–demanding
Time	9 days
Distance	82.5 miles/133km
Altitude gain	11,608ft/3539m
Altitude loss	7987ft/2435m
Status	open

For the first 5 days, as far as Lingshi camp, follow the Jhomolhari–Lingshi–Lunana trek (see Trek 3). The trek could also start from Thimphu and follow the reverse route.

This description is for a 4-day trek, but it could be completed in 3 long days. It is worth staying 1 day extra in Lingshi to explore the area (see Trek 3, day 5).

DAY 6

Lingshi camp (13,150ft/4010m)
to Shodu (13,380ft/4080m) via
Yale La (Yaley La, Yeli La) (16,235ft/4950m)

Time	8–9hr
Distance	13.6 miles/22km
Altitude gain	3085ft/940m
Altitude loss	2855ft/870m

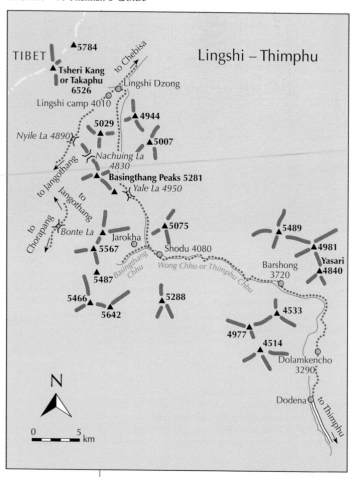

Lingshi – Thimphu

Bring sandals with you for stream crossings, or take off shoes/boots and dry your feet afterwards.

By now you should be well acclimatised and ready to cross another beautiful high pass. It is a long, hard day, so start early. Instead of crossing the Jaje Chhu (or Turquoise River) to the *dzong* take a trail through the rhododendron forest on the ridge above the camp in an easterly direction towards a small *chorten*. Turn a corner and go south into a valley with

few trees. Below flows the No Chhu or Chabey Chang Chhu (Blue River).

The climb rises steadily to reach an altitude of about 4450m, 2.5–3hr after leaving camp. Cross the main river to its right side and climb out of the main valley into a big side valley. The last part of the climb is through an area called Jimenameshing with large boulders and several switchbacks. Finally 4–4.5hr (after leaving camp) reach the big cairn on top of the **Yale La**, with views towards the snowy mountains around Lingshi and the Basingthang Peaks to the south.

Most people travelling between Lingshi and Thimphu use the Yale La, so the trail is well marked. The descent joins the Jaradinthang Chhu, which becomes the Thimphu Chhu. At around 4150m is a *chorten* from where the trail takes an easterly direction following the river. The campsite is at **Shodu** (13,380ft/4080m) just after crossing a sandy slope.

Lingshi Camp 4010m below/near Lingshi Dzong, with Jitchu Drake 6850m and Tsheri Kang 6526m in background

Side trip

Retrace your path to the *chorten*, and take the trail going west, following the Basingthang Chhu, to Basingthang (13,720ft/4183m). Basingthang means 'hidden valleys' or 'fields' in Dzongkha. This has been the base for several groups climbing peaks in the area; some commercial trekking companies arrange climbs here.

DAY 7

*Shodu (13,380ft/4080m)
to Barshong (12,200ft/3720m)*

Time	4–5hr
Distance	8.7 miles/14km
Altitude gain	426ft/130m
Altitude loss	1180ft/360m

A pleasant day
of hiking with not
too many ups
and downs.

*Lingshi villagers
prepared for the
yearly festival*

Pass a deserted military camp and follow the trail to the river through the limestone valley. Monks use the caves in the rocks; Shabdrung is said to have meditated here. Cross the bridges over the main river, which offer good views of giant rockfaces and waterfalls. Towards the end of today's trek the trail gradually ascends 130m to the Barshong Dzong ruins (12,200ft/3720m). There is a muddy campsite below the *dzong*, but you could opt to carry on for 1–1.5hr to a better campsite. **Barshong** village is very small, numbering less than half a dozen houses.

DAY 8

*Barshong (12,200ft/3720m)
to Dolamkencho (10,790ft/3290m)*

Time	4hr
Distance	9.3 miles/15km
Altitude gain	0ft/0m
Altitude loss	1410ft/430m

After crossing a side stream, Tshongjug Chhu, make a steep descent on a rocky trail ending at the Wong Chhu or Thimphu Chhu. There are several ups and downs and crossings of smaller side streams; the main river follows a very obvious, nearly perfect 90° corner, changing from west–east to the south. Reach a split in the trail; the one to the right descends to the campsite for tonight, **Dolamkencho** (Dolam Kenchha, 10,790ft/3290m). Alternatively continue up to a cairn at 11,315ft/3450m (see day 9).

DAY 9

*Dolamkencho (10,790ft/3290m) to Dodena
(8577ft/2615m) and Thimphu (45min drive)*

Time	3hr
Distance	4.3 miles/7km
Altitude gain	525ft/160m
Altitude loss	2214ft/675m

Climb back from the campsite up to the main trail to a cairn at 11,315ft/3450m, from where the route descends to a side stream (10,070ft/3070m). There are some small ups and downs followed by a couple of short steep switchbacks to descend a vertical cliff before finally reaching the last stretch to Dodena. The trail descends through bamboo forests, following the mule trail high above the river until it finally meets it again at **Dodena**. A large sign marks one of the entry/exit points of the JDNP, and a beautiful Bhutanese-style covered wooden bridge marks the path to Cheri Gompa.

TREK 6

JHOMOLHARI–LINGSHI–
LAYA–GASA–PUNAKHA

Grade	moderate
Time	14 days
Distance	125 miles/201.5km
Altitude gain	17,069ft/5204m
Altitude loss	23,042ft/7025m
Status	open

For the first 10 days up to Laya see Trek 3.

This is sometimes referred to as the Laya trek and is one of Bhutan's finest. The route starts from Paro–Drugyel Dzong and continues onwards to Jhomolhari camp. It then goes via Lingshi to Laya and exits via Gasa and Punakha. Trekking parties normally have a 1-day halt in Laya.

DAY 12

*Laya (12,465ft/3800m)
to Koina (10,627ft/3240m)*

Time	6hr
Distance	10 miles/16km
Altitude gain	0ft/0m
Altitude loss	1837ft/560m

The trail leaves Laya through fields and clusters of houses. Descend through the village entrance porch or arch *chorten* (*khonying*) – housing protective deities – and pass through

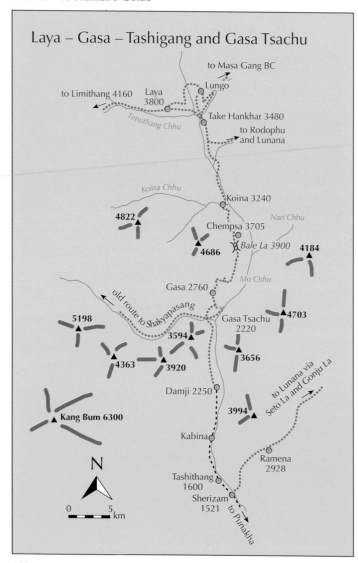

Laya – Gasa – Tashigang and Gasa Tsachu

some beautiful woodland. Cross two large rivers, Zamto Nangi Chhu and Togtserkhagi Chhu, both fed by Masang Gang glacier. With luck Masang Gang (23,600ft/7194m) will be visible; this is where the trek to Masang Gang base camp starts. The army camp **Take Hankhar** (Takchenkhar) is on the other side of the Togtserkhagi Chhu (1hr from Laya), and trekking permits are checked here.

After the army camp, descend on a good trail. Once you reach the bottom of the valley (10,496ft/3200m) a good, wide, flat trail follows the Mo Chhu. On the opposite side a bigger stream, Chhachesage Chhu, joins the main river. Turn into a small side valley and cross the Bahtlung Chhu or Rodophu Chhu (10,660ft/3250m) on a cantilever bridge. Continue on and cross another cantilever bridge at a cave (Tongshi Zam) over the Mo Chhu (10,463ft/3190m). The cave has a ladder going up to it, and is used for shelter.

Several steep climbs follow, negotiating cliffs where the gorge narrows and a huge cave is located. This area is called Chusom. The first 12m or so of the cliffs are polished smooth, with beautiful mosses and ferns above, waving in the endless fine spray of water. Some of the climbs are hard, and range between 100 and 200m.

At the end of the final climb (150m) the trail rounds a ridge into the side valley, with Koina Chhu and **Koina** camp below (10,627ft/3240m). The Koina Chhu is another tributary of the Mo Chhu and emerges in a jet from a narrow gorge.

The true Bhutanese name for Koina camp is Ku Ngel Nangsha, meaning 'body rest place', the place where Shabdrung rested; *ku* is a respectful Dzongkha form for the word body.

The campsite at Koina is muddy, with no proper space to put up tents. However there is a hut, which is clean and well looked after by a caretaker. There are also two good toilets in a separate solid-looking building. Bears and takins have been seen here.

The takin, the national animal of
Bhutan (see box Trek 3, day 8)

DAY 13

Koina (10,627ft/3240m) to Gasa hot springs/
Gasa Tsachu (7282ft/2220m)
via Bale La (Bari La) (12,792ft/3900m)

Time	3hr up + 3hr down
Distance	7.4 miles/12km
Altitude gain	2165ft/660m
Altitude loss	5510ft/1680m

After a damp night at Koina cross the Koina Chhu and start a long climb through an enormous subtropical forest. If misty the atmosphere can become very eerie, and the gorge transforms into something out of a fairytale. On the other side of the gorge is one of the few places in the world where the tiger and snow leopard uses the same territory. Around 1–1.5hr before the pass a clearing in the forest is reached where there is a camping place, **Chempsa** (12,152ft/3705m), more often used by those trekking in the opposite direction.

The valley gets a lot of rain during the monsoon, resulting in a botanical paradise.

Another 1.5hr of climbing gains **Bale La** (Bari La, Pare La; 12,792ft/3900m). Bale La is actually higher then Laya! The pass is located on a ridge and decorated with the usual cairn and some prayer flags. After a short flat trail a long descent to **Gasa** village starts. All of a sudden a magical view appears through the bamboo forest: Kang Bum mountain (c21,320ft/6500m), towering high above Gasa Dzong and village.

Gasa Dzong (9053ft/2760m) is the last district head office in Bhutan not yet connected to a main road. There are several shops in the centre of the one-street village; the first shop on the left has a telephone, and there is a restaurant on the right. For more details on Gasa Dzong see Trek 11, day 3. ▸

For trekking out to Tashithang and Punakha see Trek 11.

From Gasa it is 1hr of steep descent to **Gasa Tsachu** (hot springs).

TREK 7

MASA GANG BASE CAMP (16,480ft/5025m) FROM LAYA AND BACK

Grade	demanding
Time	3 or 4 days
Distance	18.6 miles/30km
Altitude gain	1870ft/570m
Altitude loss	2034ft/620m
Status	double check if open

This trek can be combined with Trek 3, but can also be undertaken as a separate trek starting and finishing from Punakha.

From Laya a beautiful 3- or 4-day trek (round trip) follows the Togtserkhagi Chhu valley northeast near the Tibetan border. Camping for 2 nights at Masa Gang (base) camp allows deeper exploration into the valleys and the opportunity to witness an almost 360° panorama of one the most impressive mountain scenes in Bhutan complete with jagged snow-capped peaks and hanging glaciers. (For a photo of Masa Gang, see 'Geology' section in the Introduction.)

The trail is in good condition and goes up to the Toma La/Ya La (17,550ft/5350m) and the Wagye La (17,385ft/5300m), two well-used passes crossing into Tibet.

Masang G(K)ang (22,304ft/6800m or 23,600ft/7194m or 23,615ft/7200m) is the holy mountain of the powerful Masang clan, the original inhabitants of this region who came from southern Tibet and allegedly ruled during prehistoric times. Masa Gang was climbed by a Japanese expedition in 1985 and unsuccessfully attempted in 1993 by a British–American team.

The camp used for trekking is not the actual Masa Gang base camp being used by the expeditions.

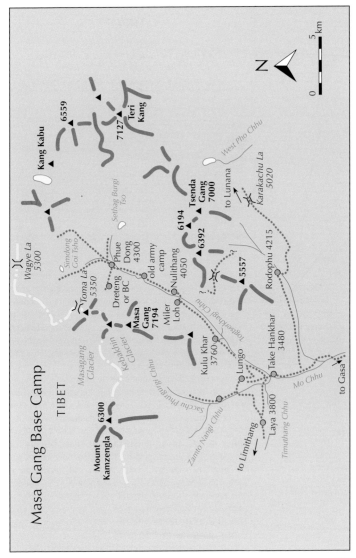

Masa Gang Base Camp

DAY 1

Laya (12,465ft/3800m)
to Take Hankhar (11,415ft/3480m)
to Kulu Khar (12,333ft/3760m)
or further to Nulithang (13,285ft/4050m)

Time	4hr or 7hr
Distance	9.3 miles/15km or 13 miles/21km
Altitude gain	918ft/280m or 1870ft/570m
Altitude loss	1050ft/320m

Alternative route: Laya–Lungo–Kulu Khar (7hr) – moderate (see below)

From Laya (12,465ft/3800m) descend through the village arch *chorten*, and on through forest, crossing the first river Zamto Nangi Chhu. Carry on to the second big river, Togtserkhagi Chhu (Takche Kar Chhu), but don't cross here. The trail to Masa Gang turns left following the right side of this river (1hr from Laya). The army camp **Take Hankhar** (Takchenkhar) is just on the other side of the second river. From here it is possible to get a first glimpse of Masang Gang mountain (23,600ft/7194m).

The Togtserkhagi Chhu is fed by Masang Gang glacier and other high mountains at the end of the valley. Follow the good trail through beautiful forest parallel to the river. The climb is steep for 1hr, to Tashi Makhang. Yaks and Himalayan blue sheep graze above the trail; beware of falling stones. About 45min after the second bridge an alternative trail appears left at 12,038ft/3670m (see below).

After 2hr walking the valley widens and an area called Yashi Mekhong is reached. In the next hour you pass through two settlements with potentially nasty dogs! Just after a ruined army camp there is a good possible campsite at **Kulu Khar** (12,333ft/3760m). If the itinerary started from Punakha/Gasa, a night here would help with acclimatisation. If the alternative route is followed this is the camp to use after a 7hr trek (see below). Opposite is a high valley with a river and waterfall, Daktir Bungi Chhu.

It will take another 2.5–3hr to reach a good campsite on a decent trail. Climb for 200m to get over a landslide area, and carry on through beautiful forest. After 2hr Masa Gang appears in a side valley to the left. There is a settlement just above the trail, Miler Loh (Zomishie; c13,285ft/4050m). The Togtserkhagi Chhu will now be out of sight; an important but indefinite split appears in the trail, and leads to a bridge. Instead of crossing a side stream, follow the trail that goes down to the river and cross the bridge in a narrow eroded valley, next to a big boulder.

The river changes its name to Lungling Thethagi Chhu (Nung Chi Tang). Camp is just 10min after crossing the bridge in a flat area with boulders, **Nulithang** (13,285ft/4050m). Masa Gang summit is just opposite the camp, and Tsenda Gang Peak (22,960ft/7000m) is visible by walking back 5min. The valley has little snow and/or rain, and is used for winter grazing by yak herders from Laya.

Sun sets at 1630hr in fall.

Alternative route via Lungo

There is an alternative beautiful trail from Laya to Kulu Khar (or Nulithang) camp via Lungo village.

Lungo village, in a valley east of Laya, looking north to Mount Kamzengla 6300m

From Laya ascend east/northeast above the last cluster of houses. Climb up the ridge and come to a high-altitude meadow. Cross this meadow (trail not always clear) and find a good trail going around a couple of ridges, and crossing some small streams. The final ridge is passed when the trail starts descending in a forest at an altitude of 12,333ft/3760m on a good trail leading north. The Zamto Nangi Chhu is flowing in the valley bottom; Lungo is on the opposite side. Descend to a bridge (11,545ft/3520m) over the river and climb steeply to **Lungo** village. Lungo is a rather big, beautiful village with a *lhakhang* and a small school. There are several big houses, some of which are newly built, and it is hardly visited by foreigners.

At the end of the valley are impressive (mainly nameless) snow-covered peaks of more than 6000m forming the border with Tibet (Mount Kamzengla 20,664ft/6300m). Going up north the valley splits: one valley follows the Kamgigi Chhu in a northwestly direction, and the Sacchu Phurgurgi Chhu goes northeast, leading to the Kebakhin glacier and Masa Gang.

From Lungo follow a good trail south through forest to a ridge. Turning a corner at 12,430ft/3790m the army camp is visible below. The trail descends into the valley in a north–northwest direction and Masa Gang and Tsenda Gang become visible. It is 45min downhill to meet the trail coming from the army camp (12,038ft/3670m). Camp at Kulu Khar to avoid the day being too long. ▸

If the itinerary starts from Gasa, goes to the army camp and then continues up to Masa Gang base camp, it is possible to trek from Nulithang in 1 day to Laya via Lungo village (7–8hr).

DAY 2

Day of exploring at Nulithang (13,285ft/4050m)

Sun reaches camp at 0900hr. There are various options for exploring:

1 **The hill opposite camp** Go back to the bridge crossed yesterday, cross the side stream coming down next to the two houses, and find an indefinite, steep, uphill trail. Climb for 2hr and Masa Gang (23,600ft/7194m) will be almost in reach! Looking back the view towards Tsenda Kang (22,960ft/7000m) is impressive.

You can opt for one more night here or trek back to the army camp. There is plenty to do to jusify an extra night or two.

2 **Up the valley** Follow the river, keeping on the same side as camp. Less than 1hr will bring you to an **old army camp** ruin on top of the moraine of the Taki Gang glacier (this can be seen from the old camp). To the east the glacier descends from the Tsenda Kang massif. The trail leads around the moraine to another good, small camp with stunning views towards Masa Gang and Tsenda Kang. About 10min later a bridge crosses the Lungling Thethagi Chhu, with a yak herders' camp on the other side. Continue for about 30min along the river to another camp site in a meadow, **Phue Dong** or Phung Dorgam (14,104ft/4300m) – possible if you want to stay longer and explore further up the valley – with old military dugouts from the time Tibetans were invading Bhutan.

2a From **Phue Dong** one trail leads to **Masa Gang base camp** (16,480ft/5025m) on a yak pasture called **Dreteng**. About 30min further, again with traces of military fortifications, a big valley on the left leads to the pass **Toma La** (5–6hr climbing with some steep sections): there are actually two passes very close to

In Masa Gang valley – Laya woman with baby

each other, Toma La (Tomu La) and Ya La. Since these are border passes, crossing is not allowed.

2b From **Phue Dong** to the north a bridge has to be crossed over the river coming down the Toma La. The trail leads to a lake, Simdong Goi Tso. From the bridge a long, steep trail leads to the well-used pass **Wagye La** (c17,385ft/5300m, 5hr), the old route to Lhasa. This valley is one of the more impressive, with amazing mountain scenery. ◂

2c Going northeast from **Phue Dong** you reach another fork going east–south and leading to a big lake, Sethag Burgi Tso (Sistiha Phugi Tso) below the enormous Tsenda Gang range. From the split after Phue Dong at c15,910ft/4850m there are a couple of trails going east–northeast, all of them increasingly less clear. Huge mountains surround you, with the Tsenda Gang range dominating to the south.

Shabdrung Ngawang Namgyal used the Wagye La pass to cross from Tibet into Laya and Bhutan. Let's hope that one day the crossing of this pass will be part of an exciting itinerary!

DAY 3

Nulithang (13,285ft/4050m)
to Take Hankhar (11,415ft/3480m)

Retrace your steps out of the valley back to the army camp (5–6hr).

YAKS

They weigh half a ton and cost a small fortune – over $500. They are nearly as tall as a man. Their tank-like bodies and stocky legs are almost completely hidden by a shaggy, luxuriant coat of long black. When they walk they hold their heads low as if they are sniffing their way through the snow, which is what they are doing. They blow hard and produce a curious grunting noise, responsible for their unattractive name *bos gruinens* ('grumbling ox'). They are shy and well-behaved animals, capable of climbing steep mountain slopes and finding their way through snow at altitudes where no other beast of burden would dare to go. The yak, despite his clumsy appearance, is a secure luggage-carrier. Yaks that get tired will dig out somewhere to rest: look out for sandy pits, like bunkers on a golf course, on the mountainsides.

At elevations over 3000m in Bhutan, yak production has been – and continues to be – the main source of livelihood for people inhabiting this rugged landscape. Yak owners/herders are known as *brokpas* in central and eastern Bhutan, *jops* in western Bhutan, *lakhaps* in the west–central region and *dakpas* in the remote *gewogs* of Merak and Sakteng under Trashigang Dzongkhag. These names all mean 'pastoralists'. The yak is the 'camel of the snows', a multipurpose animal providing milk, meat, draught and manure. It also adds to the aesthetic value of the Himalayas. Without it one cannot imagine how humans could survive in this beautiful yet hostile region.

The yak is found over a large area of Central Asia, from Mongolia to Nepal, and is well known for its ability to survive high in the mountains. It can survive sleeping out in temperatures as low as –40°C/°F due to its high fat content and is very resistant to disease, unlike lowland cattle and buffalo. Its coat has three layers: the coarse outer fur is used primarily for tent-making, the middle layer for ropes, and the soft under fur for blankets and cloaks.

Unlike Nepal, yaks in Bhutan are not usually crossbred with local cows, so most are massive animals with thick furry coats and impressive sharp horns. The name for a yak in Bhutan is pronounced *yuck* for the male and *jim* or *dri* for the female. The female is known as a *nak* in Nepal.

True wild yak are only found in Tibet. An adult male wild yak can weigh twice as much as a domesticated yak, approximately 1000kg. The present domestic yak is descended from wild yak caught and tamed by ancient Quiang people in the Quaiantang and other areas of northern Tibet about 10,000 years ago. Yaks are not herded in northwest Bhutan, where they are semi-wild.

Uses

In many parts of Tibet a good riding yak (preferably without horns) is valued at three times the price of a horse. Surefooted, able to sniff out and avoid crevasses on glaciers, immune to snowblindness, capable of bulldozing through snowdrifts, the yak's ponderous, heavy gait provides a remarkably smooth ride. The yak is used for ploughing and as a threshing machine that tramples the barley harvest with its heavy hooves, and can carry twice the load of a horse. Being ruminants, yaks have a great advantage over horses in that they need not waste hours grazing. They gulp their daily ration of hay in the morning and spend their time on the road chewing their cud. The same happens at night when they chew their dinner (sometimes rather noisily near the campsite!).

For those who can afford it, yak meat is delicious when fresh. Dark red because of the wealth of red blood cells produced at high altitudes it is, according to many experts, healthier to eat than beef. In Bhutan the best yak meat comes ▸

◄ from Haa. Most Himalayan citizens eat it dried, reduced in the cold air to a ropey substance. Yak skin is used as a blanket or carpet, but also as an emergency ration: the hairs are burnt and scraped off, the skins cooked and nibbled on.

Yak wool is used by herders to make tents, rope, carpets, awnings for monasteries, bags and boot soles. Not only are yak hides used to make shoes and other apparel, they are also sewn together and drawn over willow branches to form the hulls of coracles, the only boats found in Tibet. Yak hair is used as 'sunglasses' to protect the eyes from snowblindness.

The trimming of yaks' hair is quiet a spectacular scene. Two strong men have to get the yak on its side, holding it down, and a third person trims the hair with a big pair of scissors. Hair is of two different qualities: soft inner hair is used for sweaters, and the rough, bristly outer hair is spun by the nomads and used for making yak wool tent material.

Yaks' milk can be drunk; the *dri* produces milk the whole year through. Making butter out of milk takes about 1hr of churning. Yak butter is wrapped in either a big rhododendron leaf or those of the medicinal plant *rheum nobile*. Butter serves as fuel to light up tents and honour the statues in holy shrines. It is also meared on faces to keep the skin from drying out. Fresh butter is used in tea, which is a Himalayan staple food; yak milk contains about twice the amount of fat found in cattle milk. The butter can be rancid, giving the tea a different taste. If there is no butter available oil might be used. In Bhutan they call this *susha* or *sud-ja*. The rock-hard balls of brick-like tea come from inland China (these bricks were once used as currency). The tea will be boiled till it obtains a deep brown colour.

Smoked yak cheese, so hard a hammer can't break it, is sucked and chewed upon for hours by Tibetans; it keeps for a century when dried and smoked, and is occasionally fed to horses when the grass is running out. Fresh cheese can be a delicious snack; in hard form it can taste like strong, spicy chewing gum.

Yak butter wrapped in 'rheum noble' leaves and two yak cheeses

Smoked yak cheese: the chewing gum for Bhutanese travellers

Of all these services to man, none compares to the yak's greatest gift: its dung. All over the Himalayas yak dung is dried and burned for warmth in the extreme winter cold. The dung smells cleaner and sweeter than that of domestic cattle because the yak lives only on wild grasses.

The stomach of a yak is used to store butter and fat. The skull, complete with horns, is erected on house walls to keep bad spirits away. The horns have several magical uses; they are also used for decoration and as an emergency ration: scraped, cooked and then chewed on. The tail is used as a broom, or in a bundle as an offering attached to the summit of prayer poles. Yaks are sometimes seen decorated with small shelves. The shelves are a hiding place for the 'life spirit' in case evil spirits should appear.

White yaks are 'holy' (and more valuable) then the normal black yaks. There are several varieties of yak in Tibet and neighbouring countries, and although they have not been rigorously studied, there are at least three major types: square-headed, long-nosed yak, and miniature. There also exist various hybrid yaks crossed with regular cows, called *dzo* (female *dzomo*).

Male yaks will be sent far away, high up in the valleys, separated from the females and calves during summer. When the yaks are collected in the afternoon they will be staked out on a single rope, with side ropes at intervals. The calves will be separated from the mothers and milking will start. During the night the yaks will stay near camp guarded by the dogs, to prevent calves being taken by snow leopards.

A yak story

How the yak got his long hair and why the buffalo has so little and is always looking up.

Once, the water buffalo was hairy, and a good friend of the yak, and they both lived in the lower regions. They both loved salt, but there wasn't much around. The yak said he would go to Tibet to get some if the water buffalo would loan him his hair so he could survive the cold. The water buffalo agreed. The yak went off and never returned. To this day, the water buffalo holds his head up, searching around, awaiting the return of the yak with his hair and salt.

Note: read more on yaks in Trek 3 day 5; Trek 3 day 6; end of Trek 4; Trek 16 day 8; Trek 18 day 7; and see photo in medical section of Introduction.

TREK 8

DRUKPATH

Grade	moderate–demanding
Time	6 days
Distance	30 miles/48km
Altitude gain	7400ft/2256m
Altitude loss	6271ft/1912m
Status	open

A popular route because of its length and its proximity to Paro and Thimphu.

This 4- or 5-day trek is wonderfully varied: beautiful scenery, good views of snow-capped Himalayan peaks, a monastery high up in the mountains, and a visit to a *dzong*. There are campsites next to the monastery, and also near some beautiful lakes. There are several possible campsites besides the ones listed in the route description, so make sure that you know where your horsemen are aiming for, in case they push on to a different camp!

After the initial climb the route is not too hard and, if needed, there is access down to a road from several spots. Part of the route follows the original mule track that linked the Thimphu and Paro valleys, and eventually connected Bhutan to the Indian border.

The trek begins at high altitude. Plan some extra days in Paro or Thimphu to acclimatise.

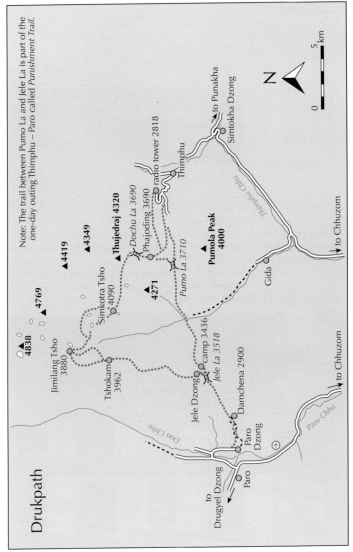

Drukpath

Note: The trail between Pumo La and Jele La is part of the one-day outing Thimphu – Paro called *Punishment Trail.*

to Punakha

Simtokha Dzong

Thimphu

radio tower 2818

Dochu La 3690

Phajoding 3690

▲ Thujedraj 4320

▲ 4349

▲ 4419

Pumo La 3710

Pumola Peak 4000

▲ 4271

Gida

to Chhuzom

Simkota Tsho 4090

▲ 4769

▲ 4838

Jimilang Tsho 3880

Tshokam 3962

camp 3436

Jele La 3518

Jele Dzong

Damchena 2900

Paro Dzong

Paro

to Drugyel Dzong

to Chhuzom

Doo Chhu

Paro Chhu

Thimphu Chhu

N

0 5 km

DAY 1

*Paro by bus to the
National Museum (8036ft/2450m) to
campsite below Jele Dzong (11,270ft/3436m)*

Time	4–5hr
Distance	5 miles/8km
Altitude gain	3503ft/1068m
Altitude loss	269ft/82m

Carry extra water since there is a major altitude gain on today's route, and no water sources.

House in Paro valley

At the museum you will meet your trekking staff, the horsemen and pack animals. At the start of a trek the staff always takes some time to get organised, so don't be in a rush to arrive early at camp – the luggage will undoubtedly be behind you!

Today's trek climbs non-stop for over 1065m, before dropping down over 80m to camp. This is a major effort at this altitude, so take your time and drink as much as

possible. The trail winds its way steeply through blue pine forest and around several farmhouses and fenced apple orchards (some royal), and crosses a dusty road – mainly used during the apple harvest – several times. The area is called Taschhugang. Along the way Kuenga Lhakhang (8660ft/2640m) is passed. **Damchena** (9510ft/2900m) marks the end of the dusty road, near a big stone house.

After 1hr or so of steady climbing there will be nice views over the Paro valley. Visible above is **Jele Dzong** (Jili Dzong), located on top of the ridge and surprisingly nearby. At 9825ft/2995m, after 1.5–2hr trekking, the route passes a long *mani* wall in a big flat grassy field – a possible campsite (Damche Gom) but with poor water sources. Near here the route joins the one coming in from Dambji on the east side of the Doo Chhu at 7544ft/2300m. Climb steadily up now through blue pine, fir and bamboo; at around 3235m a gigantic hemlock tree, over 600 years old, overshadows the trail.

The trail continues steeply up through the forest. Just before reaching a small pass (11,540ft/3518m) below the *dzong*, the route opens up a bit, and there may be some yaks with their herders and dogs. Tonight's small campsite (11,270ft/3436m) is a little way down from the pass. It can be cold here because of the wind, which often picks up in the afternoon. You may be able to hear the monks playing instruments in the *lhakhang* during one of their prayer sessions.

DAY 2

Campsite below Jele Dzong (11,270ft/3436m) to Tshokam (12,995ft/3962m)

Time	4–5hr
Distance	5.5 miles/9km
Altitude gain	1726ft/526m
Altitude loss	0ft/0m

Today is not hard – camp could be reached by lunchtime – and there are no major ascents for the rest of the trek.

From camp, climb back to the ridge and the small pass leading to the *dzong* (11,790ft/3595m).

JELE DZONG

The *dzong* is worth a visit; it's a very impressive fort, surrounded by many prayer flags, in an even more impressive and exposed location. It has been renovated recently – it takes a battering from the elements (note the iron cables holding down the roof). The views are great, looking towards Paro far below, while in the distance stand snowy peaks on the border with Tibet, including Jhomolhari (23,995ft/7315m) in the centre.

A few elderly monks and student monks live here. Do not be surprised if you are not allowed to visit the *lhakhang*, but do remove your shoes if you are allowed into the chapel. In the *lhakhang* – which is quite big, and has some huge statues – a piece of paper explains the history of the site in both Dzongkha and English. ▶

Prayer flags

◄ Leave a small donation behind. Once this is placed on the altar, you might be offered some holy water: open your left hand to receive it, sip a little and pour the rest over your head. You may be offered dice on a plate; throw the dice and the lama will say if you have thrown a lucky number – nine is best. There may be monks playing bone horns, accompanying the prayers. A good human thighbone is worth up to 30,000 ngultrum ($600) – and this is before a silver casting is wrapped around it!

The valley to the east of Jele Dzong is Gidakom or Bemang Rong Chhu (higher up, Bimelang Chhu). At the village of Gida is a hospital that traditionally treated leprosy and tuberculosis. About halfway down this valley a forestry road winds up and gets quite close to the *dzong*. At the end of the valley are several lakes.

Leaving the *dzong* walk north for about 10min on the ridge – with a beautiful view – before disappearing into forest, which looks rather bleak as a result of damage by bark beetles. Cross over to the easterly side of the ridge at 12,135ft/3700m. Go up and around a small peak, a steep 100m ascent to an altitude of 12,300ft/3750m. Looking back you see part of the Paro valley and the large Doo Chhu side valley. To the south, the Dagala range is visible (another trekking area). After 3hr pass a possible campsite (Dorjo Lakha or Jangchu Lakha, 12,365ft/3770m). After another 1hr climb, the better campsite, **Tshokam** (12,995ft/3962m), is reached, just after a small saddle.

DAY 3

*Tshokam (12,995ft/3962m)
to Jimilang Tsho (12,726ft/3880m)*

Time	6–7hr
Distance	6 miles/10km
Altitude gain	700ft/213m (or 1475ft/450m if opting for the higher trail at the end)
Altitude loss	965ft/295m

The pack animals take a different route today because there are a few stretches that would be difficult for them.

The ridge walk followed by the trekkers is about 2hr longer than the pack animals' route, and more spectacular. Weather permitting, there are several views of snowy peaks to the north and a grand view down into the valleys. Once again, we proceed in a northerly direction most of the day. Looking east tonight's camp, as well as some of tomorrow's route, is visible.

Climb gently for several hours to reach a small pass at about 13,350ft/4070m. The trail has loose stones, so watch your step. After a short descent there is a small campsite at Labanah, 'between two passes'. Continue along the ridge to the next small pass (13,380ft/4080m), with a view north to Jhomolhari (23,995ft/7315m). Down below, several monasteries are visible at the far end of the valley: Paro Dop Gensakha Gompa, Sharadango Gompa farther north, and Ragyo Chiwokha Gompa above that. Keep climbing slowly on the ridge. On the opposite side there is a view of Jimilang Thso.

At 13,695ft/4175m a small stone shelter next to a small lake is reached, with another view to Jhomolhari (a nice possible campsite). There are many small lakes here, shelters for yak herders, and yak trails. Two possible trails lead to the large sacred lake **Jimilang Tsho** (Bimelang Tsho). One is higher up and not always easy to find, and accesses the lake from the east. The other descends at first, then climbs again and reaches the lake from the west. The higher trail is a more

Little girl travelling

challenging loop and can be overgrown; despite this, this is recommended. The area above the lake to the east is especially remote.

At the east side of the lake is a good campsite (12,726ft/3880m). The lake has plenty of trout; locals are often seen standing in the cold water up to their knees, using bamboo spears to catch trout at the outlet of the lake. Ask your trekking company if they can arrange a fishing permit. There is a *chorten* at the lake.

189

DAY 4

Jimilang Tsho (12,726ft/3880m)
to Simkotra Tsho (13,415ft/4090m)

Time	3–4hr
Distance	4.5 miles/7km
Altitude gain/loss	several small ups and downs

A beautiful day of easy hiking through glorious high mountain country.

Walk around the lake to its far (western) end. There is a split in the trail. One branch is that used by pack animals; the other soon starts to climb up above the lake. There is some steep climbing through bushes, but later good views will open up. An exposed cliff trail leads to a small saddle (13,450ft/4100m). From here, you can see the next lake below (Janye Tsho or Jane Tsho; 12,975ft/3956m; 1.5–2hr), a nice campsite, which may be occupied by yak herders.

From the lake a wide stone path between rhododendron bushes traverses a valley with a small lake below. There are lakes just above, Dungtsho Tsho and Dungtsho Sama, regarded as male and female. The local people believe that the second (female) lake has a powerful spirit, who gets easily provoked if anything dirty gets near the lake. If this happens, bad weather will ensue, which only can be stopped by endless prayers.

Climb up a ridge and look for a cairn. After 1hr a viewing point at 13,610ft/4150m is reached, with a lake below, **Simkotra Tsho** (13,415ft/4090m), which has some stone ruins nearby. This is tonight's campsite.

DAY 5

*Simkotra Tsho (13,415ft/4090m)
to Phajoding (12,103ft/3690m)
or Thimphu radio tower (9245ft/2818m)*

Time	5hr
Distance	6 miles/10km
Altitude gain	755ft/230m to the viewing point
Altitude loss	1330ft/405m to Phajoding (or 4190ft/1277m to radio tower)

The trail is good, but there are seven minor climbs to small passes before you finally look down to Phajoding monastery and Thimphu. Monks frequently pass here on their way to meditate at the sacred lake Jimilang Tsho.

When climbing up pass number five – Thujedraj – Gangkar Punsum (24,750ft/7546m) becomes visible. If you are lucky with the weather, the rest of the Bhutan Himalayas can be seen. From the pass, climb 250m up to a small rocky outlook (14,170ft/4320m) on the left side. It is covered with

Tonight there is a choice: camp next to Phajoding monastery (with a view over the Thimphu valley), or continue all the way down to Thimphu.

Thimphu: left SAARC building and right Tashi Tshodzong

191

prayer flags, and there are also traces of fires on top. This place was formerly used for sky burials, and has an incredible view over the whole of the Bhutan Himalayas.

After this excursion descend a little, then climb to pass number six (13,515ft/4120m). The final pass is **Dochu La** (13,430ft/4095m), and is very windy. There is a good view over the last part of the trek: a steep descent to Phajoding monastery and finally Thimphu.

Camping at **Phajoding** (12,100ft/3690m) is definitely worthwhile.

PHAJODING MONASTERY

Togden Pajo, a Tibetan yogi looking for a place for meditation, founded the site in the 13th century. Most of the buildings were constructed by the 9th Je Khenpo, Shakya Rinchen, in the first half of the 18th century. The 16th Je Khenpo was also involved in some of the buildings, and the king's secretary has donated money for one of the more recent temples, built in honour of Padma Sambava.

Phajoding is not just one complex. The many buildings spread out over the mountainside include *lhakhangs/gompas*, monk quarters, numerous meditation centres, and even a guesthouse. The meditation centres may have a branch of a juniper tree outside, indicating that they do not want to be disturbed. There is also a sacred cave, with big ice stalactites during the colder months of the year. Phajoding is one of the monasteries visited by Thimphu people for special *pujas*, which provide funds for the monasteries. Try to visit the meditation centre, which hangs on the side of a cliff at 12,955ft/3950m.

DAY 6

*Phajoding (12,103ft/3690m)
to radio tower (9245ft/2818m)
or Mothithang (8395ft/2560m)*

Time	2–3hr
Distance	2.5 miles/4km
Altitude gain	0ft/0m
Altitude loss	2860ft/872m or 3705ft/1130m

From Phajoding monastery there are three trails to Thimphu.

- One stays high and climbs to a pass, Pumo La (12,170ft/3710m). From Pumo La a trail leads down to the Mothithang youth centre.
- The other two trails start with the same steep descent. At 10,965ft/3343m you arrive at a big split in the trail.

a) Straight down is a steep route past to the queen's compound and the wooden buildings of the royal staff, continuing on to the Mothithang youth centre. This trail descends 250m more than the alternate route b).

b) The other route goes left at the split, and follows a more gentle trail descending slowly through thick forest until Chhokhortse Gompa (9870ft/3010m) in a clearing. Just before the *gompa* there is a model of a hot stone bath in the ground. A steep, 200m descent leads to the radio tower, past hundreds of prayer flags put up by people from Thimphu. This is the transmission tower for Bhutan's radio station BBS. From here, drive down to Thimphu, passing the Thimphu Zoo, where some takins can be seen.

Get up early, and you might have a clear view of the Eastern Himalayas.

High-altitude flower Saussurea gossypiphora

TREK 9

DAGALA TREK –
AND EXTENSION TO DAGANA

Grade	moderate
Time	5 days (Dagana extension 7 days)
Distance	23 miles/37km (Dagana distance not available)
Altitude gain	7810ft/2381m (7347ft/2240m)
Altitude loss	9450ft/2881m (11,283ft/3440m)
Status	Dagala open (Dagana extension: double check if open)

This trek is also called the 'Dagala Thousand Lakes Trek' (Dagala is the mountain goddess who overlooks the lakes).

Note: ongoing road construction will shorten the Dagala trek in the Geynitsang Chhu valley.

Are there really 1000 lakes? An elderly horsemen from the area heard from his parents that there are actually 105 lakes (or maybe 108 – a holy figure in Buddhism) in the area; some stories say that there were more than 1000 in the past.

The trek has several start/end points. There are exits at: Talakha Gompa; Serbithang; Wangdi (see day 5); Dochu La; Daga in Dagana; and from after the first pass in a westerly direction into the valley Labtsakachhu and Jenjela, finishing about 2km south of Chhuzom near Lebchi.

The following two routes are described:
- From Geynikha to Simtokha: allow 4–5 days. A rest day is strongly recommended at one of the higher camps to explore the area.
- From Geynikha to Daga: allow 6 days. Again a rest day is recommended; add 1 day for driving from Daga to Thimphu: 8 days.

Both routes are rarely travelled now. The latter was formerly used by people who came over from the south, from Daga, to bring cattle to Thimphu for selling. It was also a cattle migration route. However, the track is well established due to heavy traffic in the old days.

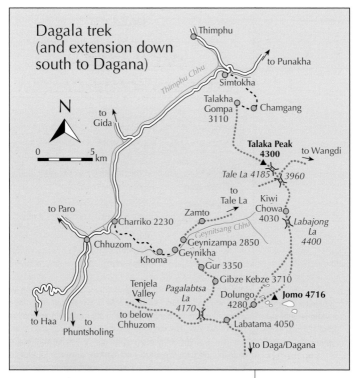

Dagala trek
(and extension down
south to Dagana)

N

0 ————— 5 km

to Thimphu

Thimphu Chhu

to Punakha

Simtokha

Talakha Gompa 3110

Chamgang

to Gida

Talaka Peak 4300

to Wangdi

Tale La 4185 | 3960

to Tale La

Kiwi Chowa 4030

Labajong La 4400

to Paro

Charriko 2230

Zamto

Geynitsang Chhu

Chhuzom

Khoma

Geynizampa 2850
Geynikha

Gur 3350

Gibze Kebze 3710

Jomo 4716

Tenjela Valley

Pagalabtsa La 4170

to below Chhuzom

Dolungo 4280

Labatama 4050

to Haa | to Phuntsholing

to Daga/Dagana

At the beginning of the Dagala trek

DAY 1

*Thimphu to Geynikha – 2hr drive from
Thimphu (7545ft/2300m)
or Paro (7545ft/2300m);
trekking to Geynizampa (9350ft/2850m)*

Time	1–1.5hr drive on feeder road (if impassable, add 2–3hr to walk) + 1hr walking
Distance	1.25 miles/2km
Altitude gain	360ft/110m
Altitude loss	360ft/110m

It takes 1.5hr to drive (and 620m of ascent) from the main road to the end of the dirt road, where the valley opens up.

The valley has many settlements and houses. Many of the houses are big, indicating wealth, and there are many *gompas* and *lhakhangs*: Chhizi Gompa; Gyemasabu Lhakhang; a *gompa* at Zanglekha; a *gompa/lhakhang* at Geynikha; Zamto Lhakhang, and a couple of *chortens*. Where does this wealth originate? Local legend tells that in the 10th century the villagers helped a wandering monk who became sick. After recovering he made a wish that these people, and future generations, should reap benefits from Mother Earth without working – and it seems to have happened! Up to halfway through the last century iron ore, lead and zinc was mined from the mountains in this valley, and remains can be still seen on a ridge called Chakola (the iron mountain). When the mining stopped, cultivation of 'matsutake' mushrooms, potatoes and apples took over in the valley.

GENYE DZONG

Close to Geynikha there used to be a big fortress called Genye Dzong; now only a ruined *utse* (main, central tower) is left. Genye Drungpa had his seat here and ruled over Geynikha and the surrounding villages. It houses a precious statue of Zhabdrung, as well as a story that the statue had 'spoken'.

After passing a small *chorten* near Geynikha primary school the feeder road continues around a mountain ridge to reach after a little while prosperous **Geynikha** village, a *lhakhang* and a beautiful valley appear. Some trekkers might feel short of breath as a result of being driven up to an altitude of roughly 9510ft/2900m; take it easy. Look for the lovely paintings on the houses – there are protecting tigers, and phalluses on each side of the front doors.

There is a short climb up to a ruin, Gepailo, (9710ft/ 2960m) from where a good trail starts descending to the Geynitsang Chhu, passing a small waterfall and an irrigation channel built on some stakes till the first campsite at **Geynizampa** (*zampa* = bridge, 9350ft/2850m) is reached. Camp is next to the main 'road', which is busy with local travellers on foot. The sun leaves camp at 16.30hr in autumn. If you arrive at camp early visit the villages Zamto (2hr) and Chhochhekha up the valley.

DAY 2

*Geynizampa (9350ft/2850m) to Gur
(10,990ft/3350m) or on to Gibze Kebze
(Gebse Kebze) (12,170ft/3710m)*

Time	To Gur about 2hr; to Gibze Kebze about 4.5hr
Altitude gain	To Gur 1640ft/500m; to Gibze Kebze 2820ft/860m
Altitide loss	0ft/0m
Distance	To Gur 2.2miles/3.5km; to Gibze Kebze 3miles/5km

Sun reaches camp at 08.00hr in autumn. Cross the suspension bridge, then keep right. Climb steeply, then more steadily, through beautiful oak forest. The trees are draped with lichen ('old man's beard', used to fill pillows and mattresses).

Along the trail there are old stone steps and resting places, indicating that it was once a busy route. At

Note: There is also a camp, Keptchin, about the same altitude as Gibze Kebze, located on the right below the main trail, but there are problems with water here.

197

*2nd camp on
Dagala trek*

10,495ft/3200m, after 1–1.5hr climb, passing a cattle gate, a group of prayer flags on a rock outcrop appears. This is Dophu Jasey Dokha, with a nice view of the valley and surrounding mountains. The trail becomes less steep, skirting around the hillside through a big birch forest that gradually gives way to bamboo.

On top of the ridge, at about 10,990ft/3350m, when the trail takes a sharp corner, look for an unclear side trail going down for about 50m to a possible campsite, **Gur**. This could also be reached in one day from Thimphu (but beware the altitude gain: Gur is about 1000m higher than Thimphu). It only takes 2 hr to get here from Geynizampa, so it's tempting to carry on – but watch the altitude. Gur camp (10,825ft/3300m) is just within the recommended height gain between campsites.

*Job-Gay-She Ru
Daga La Gey
PhuMey Choe*
'Even as a yak herder
dies of old age, he
still doesn't know the
area of Dagala.'
Old Bhutanese
saying

At 11,280ft/3440m leave the forest; the trail can be seen ahead, cutting up the hill. Ascend through ferns and flowers such as edelweiss. The possible campsite, **Gibze Kebze** (12,170ft/3710m) – rather a poor one – is on the trail and has a couple of herder huts. ◄

DAY 3

Gur (10,990ft/3350m) or Gibze Kebze (12,170ft/3710m) to near U(m)tsho Tsho (or Labatamba or Dolungo) (14,040ft/4280m) via Pagalabtsa La (13,675ft/4170m)

Time	4hr (2hr climb to the pass from Gibze Kebze)
Distance	6.2 miles/10km
Altitude gain	From Gur 2690ft/820m; from Gibze Kebze 1509ft/460m
Altitude loss	c656ft/200m

Trace your way back from Gibze Kebze camp to the main trail, which is clear and wide and runs in and out of a few small side valleys, across several creeks – no bridges, but boulder hopping. Look for wild asparagus in spring. The climb ends after crossing a little saddle at 13,450ft/4100m on a trail through a small, shallow valley leading finally to a wide, grassy area, the **Pagalabtsa La** (13,657ft/4170m), marked by four cairns. A beautiful high-altitude landscape opens up, with gentians and a fine view of the Dagala range, including some rocky peaks. ▸

Turn to the east (left); the trail can be hard to find. Very soon you should see two stone houses below at Wataching (13,450ft/4100m), a good place to stop for lunch, sheltered from wind or bad weather. Herders keep sheep, horses and yaks in the area; fresh yak cheese may be available. After Wataching traverse around a ridge and through a small valley, climb up to a small saddle, then descend into a broad main valley where there are quite a few yak herders' huts. The valley has no proper name, but is commonly called **Labatama** (Lamatamba). At the bottom is a beautiful big flat campsite (about 13,285ft/4050m). ▸

It is better to continue to the end of the valley and camp just below the cliffs, next to a stone hut at 14,040ft/4280m (near the lake Utsho Tsho, or **Dolungo**). Several good flat spots

From this pass a trail west leads into a valley called Tenjela. The trail stays above 4000m for some time and finally drops down to the road going south from Chhuzom to Phuntsholing.

If you have a permit to trek south for 3 days to Dagana, following the old trade route, this camp is a good starting point. From here you can make a day trip to Jomo (Dagala) Peak (see below).

199

Pagalabtsa pass 4170m – Dagala trek

for the tents can be found here, though it can be very windy. At 17.20hr (autumn) there is still sun in camp. Consider spending an extra day here for exploration or, if you have obtained a fishing permit, enjoy some golden trout fishing.

JOMO (DAGALA) PEAK

You could spend a day exploring the area, and also climb Jomo Peak. From camp the trail runs left of the first lake, Utsho Tsho or Imtsho Gewa ('turquoise colour'). Follow the group of lakes clockwise. The next lake, a little bigger, is Serbho Tsho ('gold'). The biggest lake is Jatsho, 'vulture', reflecting its shape. Climb up the highest peak of the area, Jomo (15,469ft/4716m). Jomo is a sacred peak; don't leave rubbish, and take incense sticks and prayer flags to offer on the summit. The Bhutanese even refrain from sleeping with their partners the night before climbing Jomo Peak in order not to upset the diety Jomo.

Jomo stands for the female deity that protects animals, and is important to farmers and nomads since cattle and horses are vital for their livelihoods. There is an annual ritual dedicated to Jomo, and the Jomo shaman is always a female who wears her hair long. When animals get sick or die the farmers believe that Jomo is upset, so carry out rituals to placate her, and never despoil her mountains and lakes.

From Jomo Peak Jhomolhari (23,995ft/7315m) and Kanchenjunga (28,160ft/8586m) can be seen. Below, to the east, are two other big lakes, Sertsho and Ngyetsho, and a small lake, Dongtsho. There is also a long lake, Dagebho, meaning 'longer than the archery range' (Batsho on one old map).

DAY 4

*Near Utsho Tsho (14,040ft/4280m) to
Kiwi Chowa (Kare Kawe) (13,220ft/4030m) via
Labajong La (low route: 14,430ft/4400m) or Jomo
(Dagala) Peak (high route: 14,825ft/4520m or
even up to 15,469ft/4716m)*

Time	low route 3–4hr; high route 4–5hr
Distance	low route 6 miles/10km; high route 6.8 miles/11km
Altitude gain	low route 390ft/120m; high route 785ft/240m or 1430ft/436m
Altitude loss	low route 1215ft/370m; high route 1610ft/490m or 2250ft/686m

The sun reaches camp early. Start climbing up the grassy ridge to reach a trail. The trail to Jomo Peak now follows an easterly direction between some rockfaces.

a) **The lower route** crosses a pass of 14,105ft/4300m. The pack animals and horsemen will use the lower trail, being easier.

Climb over the ridge 14,285ft/4355m behind camp in 15–20min. There is a small descent and ascent to a saddle in the skyline, **Labajong La** (14,430ft/ 4400m). Also visible in the far distance to the west is a famous big monastery high on a hill, Dongkha Lhakhang (12,135ft/3700m). There is a small steep descent first, then an area of flat land. Continue more steeply down on a clear trail with some loose boulders until you reach a bigger stream, Dochha Chhu, about 350m below the pass. Go back into rhododendron bushes. Soon you can look down into the valley where the trek started. Keep on trekking high above the valley and choose a good spot for lunch. This is where the 'haute route' joins the lower track.

A choice of two routes today: a lower one – easier and more obvious – across the Labajong pass; a higher one past some lakes, including a possible climb to Jomo (Dagala) Peak.

b) **Higher route** If you feel fit enough take this one, reaching altitudes of 4520m, and even higher if you wish to climb to a viewing point, **Jomo (Dagala) Peak** (15,469ft/4716m). Climb to the western side of lake Serbho Tsho/Dajatsho and cross a saddle at about 14,760ft/4500m. If the weather is fine you should be able to see Jhomolhari and Kanchenjunga. After the saddle the trail descends steeply to another lake at 14,270ft/4350m, passing several herders' camps. It rejoins the lower route at about 13,645ft/4160m near a stream called Dochha Chhu.

Walk past a very nice campsite below the trail (Panka). Looking northwest in the far distance Jili Dzong is visible – the first campsite on the Drukpath trek when starting from Paro. Talakha Peak (14,030ft/4278m) can also be seen – the climbing destination for tomorrow. There are plenty of loose stones on the trail, so take care.

Several short climbs follow in and out of minor valleys, finally reaching a small saddle with a cairn. The next steep climb leads to a clear saddle with several cairns – the last climb for the day. Just before you start the final ascent a cairn indicates a trail coming in from below. The saddle, Chole La, is at 13,580ft/4140m. In the next valley camp is near a yak herders' hut at **Kiwi Chowa** (Kare Kawe, 13,220ft/4030m) next to a little stream. There is sun at camp till 17.30hr in autumn.

Plant of the Arisaeme family (read more in the 'Flora' section of the Introduction)

DAY 5

*Kiwi Chowa (13,220ft/4030m)
to Thimphu (7,545ft/2300m) via
Tale La (Jili La) (13,725ft/4185m) and
Talakha Gompa (10,200ft/3110m)*

Time	5hr
Distance	5.5 miles (9km)
Altitude gain	505ft/155m
Altitude loss	6180ft/1885m

The sun climbs over a ridge behind camp, appearing about 07.30hr in autumn. Climb to a pass at 12,990ft/3960m indicated by several large cairns. Four trails meet here: your own from the south; to the east to Wangdi (see below); to the north to Talakha Gompa; and to the west just below the ridge, reaching another crossing point leading to Serbithang and Zamto.

Climb a steep slope to a yak herders' place, next to an enormous ruin at 13,055ft/3980m (possibly a small *dzong* to control traffic between Wangdi and Thimphu). Climb into a valley to the top of a ridge (13,725ft/4185m). Where the path leaves this ridge the locals call this Jili La; other sources call it **Tale La**. The pass, which is decorated with prayer flags, gives a full view of the Thimphu valley and, far below on the ridge, the Talakha Gompa. In clear weather there are stunning views towards the Himalayas, including Kanchenjunga (28,160ft/8586m), Jhomolhari (23,995ft/7315m), Jitchhu Drake, Tsheri Kang and in the east the mountains of Lunana. It is another 20–30min climb to Talaka Peak (c14,105ft/4300m) with an even better view.

The day starts with a beautiful view over many valleys and ridges. In summer the blue poppy grows hereabouts.

ALTERNATIVE FINISH TO WANGDI

During the climb up to Talakha Peak (12,990ft/3960m) you get to a saddle, clearly indicated by many stone piles. Descend from this saddle in a northeastly direction towards Wangdi. Follow a trail down next to the Hetsho Chhu to the *gompas* of Gikha (1–2 days) and through several villages with more *gompas*.

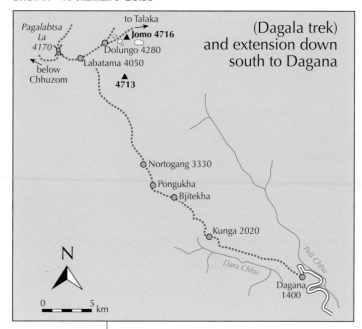

Pagalabtsa La 4170

to Talaka

Jomo 4716

Dolungo 4280

Labatama 4050

below Chhuzom

4713

(Dagala trek) and extension down south to Dagana

Nortogang 3330

Pongukha

Bjitekha

Kunga 2020

Peli Chhu

Dara Chhu

Dagana 1400

N

0   5 km

Back on the trail, descend steeply – difficult walking with lots of big loose stones, very unpleasant for the horses. The steep track leads to a large meadow on top of a ridge (12,955ft/3950m), a good lunch spot.

From this meadow turn slightly to the left, to a sandy place (known locally as 'The Beach'), from where starts the final long descent through mixed fir, juniper, rhododendron, thorn rose, bamboo, birch and spruce forest. The top part has been badly affected by fire. At 3400m bamboo forest returns.

Finally reach beautiful **Talakha Gompa** (10,200ft/3110m), surrounded by a well-looked-after garden and with a superb view over Thimphu valley. Watch the dog! Just below the *gompa* is a road, where 4-wheel drive vehicles could pick you up for a bumpy ride to Simtokha (1.5hr) and Thimphu. Alternatively you could camp here and walk down the next day through beautiful forest, and meet your transport at Simtokha Dzong.

EXTENSION TO DAGANA

The description below is not complete. The Centre of Bhutan Studies has published a booklet by Dorji Penjor, *On the Mule Track to Dagana*, describing other details of this ancient footpath.

For the first three days follow the Dagala Trek, days 1–3.

DAY 4

Near Utsho Tsho and exploring around Dagala Lakes – camp at Labatama (Lamatamba) (13,285ft/4050m)

See Trek 9, day 3, for details of an exploration day.

DAY 5

Labatama (13,285ft/4050m) to Nortogang (Nothobsawa) (10,920ft/3330m)

Time	6hr
Distance	not available
Altitude gain	1476ft/450m
Altitude loss	3935ft/1200m

During the steep climb to a pass at 14,760ft/4500m, lake Chhiba Tsho and some cliffs lie on the left. From the pass there is a splendid view north and south including Kanchenjunga (28,160ft/8586m) and Jhomolhari (23,995ft/7315m). A steep descent follows into Dagana valley. Walk next to a small blue mountain lake, Langtsho ('ox') on a well-maintained path: this has long been an important route. At 4000m you return to rhododendron shrub country. The path stays on the eastern slope of the mountainside and leads in a southerly direction.

After 1.5hr descent you reach Doma, a yak herders' camp (12,136ft/3700m). There are two houses/huts and a ruin, used in the old days as an overnight halt for the Daga Penlop (old governor's title) when he travelled to Thimphu, normally twice a year.

Nortogang is a big yak pasture at 10,825ft/3300m about 1hr from Doma. There is only a yak hut. From this campsite you can climb up a hill on the west side from where you get a view over the vast jungle forest of the Dagana region.

EXTENSION TO DAGANA (continued)

DAY 6

Nortogang (10,920ft/3330m) to Kunga (Kuengo) (6625ft/2020m)

Time	6.5hr
Distance	not available
Altitude gain	0ft/0m
Altitude loss	4295ft/1310m

The trail now leads through beautiful broadleaved forest with masses of rhododendrons, becoming denser as the day progresses.

Cross yak pastures to meet a good path through rhododendron forest. The first clearing reached is Pongukha; there is a small hut in the lower part. Keep left here and go down in the forest. A steep descent follows through an oak and broadleaved forest.

A pasture with a ruined house on the right is reached: this is Bjitekha. Again descend steeply, down to the river at 6,625ft/2020m through subtropical vegetation. Continue to twist and turn in and out of small side valleys to finally reach **Kunga** camp.

DAY 7

Kunga (6625ft/2020m)to Dagana (4590ft/1400m)

Time	4hr
Distance	not available
Altitude gain	0ft/0m
Altitude loss	2035ft/620m

The trail today leads through a floral paradise. Many orchids can be spotted on the trees, and you are surrounded by lush tropical vegetation. Beware of snakes.

EXTENSION TO DAGANA (continued)

The exposed south side of the valley is covered with dry oak forest. Today's trail is difficult for horses: the path is narrow and there are many cliffs. After 4hr of hiking you suddenly climb round a ridge and get a good view of Daga Dzong surrounded by paddy fields. The end of the trek!

DAY 8

Dagana to Thimphu via Wangdi by car (8hr)

Drive from Dagana to Sunkosh Chhu junction at Tsirang Dzongkhag (c1310ft/400m). From there drive north to Wangdi (6hr). From Wangdi to Thimphu takes 2–2.5hr via the Dochu La.

DAGANA DZONGKHAG

This district has an elevation ranging from 600–3800m. Up to 80 percent of the total area is covered with untouched forest full of wildlife. The Dzongkhag produces oranges, other citrus fruits and cardamom; dairy products are exported to Thimphu. In the 17th century the inhabitants of Dagana lived without law and order. Shabdrung Ngawang Namgyal sent in an army under the command of Donyer Druk Namgyal – who then built the Daga Trashi Yangtse Dzong in 1655 – to conquer the area.

TREK 10

SAMTENGANG TREK

Grade	easy
Time	4 days
Distance	16.1 miles/26km
Altitude gain	6117ft/1865m
Altitude loss	5215ft/1590m
Status	open

The trek is very suitable for children, especially on horseback, and is also a good trek for the winter.

One of the easier lower altitude treks in Bhutan starts in the Punakha valley and can be finished in 3–4 days. The only difficulty is that the few climbs are steep; on the last day there is a steep 2hr descent to the main road.

During the trek you may see Jhomolhari (23,995ft/ 7315m) in the west and Kang Bum Peak, located above Gaza (20,665ft/6300m). Tiger Mountain (Gangcheta 22,435ft/ 6840m) north of Laya might also be visible. The trek is especially recommended in winter, when temperatures at night are around freezing. During the rest of the year leeches may infest the trail through the paddy fields, but that is the time to enjoy watching farmers and their animals working in the fields.

The trek can be started from either end. There are several attractive villages along the route, which are used as camps. From nearly every campsite you can leave the trek and reach a road in no time.

Samtengang is mentioned again and again in old literature regarding travelling/exploring/plant hunting in Bhutan. It was the old stopping place on the first day out from Wangdi for people travelling east–west (and vice versa). The booklet *The Ballad of Pemi Tshewang Tashi: A Wind Borne Feather* by Karma Ura will tell you more about the history of the area.

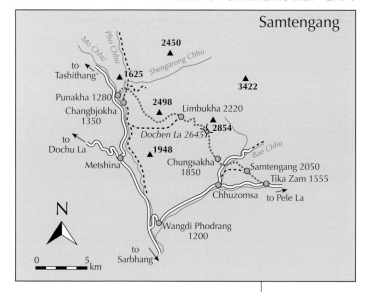

Samtengang

DAY 1

*Punakha (4200ft/1280m)
to Limbukha (7280ft/2220m)*

Time	4hr
Distance	5.6 miles/9km
Altitude gain	3080ft/940m
Altitude loss	0ft/0m

The trek starts upstream from the *dzong*, over the longest suspension bridge in Bhutan (180m) across the Pho Chhu. Climb gently on the left side of the Po Chhu through terraced fields of mustard and winter wheat. The Punakha valley is low enough to enable two harvests, so there is plenty of activity in the fields in the winter months. The valley also produces fruits like bananas and oranges.

Either overnight in a hotel in the Punakha area, or camp next to the Pho Chhu opposite the Punakha Dzong at Changbjokha (4428ft/1350m).

PUNAKHA DZONG

Punakha Dzong (4200ft/1280m) is situated at the confluence of the rivers Mo Chhu (west side) and the Po Chhu (east side), meaning 'mother' and 'father' river respectively. The Mo Chhu originates from the mountains north of Lingshi and Laya, and even from Tibet. The Po Chhu comes from the Lunana area and is mainly fed by glaciers. After the confluence it becomes the Puna Tsang Chhu or Sankosh River and continues its way south along Wangdi, leaving the Kingdom at Kalikhola and finally joining the Brahmaputra. In 1996 Punakha Dzong was hit by a flood after a glacial lake burst and sent huge waves down the Po Chhu. A couple of people died and the flood left behind a trail of devastation. Luckily only the big *chorten* in front of the *dzong* was partially damaged.

Punakha Dzong

At 6855ft/2090m (after about 2.5hr uphill through pine forest, fern, oak and some rhododendron) there is a nice clearing for lunch with a big prayer flag and a beautiful view over the valley. In the far distance the huge *chorten*, Khamsum Yuelley Namgyal, can be seen. Looking to the west the road to Dochu La can be partly traced, and if lucky some snowy peaks may be visible: Jhomolhari, Kang Bum and Tiger Mountain.

A *chorten* and some prayer flags on the skyline at 7215ft/2200m indicate the end of today's climb. From the *chorten* you can see towards Wangdi and Limbukha, where our campsite (7280ft/2220m) is located just behind the village on a beautiful green area (1.5hr). ▶

Limbuhka can also be reached by 4-wheel drive vehicles.

Limbukha has several old big houses. Some people say that this place, at the upper end of a watershed, used to be a lake. The inhabitants perform a special annual ceremony in connection with the lake, when they begin to irrigate the fields. In former times a king lived here.

Dusk arrives about 5pm in the winter. During the night tiny lights of cars crossing the Dochu La (10,170ft/3100m) are visible in the far distance.

DAY 2

Limbukha (7280ft/2220m)
to Chungsakha (6070ft/1850m)
via Dochen La (8676ft/2645m)

Time	4hr
Distance	6.2 miles/10km
Altitude gain	1230ft/375m
Altitude loss	2445ft/745m

Leaving camp climb steeply (150m) up to a small ridge (7775ft/2370m) through a cold dense forest, from which today's climb is visible. Cross this ridge, and descend steeply into a small side valley where a small stream (2230ft/2235m) is crossed. Surrounded by beautiful birdsong and oak and rhododendron forest, follow an unclear trail covered by slippery leaves.

If trekking in winter you'll have a cold start since the sun doesn't really reach the camp before departure.

After about 2hr of climbing reach a small pass, **Dochen La** (8676ft/2645m). Nearby is a spot with many prayer flags from where there is a good view towards Dochu La, Jhomolhari, Kang Bum, Tiger Mountain, part of the dust road walked yesterday, and Talo Lhakhang and Nobgang Lhakhang down in the valley.

After the pass a steep steady descent follows along a forest trail. The forest opens up after reaching Dagegon with a beautiful big old farmhouse. In the distance a ridge with Samtengang village and Chhuni Gompa is coming into view.

Just before reaching today's destination walk next to Dargyel Gompa, an old monastery of Drukpa Kinley, the 'Divine Mad Madman', whose teaching methods often shocked monks and lay people alike. On the hillside above the monastery are several small meditation cells.

At 6070ft/1850m **Chungsakha** (Chhungsekha) is reached. The village has one *lhakhang* with a simple but atmospheric chapel on the first floor. It houses a Buddha statue and a big prayer wheel. The monastery has a festival every three years with masked dances and singing. The campsite is in front of the *lhakhang*.

DAY 3

Chungsakha (6070ft/1850m)
to below Samtengang (6725ft/2050m)
via crossing the Bae Chhu (4920ft/1500m)

Time	2.5–3hr
Distance	2.5 miles/4km
Altitude gain	1805ft/550m
Altitude loss	1150ft/350m

Today's route starts with a descent through orange, banana, and bamboo trees, and many flowers, even in winter.

Sun reaches camp late. Descend to the road in 45min and find a suspension bridge crossing the **Bae Chhu** at 4920ft/1500m. The road leads to the slate mines of Tsheshinang at the end of the valley.

From the bridge start on a clear moderately steep trail through several villages. The trail goes through small deeply eroded gorges, which will be very slippery in the rain. In December, the daphne flower is already starting to flower. The climb is finished for the day when you pass Samtengang high school (established 1952) on your right. Walk through a narrow gorge to the other side at 6560ft/2000m and look down towards a holy lake, Lutshokha (Tsho Shokha), surrounded with an ugly iron fence. Turn right; walk towards a huge building, the Basic Health Unit (BHU). From this building a trail goes down straight to Chhuzomsa.

Camp is on the other side of the lake and another 20min beyond it. It is a beautiful flat campsite (6725ft/2050m) in the forest below the village of **Samtengang**.

LAKE LUTSHOKHA

The lake is said to have once been a field, owned by a farmer. A lady came with a bucket of milk, and asked the farmer if she could stay for some time. Later she poured the milk on the field, and the field changed into a lake.

After lunch there will be plenty of time either to visit Samtengang or stay in camp and enjoy the fresh wind blowing through the pines. There is a wonderful trail climbing up to Samtengang village, and a dirt road (2004). The *lhakhang* is Gonjo Lhakhang, and there is another one 2hr above the village.

DAY 4

Samtengang (6725ft/2050m)
to bridge at Tika Zam (5100ft/1555m)
and onwards drive to Chhuzomsa

Time	1–1.5hr
Distance	c2 miles/3km
Altitude gain	0ft/0m
Altitude loss	1625ft/495m

The trail, starting near camp, descends steeply through endless agricultural fields, heading into the valley of the Dang Chhu. The road will be reached next to the bridge at **Tika Zam** (5100ft/1555m).

TREK 11

GASA TSACHU
(HOT SPRINGS) TREK

For map see Trek 6, day 12.

Grade	easy
Time	2 or 3 days (including rest day)
Distance	26 miles/43km
Altitude gain	690ft/210m (1771ft/540m extra to Gasa Dzong)
Altitude loss	690ft/210m (1771ft/540m extra)
Status	open
Note	The trek is being affected by the building of a feeder road. By early 2008 another 5km road to Gay-za-pang should be in place, reducing the walk by another 2hrs. There are plans to extend the road further – by 5km to Zamay Zam.

This is the main trekking route to a popular destination: the hot springs of Gasa.

The hot springs are located below Gasa Dzong (9053ft/ 2760m) on an old trade route to Tibet at an altitude of 7282ft/2220m, one of the larger and most accessible sites. The Bhutanese visit the springs mainly for medical reasons. In the last couple of years the site has developed enormously with new showers, changing facilities and a royal guest-house. The hot water is redirected and divided among five cement-walled pools. The spring attracts more than 7000 visitors a year. Animals used the springs as well but are banned now.

To access the start of the trek drive from Punakha through a beautiful valley going north on a dusty or muddy road, which someday will go all the way to Gasa Dzong. Halfway along at Yambesa on the right at the top of the hill is an impressive *chorten*, the Khamsum Yuley Namgyel. A big stone gate marks the entrance to the Jigme Dorji National Park. Nearby is a fenced meadow and camp reserved for nature clubs and school groups.

After 1.5hr (30km) Tashithang (5250ft/1600m) is reached, the old starting point of the trek. The feeder/dirt road now climbs to the village of Damji (7380ft/2250m), bypassing the village of Kabina (6100ft/1860m). The road can be partly out of use, especially after rainfall. If so, count on some hours' trekking to Damji.

The trek is easy, being at low altitude and on a good trail parallel to and above the Mo Chhu (mother river). Allow 2hr extra to visit Gasa Dzong for the steep climb (540m altitude difference). This trek leads onwards to Laya/Lingshi and Lunana.

DAY 1

*Drive from Punakha (4200ft/1280m)
to Damji (7380ft/2250m)*

This day can be driven if the road to Damji is in reasonable condition. If the road is impassable, you'll have the opportunity to undertake a couple of hours' trekking through beautiful semi-tropical forest (takin habitat); watch the heat! Because of the altitude gain (3180ft/970m), it is best to spend a night at Damji (7380ft/2250m) (or Goen Dhamji) in order to acclimatize.

Damji village counts several houses and a good campsite at the end of the village. Shabdrung stayed here on his travels from Tibet to Bhutan. He meditated here and some precious relics can be still seen in one of the older houses: a beautiful pair of brocade, a pair of his leather boots and an image of himself. Both Damji and Gasa have letterboxes (exotic places from which to send postcards!).

In Damji is the large JDNP headquarters, opened in 2002. There is a museum in the ground floor, which is worth a visit. There is a display of maps and some stuffed animals like the red panda, and good photographs of indigenous plants and animals accompanied with explanations. A confiscated snow leopard skin and some fishing equipment complete the show. A small brochure, *Welcome to the natural beauty of Bhutan*, details the park's attributes.

DAY 2

Damji (7380ft/2250m) to Gasa Tsachu (7282ft/2220m)

Time	5hr
Distance	8.7 miles/14km
Altitude gain	690ft/210m
Altitude loss	787ft/240m

After leaving the upper campsite in Damji reach a *chorten* and the trail disappears into mixed jungle/forest with many orchids. The trail leads to a suspension bridge crossing the Lepena Chhu. A rock next to the trail carries an environmental message 'Action speaks louder then words; help keep your environment clean and green'. About 1.5hr up a steep climb from Damji, Gesapong (or Gay-za-pang; 8315ft/2535m) is reached (road planned to here for 2008). After the village, pass through some meadows (good campsite) where very large tiger tracks were observed in April 2003.

Continue through a huge landslide area, which occurred in May/June 2003. On a big trunk observe more graffiti: 'Welcome to Gasa Dzongkhag; protect forest, save the mother earth'. A picnic table at a viewing point (8070ft/2460m) is reached, from where you can see Gasa Dzong and the hot springs marked by prayer flags in the distance. Descend steeply to the Same Chhu, and cross the river by the suspension bridge (7167ft/2185m). At the split keep ahead to the hot springs at **Gasa Tsach(h)u**. Observe the orchid flowers here. ◀

From the split after the suspension bridge a direct trail to Gasa Dzong goes left towards a *chorten*.

Limited camping is possible near the hot springs. There are several houses/buildings including a dormitory and kitchen building, as well as some shops and bars with telephone.

The whole area is well organised with paths, gates, water channels, a clean toilet near the hot baths and a beautiful royal guesthouse. It can get busy, especially in winter, since Bhutanese visit for medical reasons such as curing rheumatism and treating skin diseases. There are five pools of different temperatures ranging from lukewarm to very hot, reaching 104°F/40°C. Note that plans for a new campsite on the other side of the river are being discussed.

DISUSED ROUTE

Following the Same Chhu upstream into a big side valley the river name changes into Mo Chhu. It is actually the westerly tributary of the main Mo Chhu. At 11,300ft/3445m Chhijethang Chhu comes in from the north. Following this stream you will get to the campsite Robluthang situated in the middle of the trek between Jhomolhari and Laya (see Trek 3, day 8). This route is not used any more.

DAY 3

Rest day in Gasa Tsachu

Plan a rest day here to enjoy the hot springs and/or walk up to Gasa Dzong (9053ft/2760m). The 540m steep climb is pretty straightforward and will take a maximum of 2hr partly following a stream, Chogomsa Chhu. On entering **Gasa** a signpost reads: 'Tobacco free zone. Tobacco stems from the very root of evil. So don't deal with tobacco. Dzongkhag care for your health. Say no to tobacco'. (Note: In December 2004 the sale of tobacco in Bhutan became illegal.)

Gar = wheat and *sa* = place; Gasa produces an exceptionally fine-quality wheat.

The solid-looking *dzong* is strategically located. It feels as if you have to climb forever to get there, giving the guards – in the past – plenty of time to work out whether you are friend or foe! The impressive mountain of Kang Bum (Gang Bom, Khang Bum, Khan Bhum; 20,664ft/6300m, 21,320ft/6500m, 21,405ft/6526m) towers over the whole area. Kang Bum has been climbed twice; first in 1984 by a Japanese–Bhutanese team, and again in 1991 by a Dutch team.

The whitewashed *dzong* with characteristic red-bronze stripes (*khemar*) painted high on the walls is called Tashi

Gasa hot springs

Thongmen Dzong. It was built in the 17th century (1646) by the Shabdrung Namgyal to protect the valley against Tibetan invaders, and there is evidence of cannon-ball damage on some of the outer walls. In one of the main chapels in the *lhakhang* the walls are hung with weaponry used in the old days against the Tibetans. There are many buildings inside the walls: towers (both square and round), a small inner court, stairs to the main tower, offices and quarters. It has an idyllic but powerful atmosphere. Ang Komo is the most important deity for Gasa, and his statue is in the top chapel of the *utse* (women are not allowed here). The chapel on the first floor holds the important god Dorji Tsawang

Before the *dzong* burned down there were many interesting statues of Yeshe Gönpo, the protecting goddess of the Bhutanese. It has been renovated, and now houses the Dzongkhag administration and a monastery. It is connected by telephone to the rest of Bhutan, and has e-mail facilities for officials. With some computers in the *dzong* there is even access to email for the Dzong officials.

Gasa bazaar is built around a big green field just below the *dzong*. There is a large school, with boarding facilities; children from the whole region, as far as Laya, come here. There is a BHU and RNR office located in Gasa. Gasa has a letterbox, which is visited twice a week by a mail runner; stamps are sometimes available, but no postcards.

In addition to the official and administrative people Gasa has a lot of people from whom horses can be hired. Farming is only small scale because of wild boar, bears and even tigers, which constantly raid fields.

For those with extra energy, visit the ruins from Wabsho (Wobtsho) Dzong, located on the opposite hill of Gasa Dzong (c30min walk from the main trail); once a functioning Dzong where Shabdrung spent time on his first visit to Bhutan.

From Gasa you can trek back to Tashithang, or onwards north to Laya in 2 days (see Trek 6).

Gasa Dzong 2760m and Kang Bum mountain c6500m

TREK 12

GANGTE TREK AND
SOUTHERN VARIATION

> **Note:** this trek is undergoing major changes due to the construction of a feeder road running parallel to parts of the trek and connecting Gangte (Phobjika) valley with the Gogona and Khotokha valleys.
>
> In this edition of the guidebook the original Gangte trek has been trimmed down to some limited information (see item 1). It is followed by a day hike (see 2), a half-day hike (see 3) and a 3½-day trek (see 4), which is being planned south of the original trek.

Horse riding is an attractive option for families with children on this trek.

This is 3-day trek, reaching an altitude of 11,277ft/3438m, could be combined with an extra day's stay at the start in the Phobjika valley. It is an all-season trek, with temperatures sometimes reaching freezing point in winter, and summers being hot and monsoonal.

The start of the trek is one day by vehicle from Paro or Thimphu via Wangdi. The Phobjika valley is entered via the Lawala pass (10,791ft/3290m), indicated by a *chorten,* after which the beautiful valley opens up. It has many large houses, empty in winter when their inhabitants move to warmer places around Wangdi. It is a typical glacial U-shaped valley, with marshes and the Nake Chhu running through it. Black-necked cranes congregate here when they migrate from Tibet in mid-November, and there is an annual festival in honour of the cranes. The Royal Society for Protection of Nature (RSPN) is very active in protecting the habitat, and has a well-equipped black-necked crane information centre (with telescopes) and guesthouse for birdwatchers, which include many school groups. In the valley there are also barking deer, Himalayan black bear, leopard, wild boar and red fox.

The spectacular monastery and small village near Gangte Gompa (total renovation underway in 2007) are worth a visit. The valley has a BHU, two schools, RSPN centre and four possible guesthouses/hotels. There is a limited-service satellite telephone connection in the valley. Telephone and electricity wires are banned because they would cause problems for the black-necked cranes.

There are several good day hikes, including the Gangte trail following the bottom of the valley, starting from Gangte Gompa and village; climbing the hill to Gangte Gompa; visiting the village Kumbu in a valley east of Gangte Gompa; walking south to the villages Gedachen and Khebaythang; and the Kilkhorthang trail to Kungathang Lhakhang.

Note the different names for the same area – Phobjika or Phobjikha valley, and Gangte, Gangtey or Gangteng valley. 'Gangte' actually refers to the *gompa* and village.

Four treks from and to Phobjika valley are given below.

1. Original Gangte trek

This trek is still a beauty, but be prepared to walk on (partly) feeder roads and being disturbed by ongoing road work. For

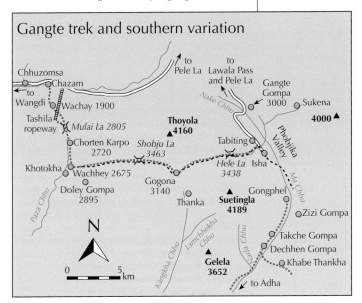

Gangte trek and southern variation

221

original trek description visit **www.bhutantreks.com**, and for an outline of this trek see below.

Day 1 – Phobjika valley (9380ft/2860m) to Gogona (Zasa) (10,300ft/3140m) via Hele La (11,277ft/3438m)
Start from near the village **Tabiting** and climb next to a stream to **Hele La pass**. From the pass keep right at the first split and descend gradually through a mixed forest into the Kangkha Chhu valley to the village **Gogona** (5–6hr).

Day 2 – Gogona (10,300ft/3140m) to Chorten Karpo (8920ft/2720m) via Shobju La (11,360ft/3464m)
Climb up through the meadow and mixed forest to the pass **Shobju La** (2.5hr). Descend into Khotokha valley. Turn right at the village **Wacchey** and climb to the campsite at **Chorten Karpo** below four big *chortens* (5–6hr).

Day 3 – Chorten Karpo (8920ft/2720m) to bridge at Tika Zampa (5100ft/1555m) or suspension bridge at Chazam (5068ft/1545m) via Mulai La (9200ft/2805m)
From the campsite climb to the top of a ridge to the last pass, **Mulai La**. A tough descent starts through a wonderful forest. Take the track to the village **Wachay**, from where the National Highway becomes visible.

2. Day hike

Walk from the primary school to the east side of the valley to **Gophu** village. Then start following the side valley upstream, next to Lolephage Chhu, until you reach **Sukena** village (10,170ft/3100m), from where a trail starts climbing up through mixed forest towards a nameless pass. During the descent into the Longte valley the National Highway between west and east Bhutan becomes visible. Some 4–6hr after leaving Phobjika valley the road is reached near **Longte** village, where prearranged transport should be waiting.

3. Half-day hike

This track follows the old route taken by inhabitants of the Phobjika valley when migrating for the winter to warmer places and crosses the **Shashi La** (11,415ft/3480m). Starting from Beyta school (below/near Gangte *gompa*), follow a track north-northwest. It leads through rhododendron forest to Shashi La, and descends to the National Highway and the village of **Khelaykha**, located 12km west from Nobding. Transport should be arranged for pick-up.

4. Three and a half day trek

This trek heads in southerly direction from Phobijka valley, following the Nake Chhu/Ma Chhu/Kisona Chhu river(s), mainly downhill, for 29 miles/47km. It then crosses over the northern part of the Black Mountains to arrive at the finishing point on the road between Wangdi and Damphu.

Trek in brief

Day 1 Phobjika (9380ft/2860m) to Gongphel (9069ft/2765m), 5 miles/8km, 4hr;

Day 2 Gongphel to Tarana (7800ft/2378m), 7 miles/11km, 5hr;

Day 3 Tarana to Adha (3936ft/1200m), 9 miles/14.5km, 6–7hr;

Day 4 Adha to Kamichu (2050ft/625m), c7 miles/11km, 5hr. Double check before you go to see if this trek is open.

Trek description

Follow the main feeder road of the valley in southern direction, a road mainly used for exporting potatoes and apples. There are some small villages and/or *lhakangs* along this road, including Damche village and lhakhang, **Gongphel** village 9069ft/2765m, Gendechhu (or Gedachen) village and *lhakhang* with Zizi Gompa nearby, Shambandi village, Takche village with Takche Gompa, and one of the last buildings in the valley before hitting mixed jungle forest – **Dechhen Gompa**.

Just after Dechhen Gompa there is a split in the trail: don't go to the southeast to the nearby village of Khabe Thankha (or Khebe Thankha). The trail to be followed leads to the southwest. The trail first stays at an altitude of c9840ft/3000m and starts to descend on reaching a gorge following the Ma Chhu (changing into Kisona Chhu). At 3936ft/1200m you reach a bridge near the village **Adha** (or Ade; 270m above the village is Photokna Gompa (or Phatakha Gompa) 1470m). Cross the bridge and follow the river till you get to the dust road connecting with the road between Wangdi and Damphu (3hr drive to Wangdi).

TREK 13

NABJI–KORPHU TREK
(THE BLACK MOUNTAINS OR
JIGME SINGYE WANGCHUK
NATIONAL PARK)

A newly opened trek.

The Black Mountains, a mysterious area of approximately 1400km² in the middle of the Kingdom, range from 700m in the south to over 4600m in the centre. Historically the area has been known either as Dunshinggang or Joedawnchey (native name), and now as Jigme Singye Wangchuk National Park in honour of HRH The Crown Prince.

Dungshinggang (or Mt Jow Durshing), the highest point of the range (15,145ft/4617m), consists of three peaks known as 'the Three Brothers Peaks'. Dungshinggang means 'fir range' or 'fir tree mountain', and locals believe there is a god living on the mountain, Jowo Dungshing ('The Fir Lord'), to whom they have built a place of worship and where, until recently, animal sacrifice was common.

Bhutanese people seldom go deep into the park because the Black Mountains have always been a very holy place, with deities living on the summits. Locals and foreigners are forbidden to visit and/or climb around the summit areas. However, this restriction does not apply to the foothills.

First birdwatchers, and now trekkers, have been allowed access. The park has a wide variety of flora and fauna, as well as cultural sites. Typical flora include fir, hemlock, blue pine, chir pine, spruce, juniper, bamboo, wild orchids and a number of rhododendron species. Among the forest fauna are Himalayan serow, goral, sambar deer, musk deer, black-capped and golden languor, black bear, red panda, clouded leopard, black panther and otter, as well as bird species such as rufous-necked hornbill, yellow-billed blue magpie, black-necked crane, nut cracker, monal- and blood pheasant, serpent eagle, white-collared blackbird and white-bellied heron. Several agricultural villages are of cultural interest.

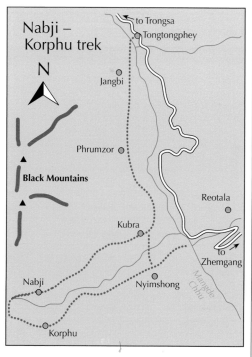

The park and surroundings provide an enormous range of trekking possibilities, and a list of 15 different treks has been produced. Trekking is best after harvesting has been completed, in winter (November – March); however it still can be hot.

The Nabji–Korphu trek is an easy–moderate low altitude trek of six days, visiting several villages (altitude range between 2296ft/700m and 5412ft/1650m). The start and finish points are two small villages on the road between Trongsa and Zhemgang, both at an altitude of about 3280ft/1000m. The trek can be walked in both directions – but is easier as described below.

Note: road construction is underway from just south of Reotala down to the river (watch out for explosions!). ▶ The

There are plans for the road to be extended; check for developments and possible changes in itinerary.

225

road will eventually take the last climb out of the itinerary, if transport is picking you up at the river.

COMMUNITY TOURISM

The Nabji–Korphu trek supports the park management in its efforts to conserve nature, which it does by raising awareness of natural and environmental issues through tourism awareness programmes and by ensuring that local communities benefit from tourism. For example, campsites are maintained by the local communities; and porters and local guides are hired in each village on the route to take the group to the next village.

DAY 1

Trongsa (7216ft/2200m) drive to Tongtongphey (c3280ft/1000m) and trek to Jangbi (4428ft/1350m)

Time	3–4hr
Distance	5 miles/8km
Altitude gain	3116ft/950m
Altitude loss	1968ft/600m

Before starting with the trek, it is worth visiting the Park Rangers office in Tongtongphey for information about the trek and the Jigme Singye Wangchuk National Park.

Drive from **Trongsa** to **Tongtongphey**; the earlier you leave the more chances there are to see any wildlife, as once a black panther was spotted. ◀ After an informative signboard with a trek map on it, posted at the trailhead, a 600m descent leads to the Mangde Chhu river and a suspension bridge. Cross, swim and climb steeply for 950m to reach the village of Jangbi (4428ft/1350m). Camp will be made near **Jangbi** village with a grand view over Mangde Chhu valley.

For two days you will be staying in the homeland of an ethnic group called Monpas, thought to be the first settlers in Bhutan. They have their own language, called Monkha. They practise a mix of animistic shamanism and Buddhism. 'Monpa', or 'the people of darkness', refers to their isolated position in the past. The term Mon refers to people without a religion, suggesting a period before the advent of Buddhism in

Bhutan. They were originally hunter gatherers, with their culture, tradition and practices intrinsically linked to the forest around them. They are traditionally cane weavers and bamboo crafters, using their skills for house construction, and making baskets and other household items.

DAY 2

Jangbi (4428ft/1350m) to Kubra (Kudra) village (c4920ft/1500m)

Time	5–7hr
Distance	8.7 miles/14km
Altitude gain/loss	couple of steep climbs/descents

Today's guide will be Guru Rinpoche! The trail is littered with stone imprints from Guru Rinpoche's footprints, and dagger and phallus symbols – all surrounded by stories about his visit to the area.

This is the most challenging day of the trek with steep (and somewhat long) climbs and descents, but in shade for the most part.

    Below a steep cliff at the Monpa village of Phrumzor, near Ugyendar, a good lunch spot is reached. Some names of holy rocks along the trail are: Phrumzor Ney, Ouzha Ney and Ugyen Drak Ney. After visiting the village *lhakhang* (time permitting) follow the trail, via Lekpogang village, to the campsite at **Kubra** (Kudra) village, which has only three households.

DAY 3

Kubra (Kudra) village (c4920ft/1500m) to Nabji (Nubji) village (4264ft/1300m)

Time	5–7hr
Distance	7.5 miles/12km
Altitude gain/loss	small ups and downs

The area travelled today is tiger and leopard country. Sightings are rare but droppings and spores can be spotted.

There is text inside that is not readable by men, only by deities, who open up the stone by reading it; only then can valuables be put in.

At the Lhakhang of Nabji (Nabji means 'promise' or 'oath') a commemorative stone pillar marks a peace agreement between King Sendhaka (Sindhu Raja; Assam) and King Na'oche (Bumthang), dating back to the eight century – one of the most ancient monuments of Bhutan.

Another day with traces of Guru Rinpoche along the trail. Thick forest with plenty of waterfalls and streams makes this day a real wilderness experience. ◄ Once you reach paddy fields the beautiful village of **Nabji** is nearby, located on a foothill. Nabji village counts about 400 people divided between 55 households. Camp is just near the village.

The village has several religious sites – a holy tree; a stone with a 'bell' in it made by Guru Pema; and, close to Nabji lhakhang, is a big stone split in two in which valuable things can be hidden in case of war. ◄

DAY 4

Nabji village (4264ft/1300m) to Korphu (4920ft/1500m)

Time	3–5hr
Distance	6.8 miles/11km
Altitude gain/loss	small ups and downs

Korphu is located on a mountain top. The village consists of 76 households (about 600 people). The climb up to Korphu is rather spectacular, with an overwhelming view of the surrounding valleys. There are sacred relics from Pema Lingpa, the famous treasure revealer of Bhutan, in Korphu's temple.

DAY 5

Korphu (4920ft/1500m) to Nyimshong (c4265ft/1300m)

Time	c5hr
Distance	6.2 miles/10km
Altitude gain/loss	small ups and downs

A pleasant day hike, through beautiful lush broadleaf forest and paddy fields, mixed with waterfalls, streams and cantilever bridges and plenty of bird watching opportunities. It is a paradise for botanists and ethno-botanists, as it is well described and illustrated by the Japanese Nishioka and Nakao in their book *Flowers of Bhutan Tokyo* 1984.

Nyimshong is the last village on trek. This village is home to about 465 people in 58 households. The campsite is located in the nearby forest.

DAY 6

Nyimshong (c4265ft/1300m) to Reotola trail head (3280ft/1000m) drive to Trongsa town (7216ft/2200m)

Time	3–4hr
Distance	4 miles/6.5km
Altitude gain	2050ft/625m
Altitude loss	2952ft/900m

Descend steeply to a suspension bridge (c1310ft/400m) crossing the Mangde Chhu river. This is followed by an easy hike along the river and then a steep last climb of 2050ft/625m (no shade) to reach the trailhead at **Reotola** (Riotala, Rayotala; 3280ft/1000m; proper village Reotola is located higher at 5478ft/1670m). A road from Reotola to the river is under construction: watch out for blasting! At the end of the trek there is transport to either Zhemgang (6232ft/1900m) or **Trongsa** town. Zhemgang is located above and nearby Reotola; Trongsa is a 3–4hr (62miles/100km) drive above and parallel the Mangde Chhu river.

Those driving to Trongsa could visit the old Kuenga Rabten winter palace.

TREK 14

NUBI/CHUTEY TREK
NEAR TRONGSA

Grade	easy–moderate
Time	5 days
Distance	not available
Altitude gain/loss	not available
Status	double check if open

Note: Not all details are available for this trek.

This trek has many interesting places along the route and can be walked in winter. Nubi and Chutey are village names, but also mean 'north' and 'source of the Mangde Chhu'.

DAYS 1 + 2

*Trongsa (7183ft/2190m)
to Gagar (11,464ft/3495m)*

Time	6–7hr
Distance	not available
Altitude gain	4280ft/1305m
Altitude loss	not available

Note: The altitude gain is too much for one day, so a campsite halfway is recommended.

Leave Trongsa from Sherubling high school and climb to the village of Yuling, where an easy hike continues to Sengibi at the foot of Lion Mountain. It is believed that a rock in the shape of a lion is gradually sinking, and that the world will end when it is gone. Continue on to Golaybji Chorten, constructed by ancestors of the people from Sengibi to keep demons from harming passers-by on this very old trail. Climb for another 1hr to reach Phurtsi Gulung pass, the highest point of today's hike. From here it's another 2hr to camp at **Gagar** ('happy village'), which has a temple to visit. Gagar is located near the Dhemla Pass (11,600ft/3538m).

DAY 3

Gagar (11,464ft/3495m) to Dongthang

Time	7hr
Distance	14.5 miles/23km
Altitude gain	not available
Altitude loss	not available

Trek down to the village of Karshong, 'the snow bowl'. En route visit the recently built Kasphey monastery. Downhill now to Pungdu Changsa ('the place where a shot-put competition was held'). Even to this day local villagers stop here during their journey and have a contest. Descend through oak forest where dead leaves are collected. ▸ Hike for another 2hr past Thrispang village to reach camp at the base of **Dongthang** (Jongda) village (known to be the domain of takins). Dongthang is the last village upstream. ▸

These are mixed with manure, collected over the winter from the cowshed, to make compost.

A new route from here leads to the Dur hot springs (see Trek 15).

DAY 4

Dongthang to Bemji

Time	6–7hr
Distance	12.5 miles/20km
Altitude gain	not available
Altitude loss	not available

Cross the ancient Dongthang bridge to reach the other side of the Mangde Chhu. Follow the trail through paddy fields to Pang (Pang Uma) village. From Pang, climb up gradually to historic **Bemji** (Bramji) village, home to many notable people from the 17th and 18th centuries. The 10th, 12th and 18th Druk Desis (temporal rulers) hailed here. Another important figure was Lama Nushey Tshering Wangchuk, the first ambassador of Bhutan to Tibet in the 18th century.

Camp is in a meadow next to the Bemji community school.

DAY 5

Bemji to Bji-Zam

Time	5–6hr
Distance	9 miles/14.5km
Altitude gain	not available
Altitude loss	not available

After breakfast visit the 'Bemji Nagtshang', home of the notable personalities mentioned on day 4. The hike is a steeply downhill to the Deoga Zam (bridge). Walk past the paddy fields to Khar Talung Chorten, built in the 17th century in the style of a gate. People were required to walk through this *chorten* to avoid being affected by the local evil spirits. It is still believed that sins get cleansed by walking through, since the *chorten* contains numerous relics blessed by many high lamas in the past.

A 2hr walk from here leads to **Bji-Zam** and the road.

TREK 15

TRONGSA–KASIPHEY–DUR TSACHU (HOT SPRINGS) TREK

Grade	moderate
Time	5–6 days one way
Distance	58.5 miles/94km
Altitude gain/loss	not available
Status	double check if open

The trek starts from the town of Trongsa (7183ft/2190m) and follows an old route through the villages of Semji, Gagar, Kashipey and Dongthang. Semji is an ancient village only 4 miles/6.5km from Trongsa. Gagar (= 'Happy') village is near the pass Dhem La (c11,600ft/3538m) (Trongsa to Gagar 13 miles/21km or 6–7hr). Kasiphey monastery is about 1.5–2hr descent from the pass. The monastery was built in 2000 by the Gangtey Tulku Rimpoche and houses over 50 monks, studying and practising Buddhism and Buddhist philosophy.

Beyond Kasiphey the trail descends and follows the river Mangde Chhu until you climb to the next and last village, Dongthang (Kasiphey to Dongthang 6.5 miles/10.5km; Gagar to Dongthang 14.5 miles/23.4km or 7hr). ▶

The new trail to Dur Tsachu starts from this village. The trail (31 miles/50km) is not suitable for pack animals all the way due to narrow passages in the gorge of the Mangde Chhu. There are a couple of stiff climbs to negotiate through a lush green forest, in order to avoid cliffs alongside the river. By day six Dur Tsachu should be reached (read more on Dur Tsachu in Trek 16). (More research on the trek is needed.)

From Dur Tsachu one trail continues north to Gankar Punsum and on to Lunana. Another goes south to Bumthang /Jakar (3 days). The latter is the normal route used for Bhutanese visiting the hot springs (see Treks 16, 18 and 19).

Note: This route should be open (2007), but is not wide enough in some sections for pack animals. See also Trek 14, days 1 and 2.

Dongthang means 'the village of takins': it is believed that this area used to be infested by takins before people settled here.

TREK 16

BUMTHANG–LUNANA
(INCLUDING THE TREK
TO DUR TSACHU)

Grade	strenuous
Time	8 days
Distance	64.5 miles/104km
Altitude gain	15,764ft/4806m
Altitude loss	11,385ft/3471m
Status	open

A trek along a remote and seldom-visited route to Lunana. For information on Bumthang see Trek 20.

This is a tough trek – but all routes in and out of Lunana are tough. There is one (major) river crossing before the final climb to the Gophu La.

Reaching Tshochenchen camp in 2 days is arduous because of the distance and altitude gain of over 1200m. An alternative would be to take 3 days, with an extra camp. Two days' hard work, however, is rewarded by a very good campsite in alpine meadows at Tshochenchen (instead of a wet, muddy jungle camp en route).

Day hikes in Bumthang Valley
1 First day of trek 20
2 From Swiss Guest House (8676ft/2645m) climb in 3hr to Petsheling Gompa (11,200ft/3415m) and descend in 2hr to Tamshing Gompa.
3 From Swiss Guest House (8676ft/2645m) cross over the 11,250ft/3430m high ridge to the east into the Tang Valley; stay high and circle the end of valley (in order to minimize the up and down) to reach Kunzangdra Gompa (10,561ft/3220m). Then descend steeply to the road, where transport should be waiting (full day).

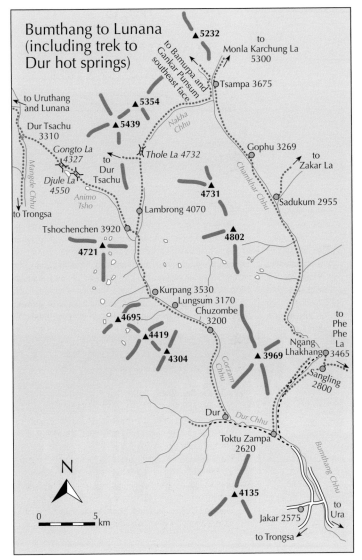

Bumthang to Lunana
(including trek to
Dur hot springs)

▲5232

to Bamurpa and
Gankar Punsum
southeast face

to
Monla Karchung La
5300

Tsampa 3675

to Uruthang
and Lunana

▲5354

Nakha Chhu

Dur Tsachu
3310

▲5439

Gongto La
4327

to
Dur
Tsachu

⚔ *Thole La 4732*

Gophu 3269

to
Zakar La

Chamkhar Chhu

Djule La
4550

Animo Tsho

Lambrong 4070

▲4731

Sadukum 2955

Tshochenchen 3920

▲4802

▲4721

Kurpang 3530

Lungsum 3170
Chuzombe
3200

to
Phe
Phe
La

▲4695

Ngang
Lhakhang 3465

▲4419

▲3969

Sangling
2800

▲4304

Gorzam Chhu

Dur *Dur Chhu*

Toktu Zampa
2620

Bumthang Chhu

N

▲4135

0   5 km

Jakar 2575

to
Ura

to Trongsa

235

DAY 1

Bumthang (8528ft/2600m) drive to
Dur trail head (8817ft/2688m) trek to Chuzombe
(10,496ft/3200m)

Time	5hr
Distance	8.1 miles/13km
Altitude gain	1968ft/600m
Altitude loss	0ft/0m

Dur is a small settlement with a monastery, several *stupas* and farmhouses. A small shop and bar sells provisions. This is a meeting place for trekkers, staff and horsemen.

Drive north from Bumthang/Jakar to **Dur** (Dhur, Duer) in 45min.

Be prepared for a muddy first couple of days. Leave the dirt road and cross a muddy meadow to find a suspension bridge – that has seen better days – across the Dur Chhu. Stay on the east side of the ridge and leave the Dur Chhu behind. Another suspension bridge soon follows, leading to Luzbi: don't cross it! Walk along the river Gorzam Chhu (Yoleng Chhu) for the next 1.5hr on easy flat ground, travelling north for most of the day. On the opposite bank,

Kurjey Lhakhang in Jakar, Bumthang

200m above, is Lurawa Gompa. About 3.5hr from the start Gorsum campsite is reached (10,170ft/3100m). If the party is feeling strong, another campsite could be reached, 1.5hr further on in an opening in the forest, **Chuzombe** (Chopchumey; 10,496ft/3200m). There are few flat, dry camping spots here, and only one roofed hut. Sun sets at 1700hr.

DAY 2

Chuzombe (10,496ft/3200m)
to Tshochenchen (12,860ft/3920m)

Time	7hr
Distance	9.3 miles/15km
Altitude gain	2362ft/720m
Altitude loss	c164ft/50m

Sun rises at 0700hr. Descend c50m through dense bamboo forest to the Yoleng Chhu from where the trail leads upstream towards the north. Today's trail crosses many bridges over streams fed by lakes high above the river. About 2hr from camp (10,660ft/3250m) the trail reaches the village of Lungsum, set in a meadow. Around 2hr later the trail reaches a possible campsite, Kurpang (11,578ft/3530m) with one big open hut. Along the trail look out for a typical feature of this trek: stones wrapped in big rhododendron leaves, placed there by herders to protect their yaks and other stock whilst migrating.

An important fork is reached 1.5hr from Kurpang, at Labi Thinla: go left. ▸

Climb a steep ridge (50m) and cross into a big beautiful alpine valley high above the river. The trail flattens out and 10–15min later reaches **Tshochenchen** camp (12,860ft/3920m), a lovely site by the river. Except for the summer, and the coldest months in winter, this area is packed with yaks and sheep from Bumthang.

A right turn here is the start of a 4–5-day trek along the Thole Chhu to Thole La (15,5210ft/4732m), which leads to Chamkhar Chhu and Gangkar Punsum Southeast Face, Bamurpa (14,530ft/4430m; see Trek 18).

Tshochenchen valley 3900m

Dur to Tshochenchen involves an altitude gain of over 1200m, and you might choose to take a rest day here, for acclimatization, gentle walking or relaxing.

DAY 3

*Tshochenchen (12,860ft/3920m)
to Dur Tsachu (10,857ft/3310m)
via Djule La (14,924ft/4550m) and
Gongto La (14,193ft/4327m)*

Time	8–8.5hr
Distance	9.9 miles/16km
Altitude gain	2065ft/630m + 449ft/137m
Altitude loss	1181ft/360m + 3336ft/1017m

Sun rises at 0730hr. Start with an easy flat hike for 1hr through a spectacular alpine valley with patches of juniper forest and wildflower meadows. A couple of sheer cliffs complete the scene. You may see yak herders rubbing the leaves of a small blue/purple flower, a member of the primula family; on them; they believe that the leaves provide protection from the bitter cold.

The end of the valley appears to be a dead end, but the trail continues on a side valley branching out to the west–northwest. The steady climb up to the pass reveals the holy lake Animo Tsho (14,350ft/4375m).

ANIMO TSHO

It is said that once a nun threw her red scarf into the lake, jumped after it and drowned. With luck, you may see the scarf in the water. Speech is forbidden at this sacred lake.

It should take 3.5hr to reach **Djule La** (Jule La; 14,924ft/4550m), a pretty pass with at least 10 cairns and many prayer flags. The views are special: looking back far below last night's campsite is visible. In the other direction is a large lake, beyond which are the Dur hot springs and tonight's camp; further again is tomorrow's camp, Warathang. In the far distance looking east–northeast is Thole La (Thogle La); ask the yak herders to point it out. The trail now enters a new watershed: the Mangde or Trongsa Chhu.

The trail descends steeply for 45min to the lake, Djule Tsho (13,743ft/4190m). Climb up again and above the lake on the right to reach the second pass of the day, the **Gongto La** (Gokthong La; 14,193ft/4327m).

From Gongto La the valleys are all heavily forested, with the mighty Mangde Chhu far below. The river leaves Bhutan through Namgyel Wangchuk (Manas) Wildlife Reserve, joining the Brahmaputra in Assam, India, which later joins the Ganges in Bangladesh.

A good trail makes a non-stop steep descent of over 1000m. About 2hr after the pass a small hut is reached in a clearing (11,316ft/3450m); 15min beyond is the campsite at Dur hot springs (Dur Tsachu). ▸

Dur Tsachu (10,857ft/3310m) has two reasonably big huts, 'guesthouses' for Bhutanese who travel a long way to enjoy the hot springs and their medicinal effect. The

Dur Tsachu counts eight pools, which are apparently beneficial for thirteen different diseases. The story goes that Dur Tsachu was created for Guru Rinpoche; look for his big footprint.

caretaker lives in a bigger complex. The one toilet facility is rather poor, and tent space can be a problem. It's been a hard day for the pack animals, so expect them to arrive late. The caretaker might offer you a cup of butter tea, and a piece of yak cheese, small hard cubes on a string, called *chugo*. Suck – don't bite – to avoid broken teeth. According to the caretaker there are 108 – a holy number – springs here, visited by 3000 Bhutanese and 20–30 trekkers every year. The pool walls are decorated with crystallized salt. Be careful – the edges of the pools are slippery.

A new trail (nearly finished in 2007) follows the Mangdu Chhu from Dur Tsachu to Trongsa (see Trek 15).

Some parties turn back at Dur Tsachu and return by the same path. An alternative (see Trek 18) is to take the Thole La pass and loop back to Bumthang, finishing in the Ngang valley. ◀

DAY 4

*Dur Tsachu (10,857ft/3310m)
to Uruthang (14,612ft/4455m)
via Nephu La (17,306ft/4495m)*

Time	6hr
Distance	6.2 miles/10km
Altitude gain	3887ft/1185m
Altitude loss	131ft/40m

Start hiking for 30min upstream on a very muddy trail before crossing a 'big' bridge high above the Mangde Chhu (10,932ft/3333m). In 1985 a yak carrying most of the money for a Japanese expedition was pushed off this bridge into the churning river by another animal. Two days later, the dead yak was found – but without the money! About 1hr beyond the bridge is a yak gate (11,267ft/3435m), marking the start of today's continuous steep climb, following a trail mainly along the stream.

The trail slowly reaches the treeline and rhododendrons take over. After about 5hr a stone marker is reached where the trail flattens out and crosses high alpine meadows. Take

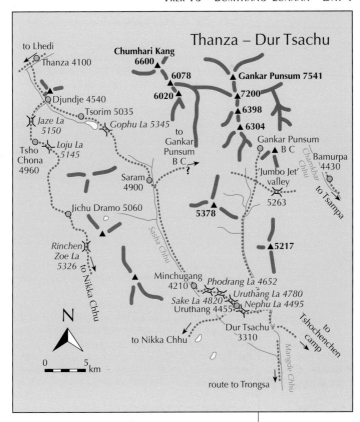

care not to get lost in mist. Around 1hr later windy **Nephu La** (Uli La; 17,306ft/4495m) comes into view, decorated with one cairn. Only 45min beyond is a good camp, reached easily by a small descent through meadows with many yaks in autumn. There are several basic herder huts in this valley surrounded by an impressive cirque of rocky mountains. The plain is **Uruthang** (Warathang, Warthang; 14,612ft/ 4455m). ▸

From Uruthang there is a difficult 3-day trail leading to Sephu Naurothang, at the Nikka Chhu bridge, crossing three passes.

DAY 5

*Uruthang (14,612ft/4455m) to Minchugang
(13,809ft/4210m) via Uruthang La
(15,678ft/4780m), Sake La (15,810ft/4820m) and
Phodrang La (15,259ft/4652m)*

Time	5hr
Distance	6.8 miles/11km
Altitude gain	620ft/190m + 574ft/175m + 112ft/34m = 1308ft/399m (3 passes)
Altitude loss	443ft/135m + 663ft/202m + 1450ft/442m = 2555ft/779m (3 passes)

From camp, a faint trail climbs east and in a few hundred metres offers a view of Gankar Punsum: the start of a 3-day trek to Gankar Punsum base camp, on the south ridge, used by the 1986 British expedition (see Trek 17).

From camp follow a rocky trail to the end of the impressive high-altitude valley, leading to a good trail climbing the first pass of today. **Uruthang La** (Warathang La, Zimmer La; 15,678ft/4780m) is followed by a short descent to two lakes and the start of the next climb. A very steep ascent to the second pass **Sake La** (Zaga La; 15,810ft/4820m) has to be tackled. From the pass a short steep descent on a rocky path with loose stones follows; be careful if the yaks are behind you. The trail traverses a geologically interesting area with glacial whalebacks and red soil – like walking through massive sand dunes.

Around 1hr beyond the second pass the trail reaches Phodrang (Phorang; 15,147ft/4618m), a good campsite with a solid hut attached to a huge boulder decorated with prayer flags. This may be too early in the day to stop; the next site will be lower. Look around for Himalayan blue sheep and pheasants.

Phodrang La (15,259ft/4652m) is the last pass for today; it takes an easy 20min to reach it. From the pass it is a long way down to the Sasha Chhu on a trail through alpine meadows.

The trail continues up the valley to the north along the Sasha Chhu. There are several camp possibilities along the way – mostly next to yak herders' huts – such as Simthang and **Minchugang** (13,809ft/4210m); the latter is a fine camp 1hr beyond the last pass with two stone enclosures.

DAY 6

Minchugang (13,809ft/4210m)
to Saram (16,072ft/4900m)

Time	7hr
Distance	9.9 miles/16km
Altitude gain	2263ft/690m
Altitude loss	0ft/0m

Today's trail runs north in one long, easy, gradual climb; at nightfall it's hard to believe that 700m of altitude has been gained. Several side streams and the main river, the Sasha Chhu, are crossed. ▶ The trail passes several herder huts. The herders report snow leopards in the area and claim to have lost yaks to them. The valley is endless with beautiful views.

After 2hr the first glimpse of the high mountains appears. There are three campsites higher up in the valley: Gechey Woma, Gechey Koma, and the highest one, close to the turning point leading to the Gophu La, is Saram. The third campsite is a good choice since it is at the foot of the final climb, right after the river crossing (be careful crossing the river late in the day), and provides a chance to dry out.

After a narrow passage a high-altitude marsh is reached. Cross it by hopping between lumps of sod. In the far distance a very pointy peak dominates the view; it looks likes the Matterhorn and is probably Chumhari Kang (21,648ft/6600m or 22,960ft/7000m). Further along the plain a big side valley branches to the right (east) towards snowy peaks and Gankar Punsum. Camping an extra day here and exploring up the valley could bring you to a viewing point close to Gankar Punsum.

Depending on the season, conditions and time of day, the river crossing could be difficult. Consider carrying sandals.

Saram camp 4900m at end of Sasha Chhu valley with border peaks in the distance

Camp is nearby below a moraine, at **Saram** (Sanam or Zaram; 16,072ft/4900m), and is quite high. Not only will trekkers and staff be tired: the yaks might simply lie down on the spot where their luggage is dropped.

COUNTING IN BHUTAN

The Bhutanese count by using all three parts of each finger (sometimes on both sides). There are some variations, but normally they use their thumb to touch each section on the other fingers, starting with the forefinger. In this way they can count up to three on each finger (or double if they us the back of the fingers as well).

The Sarchops, who live in the east of the country, have their own way of counting, only going up to 20. To indicate an age of more than 20 years they will say 'very very' old, where every 'very' stands for a 20-year period.

DAY 7

*Saram (16,072ft/4900m) to camp between
Tsorim and Djundje (15,974ft/4870m)
via Gophu La (17,532ft/5345m)*

Time	7.5hr
Distance	8 miles/13km
Altitude gain	1460ft/445m
Altitude loss	1558ft/475m

Try an early start to enjoy the views and to reach the high
pass early in case of foul weather. Today's trail can be hard if
there is snow or mist. Let the yaks go first – they smell the
trail!

Soon after leaving camp, follow a side valley to the west
towards the Gophu La. Don't cross the stream coming down
this valley. Looking back is a big surprise: a view towards the
highest unclimbed mountain massif in the world, Gankar
Punsum, the west face (24,735ft/7541m) towering up and
almost kissing the sky. The view improves as the trail
ascends.

*Looking northeast to
Gankar Punsum
7541m on the way to
Gophu La*

245

Read about climbing
Gankar Punsum at
Trek 19 day 7.

◄ The climb up the moraine is not too difficult, with only two or three steep short sections. In 3hr the pre-pass is reached, indicated by a big cairn (17,564ft/5355m). From here the last glimpse of Gankar Punsum is possible. Looking west there is a beautiful crevassed glacier leading up to a snowy peak. Look towards the Gophu La and you will see a score of small lakes. Descend to these, take a trail between them and climb back up to the **Gophu La** (17,532ft/5345m). The pass is wide, and covered with prayer flags and cairns. Towards Lunana, one big turquoise lake is visible. ◄

From the pass, a
climb east for 75m
affords one last great
view of Gankar
Punsum.

Descend on a good, sometimes rocky, trail along the right side of the turquoise lake. Around 2hr after crossing the pass and tackling a couple of small hills, **Tsorim** campsite is reached (16,515ft/5035m). This is the usual campsite for both directions; however, considering the high altitude, it might be smart to continue another 1.5hr and sleep lower. Climb out of the Tsorim valley, and 40min later the trail turns a corner on top of a moraine. The valley bottom widens and 7.5hr after Saram, at an altitude of 15,974ft/4870m, there is a reasonable campsite next to a stream.

DAY 8

*Camp between Tsorim and Djundje
(15,974ft/4870m) to Thanza (13,448ft/4100m)*

Time	3.5–4hr
Distance	6.2 miles/10km
Altitude gain	0ft/0m
Altitude loss	2526ft/770m

This is an easy day of walking, mainly downhill, on a good trail to Thanza in Lunana. The valley is narrow at first, with two moraine walls coming close together, before opening up again with some big meadows with yak herders' huts.

Around 1.5–2hr after setting out reach **Djundje** camp (14,890ft/4540m), a large meadow, the normal campsite used. Descend further for the first view of Lunana or Po Chhu valley: the big sandy valley between Chozo and Thanza is visible, the result of a glacial outburst flood (1994). Climb up again to bypass a big waterfall. The trail exits the valley at an exciting viewing point and good lunch spot (14,235ft/ 4340m), from where the three villages Dyotta, Töncho and Thanza; Chozo in the distance, Lunana valley and Table Mountain (or Singey Kang; 22,960ft/ 7000m) are all visible. From Table Mountain looking west Kangphu Kang (23,616ft/ 7200m) and part of Jejekangphu Kang (23,944ft/7300m) can also be seen.

About 1.5hr after leaving camp, the trail passes the bridge over the main river (Tsorim Chhu), leading to Jaze La (16,890ft/5150m) and following the route to Nikka Chhu. The trail joins the route coming from Chozo in Lunana that crosses the Sintia La (17,055ft/ 5200m) (see Trek 3).

Descend for 30min and cross the south leg of the Po Chhu through a deep gully to the village of Töncho (13,350ft/4070m). A good 8 or 9 days of trekking is rewarded by one of the more remote valleys of the Himalayas and Karakorams. Lunana may become less remote when an 'all-year-round-open' trail is launched, following the Po Chhu to Punakha, part of the Five Year Plan (2002–07). Since 2002 **Thanza** has had a wireless radio station, installed to warn people living downstream if a glacier outburst flood occurs again (a couple of lakes are still at risk). The Bhutanese, assisted by glaciologists from several nations (Japan, India and Austria) are studying the area intensively. ▸

A trek to Raphstreng Tsho lake – which burst in 1994 – takes about 4hr one way.

LOCAL FESTIVALS IN LUNANA

If you arrive at the right time of year you may catch one of these. In early autumn every household holds a spiritual session to ensure long life for the animals, protection against bad spirits and praise for the mountains. The ceremony can take several days, with many monastic prayers and animal sacrifice: a yak in the old days, now one or two (less valuable) sheep. The kitchen crew might obtain some blessed sheep meat to prepare for the trekking group. The Lunana area is similar to several other remote areas in Bhutan in trying to re-install some monks with pupils so that local people have easier access to religious professionals for their ceremonies.

After a rest day or two, and new pack animals (yaks), the trek can be continued: either by crossing the passes Jaze La (16,890ft/5150m) or Sintia La (17,055ft/5200m) towards Nikka Chhu in 6 or 7 days, or walking along the Lunana valley, along the east and west Po Chhu rivers, to Gaza or Laya via the Karakachu La (16,465ft/5020m). From Gaza

THE YAK HERDER'S TENT: THE *BA* OR *JHA*

The *ba* is the Tibetan/Bhutanese counterpart to the Mongol yurt. The yurt is a white, very warm, but heavy and cumbersome felt tent, stretched across a framework of willow stakes. The Tibetan *ba* is much lighter and made of 30cm strips of loosely woven yak hair, sewn together in a roughly rectangular shape.

Larger ones can measure over 8m by 11m. Two wooden posts support the tent on the inside, with 6–12 posts holding up the sides and corners on the outside. Ropes of braided yak hair, alternating with stronger ropes of yak sinew, run from the tent, over the top of the outside poles and down to the ground, resulting in something resembling a gigantic black spider. Many of the support ropes are festooned with white prayer flags of cotton cloth, printed with mantras and holy images.

In Bhutan the tents are erected over a shallow, square pit dug into the ground, with walls made of stones built up to chest level on all sides. Turf and mud are stuffed into the gaps between the stones to protect against the wind.

Entering a nomad tent is a privilege, and only by special invitation, as each tent is guarded by at least two ferocious mastiffs. Some Tibetan mastiffs are truly enormous, and nearly all are trained to be vicious. Leashed on long steel chains by day, they guard their owner's tent and livestock. Trained to attack strangers, wolves, snow leopards and bears, many are so wild that even their owners can barely enter their tents, sometimes throwing food to the dogs to divert their attention.

The tents are surprisingly bright inside, as sunlight percolates through the loose weave of the yak-hair cloth. The translucent material does not initially let in rain or snow (though after a few days of constant rain it does become waterlogged). They are remarkably warm, as the black colour absorbs solar heat

Yak herders receiving wages at the end of the trek

Yak herder's tent

by day, and a yak dung fire in a clay hearth provides heat at night. The hearth is set to the left of the entrance. In Bhutan hearths are considered the doors to the earth and the underworld, while the door to the sky is the chimney (or rather the slit in the tent's roof between the two inner poles, which can be closed by letting down flaps of cloth attached to the tent).

The tent and poles weigh some 150–200kg, and it takes two yaks to carry one tent. Every year the nomads weave three new strips of yak hair, each as long as the tent is wide. These are sewn onto the back edge of the tent, while three old and worn strips on the front are cut off. Although it may take 10 years or so for all the strips to be replaced, the constant renewal assures that the tents last indefinitely, all the while remaining in good repair. It is amazing to think that the tents seen today are the same as those seen hundreds or even thousands of years ago.

More and more nomads today are using blue (or another colour) plastic tarpaulin from India or China if they can effort it. The tarpaulins don't last as long as the traditional yak-wool tents due to the intense sunlight at altitude.

Taking down the yak tent and packing up camp doesn't take long time. The fireplace is the last spot to be taken apart: sometimes a spirit catcher is left behind.

the trek finishes in Punakha. From Laya the trek could be continued to Paro – the ultimate trek in the Bhutan Himalayas. ▸

For details on the Lunana trek in reverse, and crossing the Jaze La and Sintia La towards Nikka Chhu, see Trek 3.

TREK 17

GANGKAR PUNSUM BASE CAMP BELOW THE SOUTH RIDGE OF GANGKAR PUNSUM – VIA DUR HOT SPRINGS

Grade	demanding
Time	6–7 days one way
Distance	not available
Altitude gain	not available
Altitude loss	not available
Status	double check if open

Another possibility would be to visit base camp and Gangkar Punsum's southeast face by crossing an almost unexplored pass (see Trek 16, second map), or (further south) by crossing the Thole La and trekking up north (see Trek 16, first map).

Gaining the base camp of Gangkar Punsum is an exciting trek by itself; however, this trek can also be added to the start or end of a Lunana trek.

The trek starts from Bumthang/Jakar and follows the route to Dur hot springs, from where there are several possibilities to reach base camp (according to information picked up from yak herders and expedition reports).

From Dur hot springs

1 This route probably does not lead to base campsite itself (more research needed). It starts 1.5hr after the hot springs just before the start of the Nephu La climb (see Trek 16, day 4). Follow the Mangde Chhu upstream for 2 days until you reach Gangkar Punsum's south face (see Trek 16, second map).

2 The other route crosses the Nephu La (see Trek 16). Camp at Uruthang where a faint easterly trail crosses a ridge and leads out of the valley. According to some reports, it will take about 3 days to arrive at the south

Figures near Gankar Punsum Base Camp.
Photo: Steve Berry, Himalayan Kingdoms

ridge of Gangkar Punsum base camp (more research needed). Read about climbing Gankar Punsum in Trek 19, day 7.

After spending a day or two in the base camp area you can either go back the same way, or explore a route to the west. This leads to the upper Sasha Chhu valley below the Gophu La which leads to Lunana (there should be a route, according to unclear maps and yak herders). See Trek 16, second map, for some details on crossing Gophu La into Lunana.

TREK 18

GANGKAR PUNSUM
SOUTHEAST FACE – THOLE LA –
BUMTHANG TREK

Grade	demanding–strenuous
Time	10 days
Distance	41.5 miles/67km to southeast face, and 47.7 miles/77km return to Bumthang = 89.3 miles/144km
Altitude gain	9059ft/2762m
Altitude loss	9141ft/2787m
Status	double check if open

Gankar Punsum (24,735ft/7541m) is the highest peak of Bhutan, and the highest unclimbed massif in the world.

Gangkar Punsum and the surrounding valleys are rarely visited by trekkers, and by Himalayan standards a visit to the area is a wild experience.

This trek leads to Gangkar Punsum's southeast face and back either via the same route or by traversing Thole La. Crossing over to the base camp should be possible following a route rather difficult or impossible for pack animals (see Trek 19).

The trek description below starts from Jakar, following the Bumthang Chhu/Chamkhar Chhu up to Gangkar Punsum southeast face. The return follows the same route until a split in the trail from where you climb up Thole La (15,520ft/ 4732m). After crossing the pass descend to meet the trail between Jakar and Gangkar Punsum base camp and Lunana. Crossing Thole La from Chamkhar Chhu side is easier (less steep) than from the Dur hot springs side. You can continue up north after crossing Thole La to visit the base camp (see Trek 17) or onwards to Lunana. The description below follows the way out to Jakar. ◀

The starting point – 2–3km (in 2007) beyond Toktu Zampa (dirt road towards Zhabjethang) – is also the start for Trek 20.

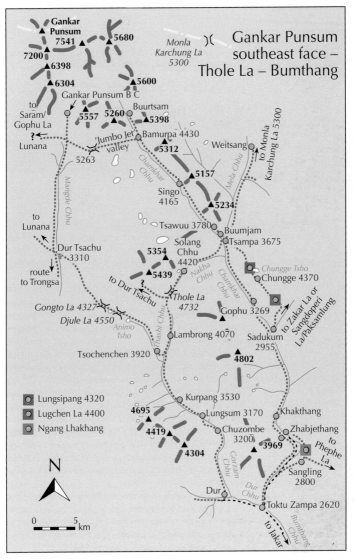

Gankar Punsum
southeast face –
Thole La – Bumthang

Gankar
Punsum
▲ 7541 ▲ 5680
▲ 7200
▲ 6398
▲ 6304
▲ 5600
Monla
Karchung La
5300
Gankar Punsum B C
▲ 5557 ▲ 5260 Buurtsam
to
Saram/
Gophu La
? Lunana
'Jumbo Jet'
valley
5263
▲ 5398
Bamurpa 4430
▲ 5312
Weitsang
Chamkhar Chhu
Mela Chhu
to Monla Karchung La 5300
Mangde Chhu
to
Lunana
Dur Tsachu
3310
route
to Trongsa
▲ 5157
Singo
4165
▲ 5234
Tsawuu 3780
Solang
Chhu
4420
▲ 5354
▲ 5439
Nakha Chhu
Buumjam
Tsampa 3675
Chungge Tsho
Chungge 4370
to Dur Tsachu
?
Thole La
4732
Chamkhar Chhu
Gophu 3269
to Zakar La or Sangdoperi La/Paksamlung
Gongto La 4327
Djule La 4550
Animo Tsho
Tashi Chhu
Lambrong 4070
Sadukum
2955
Tsochenchen 3920
▲ 4802

◎ Lungsipang 4320
◎ Lugchen La 4400
◎ Ngang Lhakhang

Kurpang 3530
▲ 4695
Lungsum 3170
Khakthang
▲ 4419
Chuzombe
3200
Zhabjethang
to Phephe La
▲ 4304
▲ 3969
Corzam Chhu
Sangling
2800

N

Dur
Dur Chhu
Toktu Zampa 2620
Bumthang Chhu
to Jakar

0   5 km

DAY 1

From Jakar (8446ft/2575m) drive 2–3km beyond Toktu Zampa (8856ft/2620m) (towards Zhabjethang) trek to beyond Khakthang army camp (9505ft/2898m)

Time	5–6hr
Distance	10 miles/16km
Altitude gain	918ft/280m
Altitude loss	0ft/0m

Toktu Zampa is a small hamlet with a couple of teahouses/bars and a forestry division checking point.

Drive north from Jakar, along Kurjey Lhakhang, to the village of **Toktu Zampa**. Start from Toktu Zampa if the drivable suspension bridge is not in use; otherwise drive onwards towards Zhabjethang. Start from Toktu Zampa with a short descent to a foot suspension bridge and cross the clear river Dur Chhu. Climb back up on the other side and walk next to a beautiful carved and painted Buddha housed in a little shrine. The valley opens up and flattens out into a northerly direction. Pass a building of the RNR (Renewable Natural Resources) organisation where the government is helping farmers with all kinds of agricultural issues. After 10min walking beside buckwheat fields reach the yellow-roofed Thankabi Gompa built in 1470 by Shamar Rinpoche. In front of this is a very long *mani* wall with more than 160 carved and coloured stones. ◀ Behind the *gompa* is the village of Thankabi. Another smaller monastery and a *mani* wall follow a little bit further on.

These bear the 'Om Mani Pad Me Hum' text ('Hail to the jewel in the lotus').

The trail continues next to fields, through an archway *chorten* with a mandala painted inside on the roof. Close by is a beautiful Buddha image carved/painted on a rock, with a little roof above.

On the west side of the Bumthang Chhu there is a choice of trails. One follows a route above the river, partly parallel with the new dust road; the other one goes down to a big suspension bridge. Do not cross the bridge, but find a good trail very close to the Bumthang Chhu.

The trek into the Ngang valley climbs gently. After 2.5hr on the opposite side of the valley a group of four houses appears, where the Ngang Lhakhang is situated, site of an annual and beautiful festival organised by the former valley headman Sherab La. The trail now takes a northwesterly direction.

About 3hr into the hike one trail goes down to the river to a 30m-long suspension bridge (9250ft/2820m); don't cross over. On both sides of the bridge there are several houses forming the village of **Zhabjethang** (Shobthang).

Soon a BHU and Choekhor Toe community primary school at Shobtang village (9330ft/2845m) are reached. There are some beautiful houses in Bhutanese style both here and further up the valley. Above, on the hillside, is a monastery – Neswy Gompa – with some meditation cells nearby. After the last house is a possible campsite, Shobtang camp (9400ft/2865m), but this might be a bit too early to stop. Walk onwards in a northerly direction, passing another small group of beautiful houses.

There are a couple of *chortens* just before **Khakthang** military camp (9505ft/2898m) is reached; one of them has a unique shape, with prayer wheels at each corner. The valley narrows here. There are campsite possibilities both before and after the army camp, which has several houses and barracks. Your permit will be checked here. There is a big meadow with a helicopter landing spot. There are also several campsites in the next hour along the Bumthang Chhu (Chamkhar Chhu).

DAY 2

1hr after Khakthang army camp (9505ft/2898m) to Gophu (10,722ft/3269m)

Time	6hr
Distance	10 miles/16km
Altitude gain	1210ft/369m
Altitude loss	0ft/0m

*Pesa 3030m – Gankar Punsum
southeast face trek*

On the other side of the bridge a long exploratory trek, Ngang valley–Zakar La–Ora La–Lhuntshi, starts by following the big side valley of the Gumthang Chhu.

Follow a good – but sometimes muddy – trail through dense mixed bamboo forest. Several small side streams have to be crossed on slippery log bridges. The military and yak herders maintain the trail because it is heavily used: enormous stone dams have been erected to keep it clear from flooding.

About 30min after camp reach a big Bhutanese-style wooden bridge at **Sadukum** (Sadrusum) (9692ft/2955m). Do not cross the bridge (just after which there is a big meadow for camping). ◄

ALTERNATIVE HIGH ROUTE

From the bridge another trail rises very steeply on the east side of the river, gaining an altitude of just under 1500m. This leads in 2 days to the same point that reached in 2 days trekking through the bottom of the valley. The high trek encounters Chameur village (14,040ft/4280m); Lugchen La (14,430ft/4400m); Chungge village (14,333ft/4370m); a lake, Chungge Tsho (14,430ft/4400m) and Lungsipang village (14,170ft/4320m).

Several side streams and a couple of log bridges are on the menu for today. It takes more than 2hr to get above 3000m, so there is little climbing. In 2.5hr Pesa or Petso (9940ft/3030m) is reached, a campsite at the end of big open swampy field, below some rockfaces and next to a big cave used by some trekking parties. There are again enormous dam constructions at the river near camp (a local legend may explain why: when Guru Rinpoche travelled to Pesa from Tibet he found a river and a lake trying to occupy the same area. He sorted out the problem, so today both lake and river 'coexist').

It is too early to camp, so 3hr more along the river through forest leads to the next campsite. In spring you may meet yak people with yaks that have taken goods up to the summer pastures.

At a narrow spot in the valley are three bamboo huts, next to the remains of an old wooden bridge: this is Bomsang Sa. There are impressive cliffs on the other side of the river. Side stream number 50 comes in just after Bomsang Sa, crossed on five big logs. A short steep climb leads to the new suspension bridge crossing the Bumthang Chhu about 15m above the water at 10,580ft/3225m. Walking now on the east side of the Bumthang Chhu the first camp, Bomsang Tang (10,760ft/3280m), is reached after 30min. Another 30min later and you reach **Gophu** or Gombu (10,722ft/3269m), via a little wooden construction spanning a small deep gorge. Watch for musk deer.

DAY 3

Gophu (10,722ft/3269m) to
Tsampa (12,054ft/3675m)
and Tsawuu (12,400ft/3780m)

Time	5–6hr
Distance	9.3 miles/15km
Altitude gain	1332ft/406m
Altitude loss	0ft/0m

Sun reaches camp around 0800hr. The trail continues through mixed forest. Watch for Himalayan blood pheasants on the trail and in the bushes. At 11,480ft/3500m a big tributary comes in from the west, the Gophu Chhu. ▸ About 3hr after leaving camp a clearing in the forest is reached, which

This valley leads to Dur hot springs but is not in use. At the end is a big lake, Upe Tso.

could be used as a campsite (11,628ft/3545m). Parties usually stop here for lunch.

The bamboo forest slowly gives way (around 3600m) to alpine forest and more open views. The valley is very narrow at first, with some impressive cliffs on the other side of the river. In the distance the valley opens up at a big split, but first an open area, Chelemmarchhu, is reached (11,800ft/ 3597m). Chelemmarchhu is dominated by a big stone, linked to the story that people from Tibet carrying butter left some here, and it transformed into stone (*marchhu* means butter).

The valley opens up with a big mountain directly ahead, Tsambar Brakhsam (14,202ft/4330m), at the confluence of the Mela Chhu and Bumthang Chhu. Confluences such as these are the homes of deities who protect travellers from evil; offerings are brought to the foot of the mountain. A pointed stone, a landmark, sits by the trail here.

CONFLUENCE OF MANY RIVERS

The names of the rivers meeting here are: Bumthang Chhu (Chamkhar Chhu) from Gangkar Punsum; Mela Chhu (Tibet River, Mela Karchung) from Monla Karchung La pass; and the Nakha Chhu from Thole La.

The army camp **Tsampa** (12,054ft/3675m) is also near the confluence. There is a wireless radio here, operated twice a day. In the old days radio contact with the next camp or headquarters in Wangdi was only possible from higher up the hill. Tsampa military camp is one of the remotest in Bhutan. Your trekking permit will be checked here, and you should be able to get information about snow conditions for crossing the Thole La (15,521ft/4732m); the trail can be seen from Tsampa.

The trek to Gankar Punsum southeast side crosses the first bridge over Mela Chhu and after that starts climbing in a northeast direction. This brings you to the foot of Tsambar Brakhsam, where there are prayer flags and several *chortens*. On your first visit you are supposed to offer something at the main *chorten* to please the mountain deities/demons. A second bridge, below the *chortens*, crossing the Bumthang Chhu, leads to Thole La.

Around Tsampa are several camping possibilities. If you feel up to it you could trek for another 30min to the next campsite up the valley towards Gangkar Punsum. Follow the Bumthang Chhu up to the first of eight settlements in this valley, Buumjan (12,333ft/3760m), a rather dirty campsite, or carry on for 30min to the next settlement **Tsawuu** (12,400ftf/3780m) with six stone huts. In the distance part of Gangkar Punsum (24,735ft/7541m) is visible (some horsemen call the mountain Kiga Ri).

DAY 4

Tsawuu (12,400ft/3780m)
to Bamurpa (14,530ft/4430m)

Time	7–8hr
Distance	12.5 miles/20km
Altitude gain	2132ft/650m
Altitude loss	0ft/0m

Start walking next to the river through a beautiful forest with lichen draping the trees. The river loses little height; there are no major waterfalls. Today there are six settlements along the trail. Early in the season they might be empty, but during summer it is very busy here with yak herders from Bumthang.

Sun reaches camp at 0700hr.

'SPRING CLEANING'

At the start of the season you might see newly erected prayer flags around the houses. This is the first task on returning to these villages after winter – as well as holding a *puja*– to make sure that the houses are blessed again and potential evil spirits are chased away.

About 30min after Tsawuu there is a steep 60–70m climb through the forest, parallel to the principal waterfall in the Bumthang Chhu/Chamkhar Chhu. The climb ends at a small Buddhist *mani* wall. The forest thins out here at 3900m.

There are a couple of yak gates here: when these are closed yaks cannot pass up or down. Just beyond a sulphur-based water source at 12,875ft/3925m the trail changes its name to 'the trail of the 1 million stones' – tiring for walking! All of a sudden an impressive part of Gankar Punsum appears around a corner.

About 3hr after leaving camp **Singo** (13,660ft/4165m) is reached, in a big open area above the treeline. On the opposite side of the valley a clear trail leads up to some houses surrounded by prayer flags.

POISONING PROBLEMS

Little grows at this altitude, so in early spring be aware that horses will eat whatever looks good, including poisonous plants. The horse becomes weak in its legs and walks around like a drunk; eventually it will not be able to move for some hours until the poison wears off. The horsemen have a remedy: water mixed with sugar is forced down the horse's throat, followed by human urine collected in a bottle! The horses soon get better.

Camp Cedi 4360m near Gankar Punsum southeast face

Before reaching Gutchen settlement go through a yak gate and pass by a *chorten*. Gutchen (13,710ft/4180m) has a few houses on both sides of the Chamkhar Chhu. In early spring there will be yaks here that belong to the Punakha

monks, and which graze here until the Bumthang yaks come up. The yaks high up in the mountains of Bhutan feed on a tough, cold-resistant grass, *lapza*. The next settlement, Cedi, is reached by two different trails: the horses take a longer trail above the river, and the trekkers follow a shorter but more difficult track next to it. Cedi has seven houses and is at 14,300ft/4360m.

If the altitude is no problem and it is not too late you could carry on for the last stretch of 1hr to **Bamurpa** (14,530ft/4430m). About 10min after Cedi there is a small stone hut, and a little bit further a small log has to be crossed (14,432ft/4400m) over a small side stream. Gangkar Punsum main peak disappears behind an enormous ice face on its east side. On the other side of the river are some houses on top of the moraine. A ridge of boulders comes down from the right, and just after that another group of four houses appears: Bamurpa (14,530ft/4430m), in a large flat area.

DAY 5

Rest/exploring day in
Bamurpa (14,530ft/4430m)

Sun reaches camp at about 0800hr. There are plenty of hiking opportunities from Bamurpa:

- Walking up closer to the big southeast ridge coming down from Gangkar Punsum: 3hr up the valley passing Buurtsam ('end of the glacier' – a new yak herders' camp, which has only been erected in the last couple of years as a result of the glacier retreating further).
- Another hike follows up the grey, grassy ridge coming in from the west, along which are a couple of prayer flags and some cairns. To get to the beginning of this ridge you have to forge the river (no bridge). The best place is just below where you can see a trail crossing a moraine slope towards a group of six houses at 14,630ft/4460m. There are several trails climbing steeply here, and after 1hr you reach Chogophu at 15,320ft/4670m, with four herder huts huddled into a flat area. From here switchback up to the top of the ridge, or carry on deeper into the valley one level

Gangkar Punsum (24,735ft/7541m), the highest unclimbed mountain massif in the world, has some impressive side valleys and ridges to explore from camp over a couple of days. (Read about climbing Gangkar Punsum at Trek 19 day 7.)

*Gankar Punsum
southeast face 7541m*

higher. This valley is enormous – you could land a jumbo jet in it; at its end are two possible passes leading to Gangkar Punsum base camp on the west side. It takes several hours to get to the end of this valley (see Trek 19).

- Climbing steeply up to the ridge mentioned earlier you will be hit by strong winds (c16,400ft/5000m). The ridge keeps climbing steadily with a couple of false summits; the view towards Gangkar Punsum gets more impressive with every metre. Look south to see yesterday's walk.

SPINNING YAK WOOL

At the end of spring you might see yak herders trimming the yaks' coats for spinning into wool. This is a rather dangerous, difficult job. The yak has to be caught and controlled. The front legs are tied with rope, and if the yak is still struggling the herders will hold it on its side. One or two herders will hold its head firmly while another will trim the tail and belly, using a big pair of scissors, to give wool with a mix of softer and coarser fibres.

DAY 6

*Bamurpa (14,530ft/4430m)
to Tsampa (12,054ft/3675m)*

Time	8hr
Distance	14 miles/22.5km
Altitude gain	0ft/0m
Altitude loss	2476ft/755m

This is the same as day 4, but in reverse, and a little longer to reach the meadow near the confluence and army camp at **Tsampa** (12,054ft/3675m). Enjoy sleeping at lower altitude!

Following the same route in the opposite direction is a totally different experience.

DAY 7

*Tsampa (12,054ft/3675m) to Solang Chhu
(Thole Tsho) (14,480ft/4420m)*

Time	6hr
Distance	8.7 miles/14km
Altitude gain	2445ft/745m
Altitude loss	0ft/0m

Most of today's ascent is at the beginning of the trek.

From the camp descend to the wooden bridge at 11,955ft/3645m and cross the Bumthang Chhu/Chamkhar Chhu for the last time on this trek. Parallel the river for a short stretch, before a steep 60m climb to a yak herders' gate leads into an opening in the forest with some yak herder huts, Tokshung. Climb steeply for 1hr through a narrow gully on a small path, through dense forest with junipers, fir, spruce, birch and rhododendrons, to reach Nagar. The small river Nakha Chhu is close to the trail now. Looking back you can see the valley leading up to Monla Karchung La. Above the treeline reach Kesi (Kesar), with a couple of herder huts, and Bopsar. From Kesi, looking back, there is a great view towards Gangkar Punsum and some other snowy peaks. After Bopsar it is 1hr to an alpine lake, **Solang Chhu** (Thole Tsho) (14,480ft/4420m). Camp just below the lake.

DAY 8

Solang Chhu (Thole Tsho) (14,480ft/4420m) to Lambrong (13,350ft/4070m) via Thole La (15,520ft/4732m)

Time	6hr
Distance	9 miles/14.5km
Altitude gain	1023ft/312m
Altitude loss	2171ft/662m

Thole means stick; the descent from Thole La to the trail between Jakar and Dhur hot springs is so steep that you need to use a stick, hence the name.

One more hour of climbing, past a herders' camp at Tiksang, leads to **Thole La** (Tholey La) (15,520ft/4732m), decorated with prayer flags and cairns. One yak herder, pointing to the west, says that it is possible to go from the pass direct to the hot springs at Dur instead of first descending south for a couple of hours. However, the trail to the west is impassable to horses.

From Thole La a steep descent follows to enter the Thashi Chhu (Tolge Chhu) valley. Carry on down to reach the herders' hut at **Lambrong** (13,350ft/4070m): a good campsite for a well-deserved night's rest. Pumbi Chhu, the river coming in from the east, has several lakes as its source.

DAY 9

—— Lambrong (13,350ft/4070m)
to Lungsum (10,400ft/3170m)

Time	4–5hr
Distance	8.7 miles/14km
Altitude gain	0ft/0m
Altitude loss	2952ft/900m

Continue down the valley along the Thashi Chhu (Tolge Chhu) for 1hr to reach the confluence with Durbichha Chhu (12,770ft/3893m). This is Labi Thinla, and also where you hit the trail between Jakar and Dur hot springs/Gangkar Punsum base camp/Lunana (see Trek 16, day 2). The river changes its name into Gorzam Chhu until the end of our trek at Dur.

The trail follows the wild Gorzam Chhu in a south-southeast direction. If you could fly high above this area you would be surprised at how many (small) lakes there are to the left and right of the trail. As a result there are lots of small tributaries to be crossed, and many footbridges.

The first habitation reached is **Kurpang** (11,578ft/3530m). The next is **Lungsum** at 10,400ft/3170m. This could be used for camping after 4–5hr trekking; trekking all the way out to Dur would be too long in one day (9hr).

DAY 10

Lungsum (10,400ft/3170m) to Dur
(8856ft/2700m) and drive (1hr) to Jakar

Time	4hr
Distance	7.5 miles/12km
Altitude gain	0ft/0m
Altitude loss	1542ft/470m

Having had a good night again at lower altitude, today's trek follows the Gorzam Chhu to Dur.

Above Lungsum is a tiny settlement called Trelshing. From Lungsum go down and cross the Gorzam Chhu. Climb a little and follow a beautiful trail through mixed forest for more than 1hr to reach a meadow below Gortshom (c9840ft/3000m).

Descend to a footbridge crossing the tributary Khamki Chhu (9250ft/2820m). On the east side, about 400m higher, is the Lurawa Gompa. Continue south for 1.5hr to reach Dur, the end of the trek (8856ft/2700m). Dur is located at the confluence of Gorzam Chhu from the north and Dur Chhu from the west. The drive to Jakar will take 1hr.

TREK 19

GANGKAR PUNSUM SOUTHEAST FACE – CROSSING OVER TO GANGKAR PUNSUM BASE CAMP

For maps see Trek 16, second map,
and Trek 18.

Grade	strenuous
Time	7 days to base camp
Distance	c56 miles/90km
Altitude gain	c8325ft/2538m
Altitude loss	c764ft/233m
Status	double check if open

This trek follows the first 5 days of Trek 18. From Bamurpa camp (close to Gangkar Punsum) a trek leads into a deep valley, crossing a pass with an unknown name. The pass is difficult for pack animals so luggage has to be carried (porters in Bhutan are rare, unlike in Nepal). In Bhutan it will be difficult to arrange for a group of pack animals and to have some supplies waiting for you on the other side of the pass, but it would make the whole enterprise easier. Crossing the second pass includes glacier travel.

The description below is based on research by the author as far as the bottom of the pass, and on first-hand advice from a Bhutanese guide who has explored beyond there.

The US expedition in 1985 to Gankar Punsum gave their expedition the motto 'Here Be Dragons', referring to the words that cartographers in the Middle Ages added to maps at the edge of the known world.

This is an 'explorer' trek – it needs more research.

DAY 6

Bamurpa (14,530ft/4430m) to the end of 'Jumbo Jet' valley (c15,910ft/4850m)

Time	6hr
Distance	6.2 miles/10km
Altitude gain	1380ft/420m
Altitude loss	0ft/0m

Bamurpa camp is located near Gangkar Punsum southeast face (24,735ft/7541m), the highest peak in Bhutan.

Follow the second hiking option on day 5, Trek 18, to reach the end of **'Jumbo Jet' valley**. From there two possible passes lead to Gangkar Punsum base camp (west side). It takes several hours to get to the end of this valley where camp should be errected.

DAYS 7 AND 8

'Jumbo Jet camp' (c15,910ft/4850m) to Gangkar Punsum base camp (16,498ft/5030m) via 'the' pass (c17,256ft/5263m) and onwards (day 8), crossing another pass to connect with the Lunana trek

The pass that looks easier is at about 5200m. There are different stories about the existence of a pass; some locals say there is nothing to be crossed; others say people from Sephu cross this pass to carry on towards Monla Karchung La and Tibet. Sonam Wangchuk, one of the excellent guides joining me, has crossed a (the?) pass from this valley over to **Gangkar Punsum base camp**.

There are loose boulders on both sides of the pass, so be careful. Along the trail are stone markers indicating that people use this route. No rope is needed to cross the pass, where there is a very old cairn. It is only 2.5hr down to camp, next to a collapsed herder's hut. This should be (near) **Gangkar Punsum base camp**. On whatever maps are available this valley should be at the source of the Mangde Chhu.

Another hard day (day 8) of exploring along the right lateral moraine for several miles, getting onto the glacier and hiking west, will lead eventually to another pass between two smaller peaks connecting to the Lunana trek (over 18,000ft/5490m).

From here you can carry on either to Lunana by crossing one more pass, including glacier travelling, or you can trek to Dur hot springs over seven passes!

CLIMBING GANGKAR PUNSUM

Gangkar Punsum (24,750ft/7546m) is the highest peak of Bhutan, and the highest unclimbed massif in the world. It is located in a very remote corner of Bhutan and virtually unmapped.

Different names and heights are given on several maps and sources: Gankar Puensum; Gankhar Puensum; Gangkhar Puensuum; Gangkar Punesum; Kangkar Pünzum (Rinchita); Kangri; Rinchita; Kiga Ri. There are various meanings: 'White Peak of the Three Spiritual Brothers'; 'Glacier of the Three Spiritual Brothers'; 'the Three Mountain Siblings', symbolising the once-peaceful coexistence between the Tibetans, Bhutanese and aboriginal Mön-pa people. The given heights range from 23,744ft/7239m to 24,750ft/7546m, with two subsidiary peaks of 24,705ft/7532m and 24,653ft/7516m.

Gangkar Punsum is the source of three major rivers: the Kuru Chhu, Chamkhar Chhu (Chomkha Chhu) and Mangde Chhu flowing through, respectively, Lhuntse, Bumthang and Trongsa valleys. The three rivers are connected to a local legend: on their very first run down the slopes of Gangkar Punsum they discussed having a race. The Chamkhar Chhu told the other two that they could race along if they wished. He was in no rush to reach the ocean and wanted to take it easy, enjoying the scenery on his trip. The Chamkhar Chhu is therefore wide and calm, in contrast to the Kuru Chhu and Mangde Chhu that plunge through steep and narrow gorges.

Gangkar Punsum has seen a few unsuccessful expeditions. In 1985 a Japanese and American team tried climbing the mountain. The American party explored the Chamkar Chhu glacier area and climbed a couple of small peaks (17,990ft/5485m to 19,500ft/5945m). They concluded that there was no passable route to Gangkar Punsum from the Chamkar Chhu valley, to which they were mistakenly guided. They asked for permission to climb Melunghi Kang instead, but were refused. In 1986 an Austrian team, followed by a British/US/New Zealand team, gave it a try. After that no one was allowed to climb the mountain. ▸

Gankar Punsum 7541m (Yoshio Ogata, Japanese Expedition, 1985)

▸ However, in 1999 a Japanese team was allowed to climb Gangkar Punsum from the Tibetan side, but the Chinese Mountaineering Association 'postponed' their permit recognising that the mountain is on Bhutanese territory. Instead they were offered the unclimbed northerly peak Liankang Kangri, just next to Gangkar Punsum. They did so, and had a close look at the knife-edge-ridge route to the summit of Gangkar Punsum.

Perhaps Gangkar Punsum will remain unclimbed; perhaps one really high mountain will remain unclimbed forever. Forbidden (unclimbed) peaks are rare and special. The Buddhist people of the Himalayas believe strongly in mountain gods dwelling around the mountains and respect fully their inviolability.

TREK 20

BUMTHANG: NGANG–
TANG VALLEYS TREK AND
EXTENSION TO URA

Grade	easy
Time	3 days
Distance	25.1 miles/40.5km
Altitude gain	3706ft/1130m
Altitude loss	3100ft/945m
Status	open

Bumthang is located in the heart of Bhutan and is one of the Kingdom's most attractive destinations for hiking, visiting interesting places or just relaxing.

Suggestions for day hikes are given in the introduction to Trek 16.

Religious rock engraving at Kurjey Lhakhang

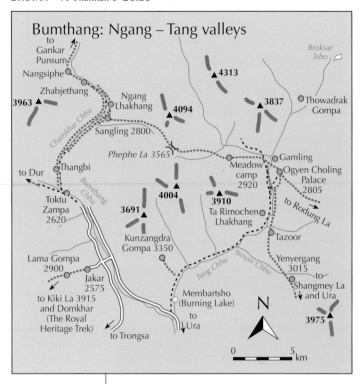

Bumthang: Ngang – Tang valleys

to Gankar Punsum
Nangsiphe
Zhabjethang
3963
Ngang Lhakhang
4313
3837
Thowadrak Gompa
Chamkhar Chhu
4094
Sangling 2800
Phephe La 3565
Meadow camp 2920
Gamling
to Dur
Thangbi
Bumthang Chhu
Ogyen Choling Palace 2805
Toktu Zampa 2620
3691
4004
3910
Ta Rimochen Lhakhang
to Rodung La
Tazoor
Lama Gompa 2900
Kunzangdra Gompa 3350
Jakar 2575
Tang Chhu
Yenyer Chhu
Yenyergang 3015
to Kiki La 3915 and Domkhar (The Royal Heritage Trek)
Membartsho (Burning Lake)
to Ura
N
to Shangmey La and Ura
3975
to Trongsa
0   5 km

Bumthang has four high-altitude forested valleys, many beautiful big houses, settlements and monasteries, and a few palaces. Bumthang is also the religious heart of Bhutan, particularly Jakar. The surrounding Choskhor valley has several good hotels/guesthouses.

Bumthang is the starting point not only for this trek, but also for many other beautiful treks (see Treks 16, 17, 18, 19, 21, 22). The Ngang–Tang valleys trek (Bumthang Cultural Trek) is an easy 3–4 days, with only one pass, the Phephe La, involving a 2509ft/765m climb. ◄

Bring walking poles along.

From Jakar (8495ft/2590m) drive north past Kurjey Lhakhang to where the road changes to dirt. Toktu Zampa or Thangbi, the starting point of the trek, is 20min further on.

DAY 1

*From Jakar (8446ft/2575m) drive 2–3km beyond
Toktu Zampa (8856ft/2620m) towards
Zhabjethang, trek to Sangling (9184ft/2800m)*

Time	3–4hr direct or 5–6hr with a loop
Distance	6.8 miles/11km or 8.7 miles/14km starting from Toktu Zampa
Altitude gain	590ft/180m
Altitude loss	0ft/0m

Just before reaching the hamlet of Toktu Zampa a 'new' dirt road descends steeply to the river, leading to the villages of Ngang valley. If there is a drivable bridge, you could start the trek somewhere deeper in the Ngang valley.

From **Toktu Zampa** a short descent leads to a suspension bridge; cross the Dur Chhu. On the other side is a beautiful carved and painted Buddha. The valley opens up and flattens to the north. Pass an RNR building; after 10min walking beside fields the yellow-roofed Thangbi Gompa, built in 1470 by Shamar Rinpoche, is reached. After the *gompa* is the village of **Thangbi**, followed by another smaller monastery with a *mani* wall. On the right, looking down, is a small well-constructed house, a BHU centre. The trail joins an unpaved road and continues next to some fields, through an archway *chorten* with a mandala painted inside on the roof (30min), just below a beautiful Buddha image on a rock.

Continue on the old trail (not the new road) to pass a water-powered flourmill. At a small *mani* wall the trail splits. The one to the right follows the usual Ngang–Tang valleys trek trail (**see route 2 below**), but if you want some extra hiking (1.5–2hr) follow the trail straight ahead and make a loop that turns back to camp via a suspension bridge (**see route 1 below**). The trail follows the dirt road in some sections.

See also Trek 18, day 1.

As dirt road has been constructed into Ngang valley since the 1st edition, the trek's starting point has been moved.

Route 1

Keep going straight ahead. The trail climbs gently into the Ngang valley. About 2.5hr after the start of the hike, a cluster of four houses on the other side of the valley indicates the Ngang Lhakhang. The trail now turns to the northwest.

About 3hr into the hike a trail descends to the river across a 30m suspension bridge (9,250ft/2820m) – cross over after a visit to the village of Zhabjethang. The village of **Zhabjethang** (Shobthang) straddles the valley here. Soon you get to a BHU and primary school at Shobtang (9330ft/2845m). Look for the beautiful Bhutanese-style houses here and further up the valley. Above on the hillside is a monastery, Neswy Gompa, and a few meditation cells.

Walk back to the suspension bridge, cross it and climb to a small flat grassy area, sometimes used as campsite (Damphay). Pass a flourmill and stream; cross this stream and hike south **to Ngang Lhakhang**. The *lhakhang* houses the Swan Temple, site of an annual festival (*tshechu*). There are two legends connected with the place: the Lama Namkha Samdrup, having dreamt how to build a *gompa*, shot an arrow; the Ngang Lhakang was built on the spot where the arrow landed. The other legend is that the valley was once only occupied by swans, giving its current name 'Ngang Yul', Swan Land.

Near the *lhakhang* is a good big campsite. Another big campsite is about 30min further at the grazing grounds above **Sangling**, next to the Sambi Chhu.

Route 2 (without the loop)

From the small *mani* wall take the trail going right. After 10min reach a big suspension bridge crossing the Bumthang Chhu. Watch for holes in the bridge and trout in the river! The trail continues on the east side of the Bumthang Chhu through meadows and a forest of blue pine and dwarf bamboo. It is a good, easy trail with the occasional muddy spot. About 1hr after crossing the bridge look up to see a big house and a small *lhakhang*. Carry on to reach a split next to a *chorten*: keep straight on to **Ngang Lhakhang**, or right to the campsite for tonight, in a big meadow (**Sangling**). A visit to the *lhakhang* before reaching camp will take 30–45min.

DAY 2

Sangling (9184ft/2800m)
to Meadow Camp (9578ft/2920m)
via Phephe La (11,693ft/3565m)

Time	5–7hr
Distance	7.4 miles/12km
Altitude gain	2509ft/765m
Altitude loss	2116ft/645m

Leaving camp cross the meadow to the east and find a trail disappearing in the dense forest. The trail is very often muddy, for the first 30min at least. Don't cross the Simbi Chhu. The climb for today follows a good trail, but the beautiful forest obscures most of the views during the climb and from the pass.

There are a couple of small streams to cross with some slippery boulders to step on; bring walking poles to help negotiate the crossing (and, if you can carry them, sandals too). One hour before the pass there is a good lunch spot in a forest clearing. After lunch the trail continues, becoming steep through a narrow gully with a small stream running through it. Make sure that the pack animals are ahead of you here.

The Phephe La (11,693ft/3565m) has some cairns and prayer flags. The first 45min descent from the pass is steep and sometimes slippery. At the bottom you reach a beautiful old *mani* wall ending at an archway *chorten* (*khonying chorten*), indicating the border between Ngang and Tang. Here the forest opens up to give the first view of the day, the wide Tang valley. From the *mani* wall it is 1.5–2hr down through meadows to a possible camp, in a large field just after crossing the last stream using a slippery log.

There are several possible campsites along the trail: **'Meadow camp'** is one of the first. A good hour later there are some other possibilities near Thakung. This part of the trail is not always clear – many other trails join the main one, so make sure you are with someone who knows the area.

Many groups take a rest day here and explore the beautiful Ngang valley upstream, a 4hr hike.

Bring walking pole(s) and sandals for some small stream crossings.

DAY 3

Meadow Camp (9578ft/2920m) to Ogyen Choling and possible drive onwards to Bumthang/Jakar (8446ft/2575m)

Time	2–3hr (not including 2hr side trip to Ogyen Choling)
Distance	7–9 miles/11–14.5km
Altitude gain	0ft/0m (optional 607ft/185m to the palace)
Altitude loss	656ft/200m or 984ft/300m

Sun reaches camp at 0600hr in spring. A grand day's hiking!

Follow the main trail through the bottom of a broad valley. Yaks and cows graze on the treeless, rounded hills. High on the left is Tahung, and above that another village, Wobtang, where the Australians have assisted with a sheep development project. Follow the trail, which soon joins a dirt road, to a substantial wooden bridge (9397ft/2865m), where a split occurs in the dirt road/trail. To the right, crossing the bridge, the dirt road continues; to the left, just before the bridge, a scenic trail brings you to a suspension bridge, crossing the Tang Chhu, and to the village of Gamling where the climb starts to the impressive **Ogyen Choling Palace** (9200ft/2805m), a good side trip (see below). The Tang Chhu is famous for trout fishing. Farmhouses are scattered all over the hills and throughout the valley. Gamling village is wealthy, with wonderful wall paintings, and is well known for *yathra* weaving, a method of weaving with wool unique to the Bumthang area. The palace and valley are best enjoyed with an overnight stay either in camp or in the palace guesthouse. Otherwise arrange to be met by transport to return to Jakar.

See photograph of the Tang valley in the 'Geology' section of the Introduction.

Side trip to Ogyen Choling Palace

To visit the palace, in the large village of Gamling follow the main trail, parallel to the Tang Chhu, till you reach a side stream (look for a mill house and a bridge). From this stream the trail climbs steeply (first on an unclear trail) for 45min,

OGYEN CHOLING PALACE – MUSEUM – GUESTHOUSE

The palace has been transformed into a museum and a guesthouse with four small and two larger rooms. It is still inhabited by a family with ancestral links to the building.

An instructive booklet – 'The Ogyen Choling Museum' (2006) – provides a brief history, dating from the 14th century when the great Tibetan master of Buddhism, Longchen Rabjam, visited the area (a comprehensive catalogue is under preparation). Besides history, the booklet also explains about the impressive permanent exhibition. The palace is said to have been built in the 16th century, but in 1897 was badly damaged by an earthquake, with only one building surviving. The palace was rebuilt and expanded, and is open to visitors.

The family living here have created a trust fund to maintain Ogyen Choling as a religious and cultural monument, preserve traditional religious ceremonies and rituals, as a place for religious studies, research and meditation, and to support local handicrafts. Funds from the museum and guesthouse go to the trust fund.

ending at four *chortens* and some large houses at 9200ft/ 2805m. The palace is just a bit further on, on top of a hill.

From the palace the trail goes around some ridges with good views back and also over the Tang valley, then descends to the picturesque village of Kizum and the Tang Chhu. A big suspension bridge crosses the river to meet a dirt road. Pre-arranged transport could be waiting here for the 2–2.5hr drive back to Jakar.

Be sure to stop at the Tang Rimochen Lhakhang, built in and around an enormous cliff. Guru Rinpoche is said to have founded the temple in the 8th century. If you walk clockwise around the temple you can see the unusual rocks carried here by devoted pilgrims. Below is a bathtub carved into a hollow in the rock, supposedly used by Guru Rinpoche; just opposite is a superb spot for a picnic next to the river.

Tang valley is the most remote of the four Bumthang valleys. It has less agricultural infrastructure than the main valley (the Choskhor valley), where the soil is richer and the altitude lower. Tang valley is exceptionally beautiful and contains several important religious sites. These include, starting from just after leaving the National Highway: Membartsho Burning Lake, Kunzangdra Gompa, Ta Rimochen Lhakhang and Thowadra Gompa.

From Ogyen Choling the Rodung La–Lhuntshi trek starts, leading east (see Trek 21).

Tang valley – Bumthang

Two-day trekking extension from Ogyen Choling Palace to Ura (grade – moderate)

Day 4

From Ogyen Choling trek to the small village of Tazoor (or Tasur; 1hr) along cultivated fields and start climbing up (2.5hr) through forest to a major split in the trail. Don't start climbing up to the left – this is the ancient mule track going east to Lhuntshi via Rodang La (see Trek 21). Turn to the right and follow a small track for 3hr, passing several yak clearings and crossing a few swampy areas. The trail is not used a lot – stay close to any locals. A large stream, called Yenyer Chhu, has to be crossed on a 'bridge' after 3hr. From here it takes another 1hr to reach camp at Yenyergang (9891ft/3015m) in a forest clearing (7–8hr in total).

Day 5

Climb, sometimes steeply, crossing some streams, and in 3hr from camp reach the pass Shangmey La, marked by an ancient *mani* wall. Weather permitting, there are some grand views from this pass. A gradual descent of .5hr to a *chorten*, followed by 1hr down through forest brings you to Yongsey (11,647ft/3550m), a small open area. After another 1.5–2hr descent the trek finishes at Somrang village, near Ura (6–7hr in total).

TREK 21

BUMTHANG:
TANG VALLEY–
RODANG LA–LHUNTSHI–
T(R)ASHI YANGTSE TREK

Grade	demanding
Time	10 days
Distance	88 miles/142km
Altitude gain	18,420ft/5616m
Altitude loss	18,099ft/5518m
Status	open

Since the 7th century this was part of the main trade route – livestock from Bumthang to Lhuntshi, rice the other way – and old steps and ruined guesthouses are visible along the way. It is a 9- or 10-day trek, with several different entry and exit points, and can be split into three sections:

A classic route that is hardly used nowadays by either Bhutanese people or foreign trekkers.

- Bumthang/Ngang valley–Tang valley: 2 or 3 days
- Tang valley–Lhuntshi valley via Rodang La: 4 or 5 days
- Lhuntshi valley–Trashi Yangtse via Dong La: 3 or 4 days

DAYS 1 + 2

See Trek 20.
For the Bhutanese palace experience stay overnight at Ogyen Choling, and start the trek from there.

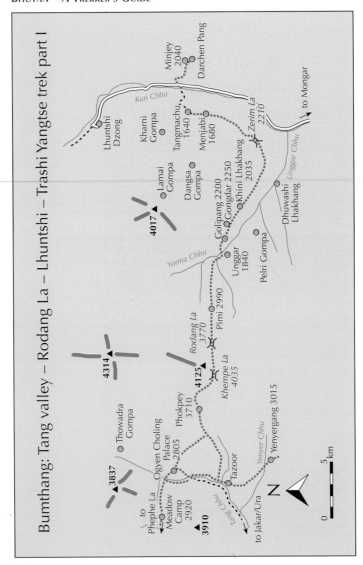

Bumthang: Tang valley – Rodang La – Lhuntshi – Trashi Yangtse trek part I

DAY 3

Tang valley/Ogyen Choling Palace
(9200ft/2805m) to Phokpey
(12,169ft/3710m)

Time	4–5hr
Distance	6.2 miles/10km
Altitude gain	2968ft/905m
Altitude loss	0ft/0m

Depending on the location of the previous night's camp either start from or pass **Ogyen Choling Palace** and climb a muddy trail (gaiters) to an altitude of 9578ft/2920m where the trail crosses a stream. Continue climbing through a marshy bamboo area to a meadow at 11,447ft/3490m (2.5hr). Stay close to the guide because the trail is difficult to find. Today is a non-stop climb to the camp. The altitude gain is great, but unfortunately **Phokpey** is about the only decent place to camp; everywhere else can be too wet. The water supply comes from a small stream about 100m from camp.

DAY 4

Phokpey (12,169ft/3710m)
via Khempe La (13,235ft/4035m)
and Rodang La (12,366ft/3770m)
to Pimi camp (9807ft/2990m)

Time	6hr
Distance	9.9 miles/16km
Altitude gain	1066ft/325m
Altitude loss	3428ft/1045m

Crossing Khempe La and Rodang La, and a long descent to camp at Pimi, makes this a hard day.

A 1hr level walk through rhododendron forest leads to the start of the 1hr-climb up a man-made rock staircase. Finally **Khempa La** is reached (13,235ft/4035m) where there is a small *chorten*. From the pass in fine weather Gangkar Punsum (24,750ft/7546m) and the Monle Karchung La (c17,400ft/5300m) can be seen. Rodang La is less than 1hr walk from Khempa La. Follow the ridge, downhill on more stone 'stairs', past a ruined 'guesthouse', used by royals on their trips through Bhutan. A 5min climb gains **Rodang (or Rodung) La** ('the width of a yak's horns'). ◄

The trail leading to Rodang La is where 'all people are equal'. A saying from the old days states that even the king couldn't stay on his horse on the steep sections and had to walk.

From here a continuous, sometimes very steep, descent starts, mainly on stone steps. These are not always in a good condition due to landslides and are sometimes narrow and steep, tricky for pack animals. Be careful on the descent.

A water supply in one of the meadows encountered during the descent determines where to camp. Normally **Pimi** is used (c3hr from Rodang La). Close by is another ruined royal guesthouse. There are a couple of meadows lower down.

DAY 5

*Pimi camp (9807ft/2990m)
to Khini Lhakhang (6675ft/2035m)*

Time	6hr
Distance	9.3 miles/15km
Altitude gain	1148ft/350m
Altitude loss	4280ft/1305m

Some houses near Unggar village are believed to be haunted by a spiritual disease that kills anyone coming into contact with the inhabitants of these houses – best to keep away!

A day of descent alternating with some flat stretches, leading from meadow to meadow with a view towards the little village of **Unggar** in the bottom of the valley. ◄ Finally the Nayurgang Chhu is reached where a bridge has to be crossed (5625ft/1715m). From here you have a choice of two trails; one muddy and wet close to the river, the other climbing up through paddyfields and close to the village. Soon another bridge is crossed (5527ft/1685m).

After all that descent a 350m climb leads to camp. There are many different routes, so make sure to follow someone.

The trail passes through the villages of **Golipang** and **Gongdar** on the way to camp at **Khini Lhakhang** (Khaine Lhakhang) (6675ft/2035m).

KHINI LHAKHANG

Khini Lhakhang is believed to be one of the oldest monasteries in Bhutan. According to old documents there are only two really ancient monasteries in Bhutan: Kitchu Lhakhang in Paro, and Jampa Lhakhang in Bumthang, constructed by King Songtsen Gampo in AD 659 as part of his project to build 108 temples around the Himalayas. But according to legend there are actually five ancient monasteries in Bhutan, and one of these is Khini Lhakhang.

DAY 6

Khini Lhakhang (6675ft/2035m)
to Tangmachu (5379ft/1640m)

Time	5–6hr
Distance	10.5 miles/17km
Altitude gain	705ft/215m
Altitude loss	1509ft/460m

A descent to a stream is followed by a climb to the village of Gortshom Meth. Continue climbing in and out of some small side valleys, passing four prayer walls and three big *stupas* through a beautiful oak forest. One of these *chortens* is located at **Zerim La** (7249ft/2210m). The trail slowly levels out and continues until a great viewing point is reached; the Kuri Chhu and Tangmachu village can be seen below in the valley. From here a descent starts to the river (5166ft/1575m in 45min), followed by a 45min climb to Tangmachu (5871ft/1790m). Just before Tangmachu, Tage La with some *chortens* and a *mani* wall is reached. At **Tangmachu** the trek can be finished (after descending to the bridge at Khuri Chhu) by driving up the valley to Lhuntshi, or down the valley to Mongar, and staying in a guesthouse/hotel. The other option is to continue the trek to **Trashi Yangtse**.

DAY 7

Tangmachu (5379ft/1640m)
to Minjey (6691ft/2040m)

Time	4–5hr
Distance	7.4 miles/12km
Altitude gain	2821ft/860m
Altitude loss	1509ft/460m

This last section of the trek is less well travelled, and the trail may be in a poor condition.

From Tangmachu descend on the dirt road to the bridge crossing the Kuri Chhu at 3870ft/1180m. There is an easy climb through rice- and cornfields passing the village of Chusa and steeply up to a campsite near **Minjey** village. Visit the beautiful garden surrounding Darchen Pang Lhakhang nearby.

DAY 8

Minjey (6691ft/2040m)
to Pemi (8331ft/2540m)

Time	5–6hr
Distance	8 miles/13km
Altitude gain	1640ft/500m
Altitude loss	0ft/0m

Climb uphill on a narrow trail through beautiful forest with few viewpoints until camp is reached at **Pemi**, a meadow with some simple herder huts.

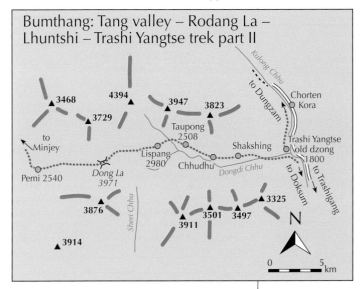

DAY 9

Pemi (8331ft/2540m) to Taupong
(8226ft/2508m) via Dong La (13,025ft/3971m)

Time	7–8hr
Distance	13 miles/21km
Altitude gain	4694ft/1431m
Altitude loss	4799ft/1463ft

A serious day of endless climbing through forest with a huge variety of flora leads to today's pass, **Dong La**. The area around the pass is called 'Nine Sisters', meaning there are nine passes to be tackled (including Dong La) before the start of the descent into the last valley of this trek. From Dong La there are some nice mountain views.

The Dong La range is the mountain ridge that runs from Tibet, dividing the Trashi Yangtse valley in the east from the Lhuntshi valley to the west. Further north is another pass, Pang La (c14,000ft/4270m), described by the two botanists Sherriff and Ludlow who crossed it in 1933.

After the pass a couple of ridges are crossed before reaching a meadow at 11,424ft/3483m, Sher Lapche. From here descend past another meadow at **Lispang** (9774ft/2980m), crossing Tongdala Chhu on a small bridge at 8908ft/2716m (changing later to the Dongdi Chhu). After many hours on very often slippery and muddy trails through jungle a campsite in a forest clearing, **Taupong** (Taupang), is reached (8226ft/2508m).

Two unicyclists have cycled this whole trek and produced a worthwhile DVD of it; see bibliography.

DAY 10

*Taupong (8226ft/2508m)
to Trashi Yangtse (5904ft/1800m)*

Time	6–7hr
Distance	11.2 miles/18km
Altitude gain	0ft/0m
Altitude loss	2322ft/708m

It is downhill now on muddy trails, passing the grazing grounds of Sana and **Chhudhu** below the village of **Shakshing** and finally crossing the Dongdi Chhu on a large bridge (6166ft/1880m). From here it is an easy hike to the old *dzong* of **Trashi Yangtse** (5904ft/1800m). There is an old Bhutanese-style cantilever bridge at the old *dzong* (see Trek 23). The end of the trek is reached after crossing the main river Kulong Chhu at 1745m, and a small climb up to the road from where pre-arranged transport should relieve tired legs.

TREK 22

ROYAL HERITAGE TREK:
BUMTHANG–KIKI LA–TUNGI
LA–KUENGA RABTEN–TRONGSA

Grade	moderate–demanding
Time	3–4 days
Distance	28 miles/45km
Altitude gain	c8100ft/2470m
Altitude loss	c10,725ft/3270m
Status	open

The Royal Heritage Trek traces the historical route travelled by the royal family when moving between their summer and winter residences in Bumthang and near Trongsa. In 2007 the monarchy was 100 years old, and to commemorate this fact the old route was 'rediscovered'. The trek includes two long climbs to passes of around 4000m on days 1 and 3 and one long descent.

Along the trail several palaces, monasteries and *dzongs* can be found.

DAY 1

Bumthang (8446ft/2575m) to Duegang Chhu (9538ft/2908m) via Kiki La (12,841ft/3915m)

Time	7–8hr (see note)
Distance	9.9 miles/16km
Altitude gain	4395ft/1340m
Altitude loss	3303ft/1007m

Note: in order to shorten this day, transport could be organised to drop off near Lama Gompa and pick up near Tharpaling Gompa.

287

Take your time to acclimatize before starting the trek.

Wangdichholing Palace, located in Jakar town, is the starting point of a long day trekking on a good trail. Climb up to Jakar Dzong and onwards to Kiki La. After passing Lama Gompa (c9512ft/2900m), it takes around 4hr to reach the royal lunch spot, called Soe Zheysa or Sew Zhaysa.

The gompa was founded by the philosopher Nyingma and the saint Longchen Rabjampa (1308–1364). It houses several temples and about 100 monks.

After lunch it takes one more hour to the pass **Kiki La** (or Keke La; 12,841ft/3915m). There are some good views from the pass. After the pass a steep descent of 2–3hr passes Choedrak Gompa, Tharpaling Gompa (which can be reached by a feeder road from Chumey valley), Samtenling (with an archaeological site; 10,175ft/3102m) and Buli Lhakhang (9512ft/2900m), and finally reaches Domkhar and Gyatse village (Gyetse or Gyatsa; 9679ft/2951m), where there is a suspension bridge. Tharpaling (Tharpoling) Gompa, with its red roof, is located on a cliff. ◀

The campsite (Makhang Thang) is located alongside the **Duegang Chhu** (9538ft/2908m), near (½km) Domkhar Tashichholing Palace.

DAY 2

Duegang Chhu (9538ft/2908m) to Jamsapang (13,182ft/4019m)

Time	6–7hr
Distance	8.7 miles/14km
Altitude gain	3644ft/1111m
Altitude loss	0ft/0m

Cross the **Duegang Chhu**, pass a guesthouse and continue up to Domkhar Tashichholing Palace (9742ft/2970m). From the palace start climbing, pass the royal lunch spot at Pangt-Tsam Bung Tsam (10,906ft/3325m), and in 3½–4hr Dungmai Jab lunch spot (12,064ft/3678m) is reached.

In 2–2½hr **Jamsapang** campsite (13,182ft/4019m), near a yak herder's hut, is reached. Tungi La pass is nearby. From the camp and its surroundings there are good views to the lowlands of India, Black Mountains and the Greater Himalayas. ◀

Jhomolhari can be seen.

DAY 3

Jamsapang (13,182ft/4019m) to Kuenga Rabten (5819ft/1774m) via Tungi La (13,248ft/4039m)

Time	8–9hr
Distance	9.3 miles/15km
Altitude gain	66ft/20m
Altitude loss	7429ft/2265m

Start with a small climb of 66ft/20m to a *chorten* at **Tungi La** (or Tongle La; 13,248ft/4039m), with some great views of the Bumthang and Trongsa area and the Black Mountains range. ▶ More than one hour after the pass is a possible campsite, called Jobchisa. After 4hr of descent, Saphay Pang (or Zangro Pang; 9387ft/2862m) is reached, a good lunch spot. Here another trail joins the route, coming down from Nada La (Saphay Pang is used as campsite).

Just south from Tungi La (on the same ridge) is another pass located at about the same altitude, called Nada La.

Another 4hr descent follows, sometimes parallel to a stream called Nikha Chhu, through a forest of oaks and rhododendrons. It leads finally to **Kuenga Rabten** Dzong/Palace (5819ft/1774m). ▶ The buildings are well preserved. The courtyard, surrounded by a gallery, has a well-decorated central tower (*utse*) of three floors. On the top floor is part of the collection from the National Library, the private room of the King and a chapel. The other floors were used as a granary and military garrison. The campsite is on the archery field!

The palace, the winter residence of the second king of Bhutan, King Jigme Wangchuk, was constructed in the 1920s by Droka Mingyur.

DAY 4

Kuenga Rabten (5819ft/1774m) drive to Trongsa (7183ft/2190m) (14.3 miles/23km; 1hr)

After visiting the palace either drive back to **Trongsa** or hike for some hours from the palace to Samcholing on the motor road. It is an easy hike with beautiful views over Dakten Geog, Kela village and the Mangde Chhu.

TREK 23

URA–BULI/ZHEMGANG TREK

Grade	easy–moderate
Time	6 days
Distance	44 miles/71km
Altitude gain	5429ft/1655m
Altitude loss	10,114ft/3083m
Status	double check if open

A combination of pack animals and/or porters – rare in Bhutan – is used on this trek.

Zhemgang is roughly divided into three areas: Upper, Middle and Lower Kheng. Two major rivers, Chamkhar Chhu and Mangde Chhu, unite in the central part of the Dzongkhag to become the Manas Chhu. The landscape is characterised by deep river-cut gorges and valleys. The altitude ranges from 200m to 3600m, giving both a temperate and subtropical climate. A largely untouched forest covers 85 percent of Zhemgang – fir, mixed conifer, blue pine, chir pine, oak and rhododendron, one of the most diverse collections not only in Bhutan, but in the world. Zhemgang is also known for the Royal Manas National Park, which has been declared one of 10 internationally recognised 'hotspots'. The Black Mountains (Jigme Singye Wangchuk National Park) also extends into Zhemgang.

There are plans to construct a farm road beyond Buli, which will affect the trek.

The Ura–Buli trek passes mainly through the Upper Kheng, dotted with 11 villages (Nyimzhong, Thazong, Zangling, Thrisa (or Thriso), Bardo, Khomshar, Langdurbi, Digala, Radhi, Wamling and Shingkhar). ◀

While this trek could be done at any time of year, monsoon rains and leeches, fleas, and mosquitoes make it more challenging in the summertime, though the reward is the stunningly beautiful flora.

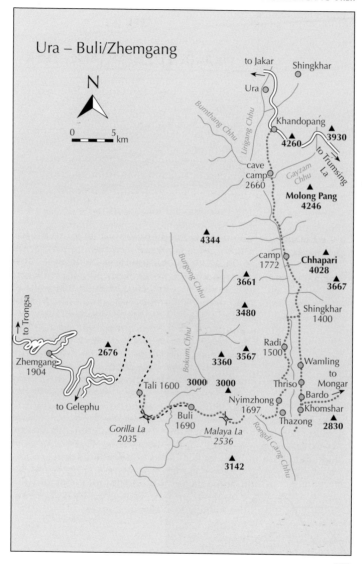

DAY 1

Jakar by bus to Ura and Khandopang
(10,825ft/3300m), trek to Gayzam Chhu
(8725ft/2660m)

Time	2hr trekking in the afternoon
Distance	3 miles/5km
Altitude gain	0ft/0m
Altitude loss	2100ft/640m

En route to the start at Khandopang, visit Ura and the Trumsingla Park Centre.

Jakar (8460ft/2580m) to the town of **Ura** at 10,170ft/3100m is a 1.5hr (30miles/48km) bus journey. The starting point of the trek is at **Khandopang** (10,825ft/3300m; 7.5miles/12km from Ura) on the lateral road.

The trek begins through beautiful forest dominated by rhododendron, lichen, asters and orchids. The trail is level for the first 30min, then continues steeply down to the Gayzam Chhu via two small passes (Hohomi and Melong Pang). At the river, the campsite **Gayzam Chhu** (Gezam Chhu, Ghijam Chhu) is beside a cave at an altitude of 8725ft/2660m.

During the descent you may encounter local farmers moving their cattle to the Bumthang grazing areas. Many ties exist between the Khengpa and the people from the Bumthang valley. The old nobility of Bumthang owns land in the Kheng region where they graze their herds in winter. The Bumthang weavers get their raw materials for making vegetable dyes from the Khengpa.

Bumthang Chhu in the Upper Kheng

DAY 2

Gayzam Chhu (8725ft/2660m) to a site next to Bumthang Chhu (5812ft/1772m)

Time	7hr
Distance	13 miles/21km
Altitude gain	0ft/0m
Altitude loss	2910ft/888m

Hike south through a steep dramatic gorge cut by waterfalls. At one of the falls, Bashja Darma, water is forced through a hole like a jetstream. Today we will cross the Bumthang–Zhemgang Dzongkhag boundary.

A beautiful but long hike.

This area is beautiful all year round. Summer rain can make the trail rather muddy and slippery, but nature is at its best at that time of year. Look out for the spectacular rufous-necked hornbill. As the day wears on, the mighty Bumthang Chhu (Chamkhar Chhu) gets closer and closer. Camp is at an opening in the forest at 5812ft/1772m.

THE ANCIENT REGION OF KHENG (KHYENG)

This region, which stretched east to Mongar and south almost to Gelephu, was divided into a multitude of little kingdoms until the 17th century. The most important were Buli and Nyakar. The Nyingmapa saint, Pema Lingpa, who founded a temple there, visited Buli in 1478 and 1479. After the Drukpa conquest in the mid 17th century the kings lost whatever importance they may have formerly enjoyed, but their descendants still call themselves 'king', a purely honorific title.

In 1963 the region of Khyeng was divided into the districts of Mongar and Zhemgang.

DAY 3

Next to Bumthang Chhu
(5812ft/1772m) to Shingkhar (4590ft/1400m)

Time	4hr
Distance	8 miles/13km
Altitude gain	2115ft/645m
Altitude loss	1425ft/435m

Follow the river down till the valley starts to widen. The trail climbs out of the gorge (656ft/200m). After 3hr hiking the maize fields of Changkhar village (5870ft/1790m) come into view, the first sign of habitation. Break for tea at one of the local farmhouses. From Changkhar there is a 1hr hike through agricultural land to reach the village of **Shingkhar** (4590ft/1400m).

Shingkhar (and Changkhar) are villages in the Upper Kheng. The people here speak their own language, Khengkha. Shingkhar is still very Bumthang-orientated because of historic and religious ties. The royal family has grazing rights for their cattle in the Shingkhar area, and one of the higher lamas from Bumthang visits Shingkhar occasionally. Shingkhar has over 40 households, a school, several *lhakangs,* a BHU with a wireless radio and basic veterinary services.

LOCAL ACCOMMODATION

Accommodation with a local family means normally that the best room in the house is offered for guests, being the altar or chapel room – a special experience. Try the local beer, *bangchang,* usually served warm and mixed with fried egg. Traditionally it is served at every meal, even breakfast.

DAY 4

Rest day at Shingkhar (4590ft/1400m)

Besides relaxing, reading or writing, and catching up on laundry, take some time to look around the village. You could help to prepare some of the local dishes and drinks. Another option is to hike above the village to a viewpoint where Gangkar Punsum (24,735ft/7541m) is visible. Alternatively, visit one of the *lhakangs*, bring some offerings and meditate with one of the monks. Visit one of the local schools and talk to the children. Watch an archery game. It is also possible to learn about the local medicinal practice and how certain diseases are treated. If visiting Shingkhar in December, the *tsechu* festival is well worth attending.

There are plenty of options to make your stay at Shingkhar special.

DAY 5

Shingkhar (4590ft/1400m) to Nyimzhong (5566ft/1697m) via Radi (4920ft/1500m)

Time	6hr
Distance	7.4 miles/12km
Altitude gain	2020ft/616m
Altitude loss	1045m/319m

A steep 30min descent leads to the river below the village. Cross the Bumthang Chhu (Chamkhar Chhu) on an old bridge (3545ft/1081m). Walk below enormous cliffs to a spot where nearly 20 rock bee nests are located. Climb steeply for 1.5hr to the village of **Radi** (4920ft/1500m). Shingkhar porters/pack animals will be exchanged while you rest and enjoy lunch.

After Radi the trail climbs to an amazing viewpoint with a 400m drop down to the river. In the distance, the last village of the Shingkhar *gewog* (Sangling) can be seen. On the opposite side of the river the villages of Wamling, Thriso, Bardo and Khomshar are visible. In the future these villages could, according a Road Sector Master Plan, be connected to

View looking south from Radi

the National Highway network – coming in from the north from Ura, from the east from Mongar and joining the road in the south from Zhemgang – Tingtinbin – Panbhang (Manas National Park).

After a steep descent to the river, cross a side stream (Sibdi Gong) and pause at this beautiful spot for a swim. Climb again for 2.5hr to **Nyimzhong** village (Nimjong) (5566ft/1697m) to camp.

DAY 6

*Nyimzhong (5566ft/1697m)
to Buli (5545ft/1690m)
via Malaya La (8318ft/2536m)
and possible drive to Zhemgang*

Time	7hr
Distance	15.5 miles/25km
Altitude gain	2752ft/839m
Altitude loss	2775ft/846m

While trekking through the Upper and Middle Kheng area you will see beautiful old *mani* walls at the passes surrounded by prayer flags. *Mani* walls, so plentiful in Nepal, are rare throughout Bhutan.

Soon after leaving Nyimzhong, the next village, Thazong, appears below the trail. At this point the trek changes from a southerly to a westerly direction. After crossing a bridge over Rongdi Gang Chhu (Raidi Gong Chhu; 6445ft/1965m) there will be 2.5hr of easy climbing. Water bottles should be filled at the river because no water is available until camp is reached after **Malaya La** (8318ft/2536m), approximately 5hr later.

From the pass descend to **Buli** (5545ft/1690m) in 2hr on a good trail through forest. Buli is a large, rich village with more than 70 households and an old impressive *lhakhang*. Buli is supported financially by ex-residents who have moved to Thimphu. Camp at Buli or drive the (farm) road to Zhemgang in 3-4hr. ▸

A farm road has made the trek over Gorilla La to Tali unnecessary; however it is a beautiful trek.

DAY 7

*Trek from Buli (5545ft/1690m) to
Tali (5248ft/1600m) or drive from Buli
to Zhemgang 3–4hr*

Time	4hr
Distance	5 miles/8km
Altitude gain	656ft/200m
Altitude loss	1280ft/390m

From Buli, descend to a bridge crossing the Bokum Chhu (Burgong Chhu) at 4560ft/1390m. This is followed by a steep, steady climb to the **Gorilla La** (6675ft/2035m), with a beautiful old *mani* wall. About 30min after the pass the trail turns to the north to the village of **Tali** where a visit to the important Tali Lhakhang can be arranged. From Tali it will take 1.5hr to drive to **Zhemgang** (6245ft/1904m). Zhemgang is situated on an open ridge, which provides an unbroken view over the entire region. Despite its low altitude it is a cold and windy place.

TREK 24

BUMDELING WILDLIFE SANCTUARY TREK (BUMDELING IRON BRIDGE TREK)

Grade	easy–moderate
Time	7 days
Distance	not available
Altitude gain	not available
Altitude loss	not available
Status	double check if open

This trek can be done all year round.

Bumdeling Wildlife Sanctuary, located in the northeastern corner of Bhutan, is one of nine protected areas in the country. The sanctuary covers 1538km^2 and has more than 2200 inhabitants, mainly farmers growing food crops, and rearing livestock as a secondary business.

In the winter black-necked cranes can be seen in the Bumdeling wetlands or at their roosting site on the sand and gravel banks of the Kulong Chhu below Ngalimang.

DAY 1

Chorten Kora (6265ft/1910m) to Solomang (c7872ft/2400m) (Dechhenphodrang Gompa)

Time	5–6hr
Distance	6.6 miles/10.7km
Altitude gain	1640ft/500m
Altitude loss	c984ft/300m

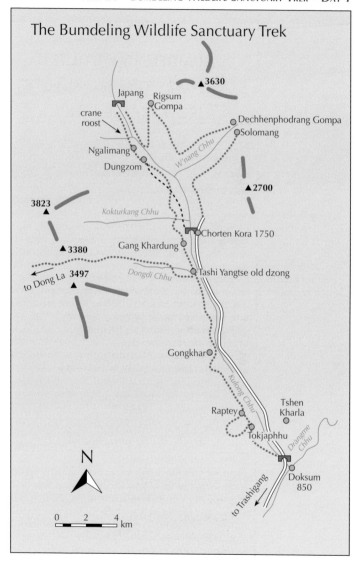

The Bumdeling Wildlife Sanctuary Trek

Japang

▲3630

Rigsum Gompa

crane roost

Dechhenphodrang Gompa
Solomang

Ngalimang

W'nang Chhu

Dungzom

▲2700

3823
▲

Kokturkang Chhu

▲3380

Chorten Kora 1750

Gang Khardung

← to Dong La **3497**
▲

Dongdi Chhu

Tashi Yangtse old dzong

Gongkhar

Kulong Chhu

Raptey

Tshen Kharla

Tokjaphhu

Drangme Chhu

N

Doksum 850

0   2   4 km

to Trashigang →

CHORTEN KORA

During the Chorten Kora festival, villagers come from as far away as Tawang in Arunachal Pradesh (India). It is said that during the construction of the dome of the *chorten* an eight-year-old girl from Tawang, believed to be an angel, volunteered to enter it and be buried there. After consecration of the *chorten*, the demon that harmed the local people was subdued, leading to peace and harmony in the valley. The *chorten* is a replica of one in Bodhnath near Kathmandu, but smaller. Lama Ngawang Loday constructed the *chorten* over 12 years in the late 18th century. He carved the design into a radish, but during the long trip from Nepal to Trashi Yangtse the radish dried out and shrunk, making the *chorten* in Bhutan smaller.

Chorten Kora is the area around the *chorten*.

Drive or walk up the road past the *dzong* and Rinchhengang village towards the new high school near Belling. From the *chorten* at 6265ft/1910m follow the track northwards through paddy fields. Black-necked cranes may hang out here, often in big numbers in January or February. Continue past a couple of *mani* walls above the village of Sep (6888ft/2100m), ignoring smaller trails that snake back down the mountain. After 2–2.5hr reach a *khonying/kakali* (archway *chorten*) and *mani* wall on the ridge separating the Kulong and the Womenang valleys at 7183ft/2190m. The ridge offers views of the mountains higher up in the Kulong Chhu valley (north-northeast).

Follow the main trail – with good views of the high mountains at the end of the Womenang valley – for some 1.5hr. This undulates past a *chorten*, across a creek and past a side trail (stay high) to Shiling village, where there is a daphne paper maker.

After a further 1hr Womenang community school (7544ft/2300m) is reached. After a short climb pass an area with some big dead trees. It is forbidden to cut trees in this protected area so as not to displease the local deities. Such deities, which reside in high places, rivers and other special areas, are part of the original Bon religion and have been integrated into local Buddhist beliefs. About 30min on, past the village of Kilinbaling (three houses and a ruin), the trail splits (c7708ft/2350m). Turn left and within 30min reach a rhododendron-fringed pasture just below the hamlet of **Solomang** (c7872ft/2400m). There is a creek nearby.

In the afternoon walk to the idyllically located
Dechhenphodrang Gompa.

TIGERS

In early 2002, just above Solomang, a tiger and cub killed a big bull. Don't count
on seeing tigers; the chances of getting dragged out of your tent at night by one
are negligible. There used to be a trail for traders, smugglers and poachers up the
valley and across the high ridge into Arunachal Pradesh.

DAY 2

*Solomang (c7872ft/2400m)
to Rigsum Gompa (9643ft/2940m)*

Time	6–7hr
Distance	6.8 miles/11km
Altitude gain	1771ft/540m
Altitude loss	0ft/0m

From the campsite follow the trail towards the monastery.
Take a left at the highest junction. Walk past the fields and
sokshing forest of Phanbu and Bomdir (c7872ft/2400m), with
rather inaccessible waterfalls above (*sokshing* = plots of
forest from which farmers collect leaf litter to put in their
stables; mixed with dung this produces manure, used to fer-
tilise the fields for crops). At each junction take the trail that
goes on or up, normally the largest one. The main crop in the
dry fields in Bumdeling and Yangtse is millet. The seedlings
are grown in *tseri* (shifting cultivation/slash-and-burn) fields,
and transplanted around June/July. At a junction past the
village of Koulong, take the right trail up. After a short climb
the trail reaches a *chorten* on a ridge at 8120ft/2475m. This
part of the walk should take 3–3.5hr. A bit further on Jingbu
Gompa (8200ft/2500m) is reached. From here the trail
continues to climb, occasionally descending to a creek, and
leads to a small ridge where an aquaduct used to cross the
way at 9742ft/2970m (another 2.5–3hr).

From the ridge it is about 1hr to the highest point, around 9840ft/3000m. From here the trail runs gently down to **Rigsum Gompa** (9643ft/2940m). The vegetation is scrubbier here, dominated by gaultheria, which has purple, edible – but rather sharp-tasting – fruit. Just beyond the *gompa*, at the edge of the wildlife sanctuary, there are a number of terraces where you can camp. Water can be collected from the tap at the *gompa*. There are often people meditating here – do not disturb them.

DAY 3

Rigsum Gompa (9643ft/2940m)
to Japang/Dungzom (6363ft/1940m)

Time	3hr

From Rigsum Gompa take the trail down to the right. The trail descends first through shrubs, mainly gaultheria, then broadleaved forest. Carry on down a few open ridges to the *sokshing* and agricultural lands of Lamdrawog. This trail has been designated as an orchid trail. Eventually, after some 3hr, reach a small ridge, at the bottom of which is the suspension bridge to **Dungzom**.

DAY 4

Dungzom (6363ft/1940m)
to Gang Khardung/Tashi Yangtse
Old Dzong (5904ft/1800m)

Time	6–9hr

From wherever you camped, make your way to Dungzom. Follow the dirt road past Dungzom lake/marsh and the school – which has an interesting, but not prehistoric, rock painting – to a trail that goes off left near the end of the *sok-shing* forest. Follow this trail, mostly down, past the hamlet of Badigang, to a river terrace at the confluence of the Kulong Chhu and the Womenang Chhu. Badigang often offers a good range of butterflies, including common species such as cabbage white, Indian tortoiseshell, painted lady, hill jezebel, yellow coster, azure sapphire and chocolate soldier; and less common ones such as blue admiral, common white commodore, Bhutan sergeant and yellow woodbrown. This stretch takes some 1.5hr from Dungzom.

Next, a climb to the village of Tshaling is followed by a right turn up the ridge on a somewhat vague trail and then onwards slowly, before descending towards the Kokturgang Chhu. From the trail head at the farm road it may take 2hr.

Cross the bridge at 6183ft/1885m and start climbing to a cluster of houses. Turn left just above the first house of lower Gang Khardung (c6560ft/2000m). Continue, until after 1hr you reach a larger trail, the mule track. This is a pleasant trail, augmented by views across the Kulong Chhu valley.

Next, turn sharply right into a parkland-like area, a *sokshing* forest, mainly deciduous oaks and smaller tree rhododendrons. At the next junction keep left (although this trail is much less used) and climb along the ridge from which the views to the north and east are excellent. Dry fields and a lone goli tree lie to the right, with the village of **Gang Khardung** (7134ft/2175m) just ahead. Villagers here grow millet and some rice and raise cattle. The main source of cash for the villagers of Bumdeling *geog* is the sale of potatoes, which are carried on their backs – or, for the lucky ones, on horses – to the nearest road head, up to 6hr away. It may be possible to camp on the odd piece of level ground on this ridge; if not, spending a night in one of the farmer's huts would be a novel experience. Move through the village, past howling dogs, up to a high point of 7298ft/2225m that can be reached within 1hr.

The trail runs along the slope for a while through oak forest with rhododendron. The next *sokshing* forest is easily reached within 1hr and provides a good camping spot at 7052ft/2150m. Water has to be collected from one of the small streams nearby.

In the *sokshing* area keep to the left and follow a trail steeply down. Pass a point with a good view of the **Tashi**

Yangtse Old Dzong 5904ft/1800m. The ridge with the Old Dzong is reached in about 2–2.5hr, a pleasant spot to camp. There is a water tap near the house.

TASHI YANGSTE OLD DZONG

This was built around 1500 by Pema Lingpa, Bhutan's best-known *terton* (discoverer of religious treasures hidden by Guru Rinpoche). It is located at the spur of the ridge between the Kulong Chhu and the Dongdi Chhu, at 1800m. It always looked like a big *gompa*, until in 2002 the Dzongkhag constructed the surrounding buildings to house monks, giving it a more *dzong*-like appearance.

DAY 5

Tashi Yangtse Old Dzong/
Gang Khardung (5904ft/1800m)
to Gongkhar (c6396ft/1950m)

Time	5–6hr

Just a bit upstream from the bridge there is a medicinal hot stone bath. There are plenty of rocks around to heat up, and if you manage to get some hot water it can be quite enjoyable.

From Old Dzong follow the road down to the right to the bridge across the Dongdi Chhu. Cross the traditional covered bridge or the new logging truck bridge, the lowest point for the day (c5576ft/1700m).

Start working your way up to higher ground by following the trail to the left at the first bend in the road. Cross a creek and start climbing again. Having gained about 100m, the trail descends somewhat and then stays between 1950m and 2000m. Few people travel along this stretch, as indicated by the evidence of boar diggings and frequent heaps of droppings of barking deer. Pass a ruined *chorten*, then take a steep trail down to a suspension bridge and the main road. Take the right-hand trail at the next junction, shortly after which the campsite, in a pass just before the village of **Gongkhar** (c6396ft/1950m), is reached. This last stretch takes 3–4hr. To find water, stroll 10min to the village along a level trail.

DAY 6

Gongkhar (c6396ft/1950m)
to Raptey (6757ft/2060m)

Time	4–5hr

Return to the last junction and take the trail down, then turn right into the valley and continue through or just above the village of Pam until you reach the community school. Avoid the steep trail further back, which leads to a suspension bridge and then onto the main road near the cliffs south of Buyang. Continue to Gongkhar; turn left after the first two houses and follow a trail down a ridge.

Follow the large and eroded trail from the school down through *sokshing* and past a *mani* wall to a suspension bridge at 5166ft/1575m, the low point of the day. The next part of the trail is infrequently used, as evidenced by signs of wild boar, barking deer and occasionally *dhole* (wild dog).

Pass a robbed *chorten* in an area dominated by chestnuts. Eventually, a couple of houses and fields appear on the ridge above. A bit further along, some 2–3hr from Gongkhar, pass Shung village (5970ft/1820m).

Eventually you enter the wheat and barley fields of **Raptey** (6757ft/2060m), a village with a small community school. You can camp here on the smallest football field in Bhutan!

Monkeys – capped langurs or Assamese macaques – may be encountered after the suspension bridge. The langurs are usually in the trees, the macaques in the trees or village fields.

Fern

DAY 7

Raptey to the Doksum iron bridge (2788ft/850m)

Time	5–6hr

A fairly easy day, trekking back and down towards warmer regions through agricultural areas and along a windy ridge.

Within 1hr of leaving camp reach a stretch with views over the hamlets and rice, maize, millet and wheat fields that make up Tomizangtsen. The road to Tomizangtsen from the Drangme Chhu valley stops here for the time being.

The long and dusty descent to **Doksum** starts here.

THE IRON BRIDGE

This trek is also called the Bumdeling Iron Bridge Trek because before 2005 the only remaining iron bridge still functioning in Bhutan could be seen at the village of Doksum. This bridge has now being removed, renovated and installed at the foot of Tamchong Lhakhang, located next to the Paro Chhu between Paro and Chhuzom. It was the only functioning iron bridge out of a total of 108 built in Tibet and Bhutan by the 'great magician' Thangtong Gyalpo.

TREK 25

MIGOI (YETI) NATIONAL PARK (MERAK–SAKTENG) TREK

Grade	moderate
Time	5 days
Distance	not available
Altitude gain	not available
Altitude loss	not available
Status	double check if open

In eastern Bhutan the Sakteng Wildlife Sanctuary, or Migoi National Park, covering 650km², was set up specifically to look after the *Migoi* (or Yeti). Surveys are being carried out to determine how many species exist there; no *Migoi* have yet been spotted. Besides the Migoi National Park *Migoi* may be encountered between the Tang and Lhuntshi valleys (Rodang La).

As in other parts of the Himalaya, the people of Bhutan have a strong belief in the *Migoi*.

This trek involves a couple of days' driving. If a domestic airport is opened in the east, it will provide an option to fly. Trashigang is the last big town before a 20.5mile/33km drive along the Gamri Chhu valley brings you to the starting point at the village of Phongme (2hr drive). A couple of villages along the road are worth a visit.

This 4–5 day trek visits the isolated valleys of Merak (c11,536ft/3517m) and Sakteng (9709ft/2960m), with a crossing of the Nyuksang La (Nyakchung La) (13,579ft/4140m). Allow some extra days so that you can make the most of this special area with its unique culture, rich history and very friendly people.

Being a loop, the trek can be started from both directions; however, crossing the Nyuksang La from the Merak side is less steep.

At the time of writing the trek is closed, but there are rumours that the area will be opened again for trekkers. It has been closed to protect the cultural heritage of the Brokpas (or Takpas), the valley inhabitants who are semi-nomadic yak herders, and also to give the *Migoi* some peace.

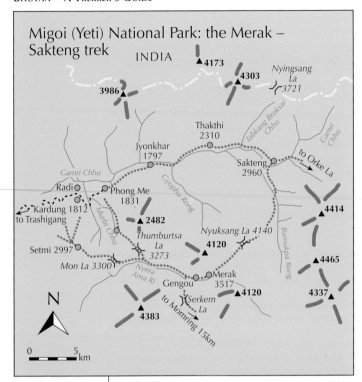

Migoi (Yeti) National Park: the Merak – Sakteng trek

INDIA

THE BROKPAS

These people wear an outfit that is completely different from the other Bhutanese: a felt hat made of yak hair and shaped to the head, with tails made of the same material hanging down in three or four places round the edge. The tails serve as an umbrella to drain off rainwater. On their bottoms they wear a little felt patch to sit on. They do wear a *gho*, but it is different from other Bhutanese. Women wear red dresses. Except for salt – and perhaps Bhutanese tea – they appear to be absolutely self-sufficient. They have a darker complexion than other Bhutanese, and curlier hair. They are farmers and own herds of cattle and yak. There are 6000 Brokpas living in the area.

DAY 1

Drive from **Trashigang** (3739ft/1140m) to **Radi** and **Kardung** villages (5943ft/1812m) and the starting point. It is a steady climb today on a slippery footpath through forest, occasionally along the Murbi Chhu, finishing in 3–4hr at Charbaling (Charbiling) winter grazing grounds (9305ft/2837m).

DAY 2

A 2hr climb to **Thumburtsa La** (10,735ft/3273m) from Charbaling, from where another 3–4hr of easy hiking leads to **Merak** village (c11,536ft/3517m) via **Gengou**.

DAY 3

Spend a day or two in Merak. You can visit the *lhakhangs*, explore the village, watch weaving, take a 4hr hike to the lake where the local deity, Aum Jumo, resides, or a 5–6hr loop to visit Bujla grazing area (13,373ft/4077m).

Or you can keep going from Merak village to Sakteng (9709ft/2960m), including crossing the **Nyuksang La** (13,579ft/4140m). A steady climb of 2–2.5hr leads to the pass, from where a steep 3hr descent, with 1hr along a river, gains Sakteng. At the end of the day a steep climb of 1hr leads to a *chorten*, from where it is 30min down to **Sakteng**, located in a big open space surrounded by heavily forested mountains. ▸

Beyul Tama Jang, another name for Sakteng, means 'the Hidden Paradise of the Rhododendron Blossom'.

DAY 4

It's worth spending an extra day in Sakteng to explore. Sakteng had about 60 houses in the 1930s, and the village has grown a little since then. The inhabitants are very religious, and north and east of Sakteng – in India – are many important Buddhist temples. Three routes leave Sakteng village. One to the north, crossing the Se La range via the Nyingsang La (12,200ft/3721m) into India; one to the east, crossing the Orke La or Arka La (13,900ft/4240m), very close to the border with India; and finally the Nyuksang La (13,579ft/4140m) to the southwest.

If you don't want to stop, carry on to Jyonkhar (Jongkhar; 5894ft/1797m) crossing a small pass, Munde La (9604ft/2928m). There are a couple of small ups and downs before reaching **Jyonkhar** after 5–6hr.

DAY 5

Jyonkhar (5894ft/1797m) to Phong Me (6006ft/1831m) in 2.5–3hr, including one stiff climb of 1hr before reaching **Phong Me**.

YETI

In this gloomy age of materialism, what could be more romantic than Abominable Snowman, with an Abominable Snow-woman and, not least Abominable Snow-baby? Yeti – or 'Abominable Snowmen' – large, h creatures like a man or bear (but bigger) with small, sharp eyes, are reporte live in the highest part of the Himalayas.

'There are far more people-sightings by Yeti than there are Yeti-sighting people,' says Ang Nima Sherpa from Thame village in the Everest reg Whenever there is new evidence about the existence of the Yeti – footprint alleged scalp, supposed droppings – excitement peaks but quickly dies dc The media has an enormous influence. 'For most people from the Himala belief in the existence of the yeti and attitudes related to it are beyond scien judgement or analysis. The belief in the existence of the elusive creature, inc ing yeti-like creatures, is so widespread that it is known by different name different regions of the Himalayas' (Kunzang Choden; see below). For insta Yeti in 'tourist' language, Yeri in China, Migoi (Strong Man) or Migyu or Gre in Bhutan, Metoh-Kangmi or Gangs mi (Glacier Man) or Mi shom po (String M or Mi chen po (Great Man) in Tibet. The Lepchas call it Chu mung (Snow Go or Hlo mung (Mountain Goblin). It is Nyalmu or Ban Manche to the Nepa Barmanu (Big Hairy One) in the Hindu Kush of Pakistan. Outside the Hima it is: Almos in Mongolia, Chuchuna in Siberia, Sasquatch or Big Foot in Ca and North America, Ukuma Zupai in the Andes in South America, Yow Katoomba in Australia and the Long Grey Man in Scotland.

It is amazing how much has been written about them, yet we know so littl

◂ We do know that we should learn to leave them alone, but would all like to know just who does leave those footprints up in the Himalayas.

The Yeti in Bhutan

'It is believed that the *Migoi* or *gredpo*, better known as the 'Abominable Snowman', or Yeti, inhabits the high altitudes ranging probably between 3500m to well over 5000m, the same areas as yak pastures. The *Migoi* is known by all accounts to be a very large biped; something as big as "one-and-a-half yaks" or occasionally even as "big as two yaks!" Or about 2.5m tall and has a foot some 30cm long and 15cm wide. With a nearly human, hairless face and a body totally covered with brownish/red/black hair, the *Migoi* is not a creature to get too close to. The head is conical, with an extra air cavity inside the skull, making him immune to high-altitude sickness. The female has enormous, drooping breasts, while the male is rather well equipped. The Bhutanese *Migoi* has two special features: it has the ability to turn invisible, and their feet face backwards, making it difficult for people to track them.

'Unlike other wild creatures the *Migoi* is apparently not afraid of fire, in fact it is often attracted to it and approaches it seeking warmth. Apparently the *Migoi* manifests a peculiar eating habit in that it grasps its food in its hands and eats only what protrudes on either side of its fists.' (Kunzang Choden).

They like eating chocolate and garlic, and are particularly fond of a wild shallot; fistfuls of discarded shallots, eaten from both ends, are a clue to their prescence. The *Migoi* carries a rather unpleasant stench. They seem to be extremely curious about human beings and perhaps this makes them vulnerable to human treachery, sometimes costing their lives.

The *Migoi* is believed to exist throughout the northern part of the country. The Sakteng Wildlife Sanctuary has been set aside to protect a likely habitat; they are sighted frequently around the Rodung La, the pass between the Tang valley in Bumthang and the valley of Lhuntshi. The government of Bhutan has employed Yeti watchers.

Bhutanese Tales of the Yeti by Kunzang Choden can be highly recommended. If, for whatever reason, the Yeti is not sighted, visit the Benez bar in Thimphu where Yeti milk can be ordered: an especially tasty, strong alcoholic drink based on the famous Bhutanese rum and ginger. Availability – of course – depends on bar staff being able to collect the milk!

Yeti illustrations on Bhutanese stamps (courtesy of Bhutan Post)

TREK 26

KHARUNGLA APEMAN TREK

Grade	easy
Time	5 days
Distance	not available
Altitude gain	not available
Altitude loss	not available
Status	double check if open

An easy 2-day trek (possible in 1 day) at low altitude, which can be walked in winter, spring and autumn.

The trek is located in eastern Bhutan around Khaling, south of Trashigang. During the trek Kharung La Peak 1 (9440ft/2878m) is climbed on the old mule route between Khaling and Womring.

DAY 1

Arrive from Mongar and overnight in Khaling (6166ft/1880m) at Uling Lodge (7708ft/2350m) (Rashung) located 1.1km off the National Highway.

DAY 2

Local sightseeing in Khaling, and overnight at Uling (7708ft/2350m).

- The Uling botanical garden
- The Womrong Zangtopelri Lhakhang
- The National Handloom Development Project: the project trains Bhutanese women in the traditional art of hand weaving and (vegetable) dying.
- Gyalsey Ganapati Lhakhang: the Tibetan saint Gyalsey Ganapati visited this temple and left behind a large *thangka* painting in the early 15th century. This is displayed every year in October during Khaling *tsechu*.

- The National Institute for the Disabled: the country's only institute (besides a centre for special children in Thimphu) for the disabled has both blind and visually impaired students.
- The medicinal fountain at Donfangma–Khandro Drupchu (6166ft/1880m), 'a goddess deity's fountain'. The sulphurous water, which emerges from a huge rocky cliff, is believed to cure many diseases, and faithful devotees visit from all over the country.

DAY 3

Khaling/Uling (7708ft/2350m)
day trip to Jirizor (5379ft/1640m)

Time	6hr

Drive from the lodge south for 6.2miles/10km to Kharungla Peak II (7872ft/2400m). From this peak, hike down through the thick forest and visit the mineral water source. Descend further through an orchid forest to Jirizor, to visit the ruins of a fort (5379ft/1640m).

JIRIZOR

Jirizor is one of the most important battlefields in the history of Bhutan. According to Bhutanese history, Lam Namsey, one of the Shabdrung's generals assigned to govern over the eastern chieftains, built the fort here.

From Jirizor, continue trekking and visit en route the villages Kholdung (5576ft/1700m), Bremang (5576ft/1700m) and Dausor (5904ft/1800m) before heading back to the lodge (c6hr leisurely hiking). These are some of the oldest villages in the east, once ruled by their own kings – Gyalpo Jadrung, Gyalpo Dewa and Gyalpo Changlopey.

DAY 4

Drive from Khaling/Uling to Khola camp village (6166ft/1880m) and start trekking to Kharungla base camp (5904ft/1800m)

Time	6hr

The real Apeman trek begins here. In the past there have been several encounters with an ape-like species on this route, and many cattle herders living in these remote areas will share their tales of encounters with the mystical apeman (or apewoman?). On this part of the Apeman trekking route – particularly in the winter months – it is not so rare to hear the mystical Apeman's shrieking calls, recognised as authentic by local inhabitants. These mystical animals, locally known as 'Mirgula' (or *Migoi*) were frequently encountered in an isolated dense forest near a pond in misty or foggy conditions.

DAY 5

Trek to Kharungla Peak I (9440ft/2878m) and onwards to Womrong; visit Tashi Chholing Gompa and finish the last stretch by bus/car to Khaling/Uling (7708ft/2350m)

Time	7hr

The descent is through dense temperate broadleaved jungle, an excellent opportunity for birdwatchers to capture endless glimpses of birds, but also to enjoy other fauna and flora. There are countless Himalayan orchid species.

Finish the trek at Womrong.

TREK 27

MANAS NATIONAL PARK TREK

Grade	easy
Time	probably less than 5 days
Distance	not available
Altitude gain/loss	not available
Status	double check if open

Manas National Park, also called Namgyal Wangchuk Wildlife Reserve, is connected to the Manas Park in Assam, India. Bhutan's Manas National Park is currently closed to trekkers (but with strong rumours – 2007 – that it will be opened up again).

In this, the oldest of Bhutan's parks (1966), several routes cross areas of dense forest and jungle, such as along the Mangde Chhu, and lead to the Wildlife Sanctuary of Manas Park near the Indian border. One of the older routes starts near Zhemgang. The park is one of the richest biodiversity spots in the entire Himalayas.

The park, home to about 3000 people, is partly inhabited by farmers of the Khengpa ethnic group.

There are two powerful local deities ruling the park, Tewaraja and Dewaraja, who live on a hill overlooking the park's guesthouse.

The park is characterised by rugged, mountainous terrain with moderately steep slopes and a forest vegetation of 92%, including areas of tropical monsoon forest mixed with patches of Savannah grasslands and some wide riverbeds. More than 900 types of plants have been identified.

The park contains numerous large and smaller animals including elephant, rhinoceros (probably extinct), Bengal tiger, slot bear, leopard, gaur, buffalo, deer, sambar, golden langur and wild dog. Over 360 species of birds have been confirmed, including pelicans, peacocks, large cormorants,

It has been said that Manas National Park is what the earth looked like before the arrival of man, 'a jewel encrusted on land reflecting nature's varied and brilliant colours'.

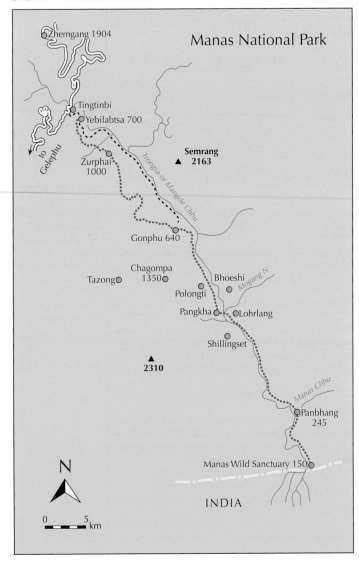

white-capped redstars and great pied hornbills, with an additional 200 species believed to be in residence.

DAY 1

From Yebilabtsa (c2296ft/700m) via Tshanglajong to Zurphai (c3280ft/1000m) – 3hr

DAY 2

Trek to **Gon(m)phu** (2100ft/640m) – a dirt road is planned towards Gonphu – 7hr

DAY 3

Trek to below **Pangkha** along the river to an altitude of 100ft/30m – 7hr

DAY 4

Trek to **Panbhang** (800ft/245m) after crossing the river on bamboo bridges, to the confluence of the Tashigang (or Manas Chhu) and Mangde Chhu rivers – 6hr

DAY 5

Last day trekking along the river to the plains of Manas. Cross the river using a ferry to reach **Manas Wild Sanctuary** (500ft/150m) – 5hr. Safari tour on elephant, and drive out to Siliguri in India.

Note: This trek is seeing some major changes with a surfaced road reaching Gonphu in 2005 and there being plans to extend the road to Panbhang.

Rafting the Mangde Chhu river down to Manas is an option being studied.

ACKNOWLEDGEMENTS

As one of the many contributors said 'I will be happy to add to the confusion involved in writing a trekking guidebook'. That hasn't actually been the case at all, because without all the superb input and help I have received this book wouldn't be what it is. There are many people to whom I owe enormous gratitude and appreciation (please accept my apologies if I have forgotten somebody).

Her Majesty the Queen of Bhutan, Dorji Wangmo Wangchuk, who kindly contributed the foreword.

Very warm thanks are due to all the Bhutanese who accompanied me and shared their knowledge. Sonam Ongdi took me around the first time I visited Bhutan. Since then I have been on trek in Bhutan either leading groups or on my own with excellent staff. Thank you especially to Yangphel, Yu-Druk, Etho Metho, Lhomen Tours & Trekking, Intrek and Bhutan Expeditions. On smaller trips I had excellent guides like Karma Tanzing.

I also travelled with non-Bhutanese and would like to say thank you for some very pleasant trekking days in the Bhutan Himalayas.

Many people and organisations helped me in the preparation of this book: Reinhard Wolf and Sabine; Frederik Sjösten Björn and Katrin Leo; Gavin Jordan; Grant Bruce; Thomas Slocum; Dorthe and Kjeld Poulsen on finding the 'dansker sti med Seje Sild slik poser'; Stefan Priesner; Ugyen Tshering; Pete Royall; Tshering Tashi; Chheda Dukpa; Pasang Dorji from Paro valley; Anke Sonnemans and Reindert Augustijn; the Department of Tourism (DoT) of the Royal Government of Bhutan; Association of Bhutanese Tour Operators (ABTO); Jack from Snow Leopard Trekking; Robert Dompnier; Peter Newsum; Sangay Wangchuk from Etho Metho; Karma Lotey from Yangphel; Piet van der Poel; Rogier Gruys; Baiba and Pat Morrow; Nima Sherpa for her endless and prompt cups of coffee; Francis Turkelboom; Bhutan Trust Fund; Rebecca Pradhan from the RSPN; Peter Kok; Tshewang Wangchuk from JDNP; Roy Cameron; Gyamcho Wangdi; Harry Marshall; Dorjee Lhatoo; Adam Pain; Marion Hass; Brad Rutherford from the International Snow Leopard Trust; Helge Westbye in Oslo; Claes Clifford as a courier; Christof Hahn; Aum Chime Wangdi; Steve Berry; Peter Kurt Hansen; Hans Beukeboom; Michael Rutland; David Annendale; Koert Sijmons; Nanda Ritsma from SNV; Damcho Rinzin from DoT; Tashi Tshering WWF; András Darabant; info on Nabji-Korphu trek via ABTO, DoT, SNV; and many more people.

Special thanks to Dasho Dzongkhag Chencho Tshering from Gasa who made the survey of a route possible.

Isabel and Austin Hutcheon deserve not only a sincere thank you for their input but also a compliment for their achievement in the Himalayas of Bhutan – good on you! Thanks also to Kristian Lørup, Jette Arildsen and their children Anna, Rasmus and Sofia who organised some brilliant family treks.

For their help with the Dagala trek: Alex Ergo and Laurence Ergo-Levaque; Dieter Zürcher and Maria Känzig (and for finding the Dagana extension route); Beth Dutson (aged seven) and her mother Anna for the Dagala trek diary; Dorji Penjor from the Centre for Bhutan Studies who wrote a useful booklet on the Dagana area. Tashi Tshering or Khaling from Uling Resorts for much input on eastern treks. Garab Dorji and Bill Jones for the trek from Haa to Paro. Edwin and Tineke Ruigrok from Zhemgang for a warm reception at their home and Edwin's input on the Ura–Buli/Zhemgang trek; we did the trek together and survived. Tsewang Nidup from Bhutan Expeditions who contributed information on Haa and is a superb guide.

Thanks to Peter Spierenburg, Marleen de Kok and Ugyen Namgyel for Black Mountains input, and to everybody who helped me on Lunana details: Professor Chris Duncan from the University of Massachusetts; Yannick Jooris; Hans Hessel Andersen for his mysterious Lunana contribution. Special thanks to Sämi Moser who pulled me over some high passes visiting a 'new' route into Lunana and who wrote a very informative paper on the Lunaps together with Gyembo Dorji; also thanks to Jacky and their children Viviane and Anina, with whom we had some very nice family treks (though Sämi, being Swiss, had a hard time with my yodelling).

Without access to many articles, papers and books, this guidebook would be incomplete. Many thanks to Dr Pema Gyamtsho for his paper 'Economy of yak herders'; Prof Dipl-Ing Manfred Gerner for papers on Lingshi Dzong (and who is in the process of renovation work on the Dzong); the Inventory of Glaciers, Glacial Lakes and Glacial Lake Outburst Floods in Bhutan by ICIMOD Nepal; the *Atlas of Bhutan* by the Ministry of Agriculture in Thimphu; Doug Scott for climbing history and details of Bhutan; Christian Schicklgruber's *Gods and Sacred Mountains*; Françoise Pommaret's excellent guidebook on Bhutan (as well as constructive discussions on writing a guidebook); Stan Armington's and Gyurme Dorje's guidebooks to double-check some references.

The following helped me and sent me numerous copies of published articles regarding Bhutan: the Royal Botanical Gardens (Kew) in the UK and Craig Brough; the Royal Botanic Gardens (Edinburgh) in Scotland and Graham Hardy; the Japanese Alpine Club and Tamotsu Nakamura; the British Mountaineering Club and Stuart Ingram; the Alpine Club in London and Margaret Ecclestone; the American Alpine Club Library and Francine Loft; the British Ornithologists Union at the Natural History Museum in Hertfordshire and Gwen Bonham and Steve Dudley; the Royal Scottish Geographical Society and David Munro; the Royal Geographical Society in London and Julie Carrington; Charles Dufour and Hanke Roos from Dufour Book Antiquarian in Leiden (the Netherlands); Chris Bartle from Glacier Books (Scotland).

Extensive use from the book *A Quest of Flowers* by H. R. Fletcher, who worked on the diaries of George Sherriff and Frank Ludlow, two botanists who explored Bhutan extensively in four expeditions in the beginning of the last century. Quotes from other books: *The Valley of Flowers* by F. S. Smythe; *Tales of the Yeti* by Kunzang Choden; *The Last Barbarians* by Michael Peissel; *Flowers of Bhutan* by Sasuke Nakao and Keiji Nishioka.

Thank you to Carol and Tim Inskipp, Richard Grimmett, A&C Black Publishers and illustrators for permission to use some bird images from *Birds of Bhutan* (1999). And thanks to Dr Kåre Hellum for the plant and flower sketches.

Special thanks go to Dr Peter Steele, on whose book (*Medical Handbook for Walkers & Climbers*) I have leaned heavily, and whose words I have often used, with his permission. Another medical contribution came from the outstanding trekker Rick Kutten from California, who wrote the stretching section. Thanks (and you were lucky you beat me once at chess!). On medicinal plants and Lingshi my sincere thanks go to Ugyen Paljor and Irmela Krug, whose research paper didn't make it into the book.

On white water sports special thanks to Sonam Tobgay and Ugyen Dorji from Lotus Adventures Bhutan, and the information on the combined trek/rafting destination in Haa by Maria Noakes and Nick Williams from Needmore Adventure. Also thanks to Gerry Moffatt on this section. Several people contributed on mountain biking: Rinzin Ongdra Wangchuk from Yu-Druk Tours & Treks; Piet van der Poel; Penny Richards and John Weiss and the Bhutan Mountain Biking Club. My introduction to rock climbing in Thimphu was by Stefan Priesner, Dilu Giri and Robin Pradham. Thanks – and I wish the Thimphu rock-climbing club a successful future.

Very special thanks to Professor Augusto Gansser from Switzerland who has been exploring the Bhutan Himalayas like no other foreigner and who generously offered me his materials. Very special thanks too to Dr Michael Ward who gave me an update on the Bhutan Himalayas and who generously offered me the use of his materials; he is by far the most knowledgeable person (outside Bhutan) regarding the mountains there. Thanks to Mike Searl from Oxford University on the geological section.

Respect is due to all my trekking colleagues, especially Rex Munro, Steve Razzetti, Val Pitkethly, Karl Farkas, Kate Harper, Tom Gilchrist, Pete Royall, Tim Greening, Glenn Rowley, Kit Wilkinson, Mark van Alstine, Andy Crisconi, Michael Steigerwald, Rahul Sharma, Brent Olson, Sean Morrissey and Andrew Sanders.

The text has been proof read by many people: many thanks to Isabel and Austin Hutcheon, Adam Paine, Richard Allen, Helene Bjerre Jordans, Lisa Pelton, Jim Mork, Sherry Teefey, Adrian Bland, Julie and Spencer Nicholls, George Cook, Alison Chubb, Per Sørensen, Ken Phelps, Chona and Doug Hirsch, Annette and Keith Ehrman, Emily Ennis, Gary Hirschkron, Mary Ann Walsh, Jock Martin, Margot Snowdon, Andrea Ronzani and Brian Clark, David Song, Ron Silberman, Steve Kilgore, Liliane and Peter Townshend, Donna and Mark Blum, Paul Ezatoff, Joe DiNunzio, Baiba and Pat Morrow, Cindy Hall, Kenneth Hanson, Bob Dickinson, Richard Farnhill and Brent Olson.

Kent Klich helped with selecting the slides for the book.

Most of all, thanks to Hazel Clarke, Lucy Histed, Sue Viccars and others from Cicerone Press for their expert and patient work on my Dutch–English. Publisher Jonathan Williams of Cicerone Press for allowing me to use more words then was agreed.

My guru in writing this book was Kev Reynolds. Thanks for the encouraging words during the process and the Mars bar in 1989.

The background of my love for the mountains goes back to many visits to the Alps with my parents – many thanks.

Finally, the biggest thank you is for all the support, stimulus and endless patience from my love Helene and our great children Laura and Max – I am always indebted.

APPENDIX 1

LIST OF MAPS

APPENDIX 2

LIST OF TREKS

Information for each trek covered in the book, regarding grade, duration in days, total distance, total altitude gain, total altitude loss and if the trekking area is open or closed; see also list of approved treks (see page 60) and check **www.tourism.gov.bt**.

Notes
a   Distances indicated in miles/km are approximate: actual hiking hours are much more useful than distance!
b   Figures of site trips (on rest days) are not included
c   Complete details are not available for a couple of treks

The Treks

1   **Haa Valley–Saga La–Drugyel Dzong**
     Grade: easy; 2–3 days; distance 14.3 miles/23km; altitude gain 3306ft/1008m; altitude loss 3739ft/1140m; double check if open

2   **Haa Valley–Nub Tshona Patta Tsho–Rigona**
     Grade: moderate–demanding; 6–7 days; distance not available; altitude gain 8443ft/2574m; altitude loss 8567ft/2612m; open (also summary of trek and raft descent Haa–Amo Chhu–Phuentsholing)

3   **Paro–Jhomolhari–Lingshi–Laya–Lunana–Nikka Chhu**
     Grade: strenuous; 24 days; distance 216.7 miles/349.5km; altitude gain 31,429ft/9582m; altitude loss 23,770ft/7247m; open

4   **Jhomolhari–Bonte La–Tagulun La or Lalung La–Drugyel Dzong Circuit**
     Grade: moderate–demanding; 9 days; distance 72.9 miles/117.5km; altitude gain 10,772ft/3284m; altitude loss 10,772ft/3284m; open – check for changes

5   **Jhomolhari–Lingshi–Thimphu**
     Grade: moderate–demanding; 9 days; distance 82.5 miles/133km; altitude gain 11,608ft/3539m; altitude loss 7,987ft/2435m; open

6   **Jhomolhari–Lingshi–Laya–Gasa–Punakha**
     Grade: moderate; 14 days; distance 125 miles/201,5km; altitude gain 17,069ft/5204m; altitude loss 23,042ft/7025; open

7   **Masa Gang Base Camp from Laya and back (not including side trips)**
     Grade: demanding; 3 or 4 days; distance 18.6 miles/30km; altitude gain 1870ft/570m; altitude loss 2034ft/620m; double check if open

8   **Drukpath**
Grade: moderate–demanding; 6 days; distance 30 miles/48km; altitude gain 7400ft/2256m; altitude loss 6271ft/1912m; open

9   **Dagala and Dagana extension**
Grade: moderate; duration Dagala 5 days, Dagana extension 7 days; distance Dagala 23 miles/37km, Dagana extension not available; altitude gain Dagala 7810ft/2381m, Dagana extension 7347ft/2240m; altitude loss Dagana 9450ft/2881m, Dagana extension 11,283ft/3440m; Dagala open, Dagana extension double check if open

10   **Samtengang trek**
Grade: easy; 4 days; distance 16.1 miles/26km; altitude gain 6117ft/1865m; altitude loss 5215ft/1590m; open

11   **Gasa Tsachu (hot springs)**
Note: details are due to alter with the building of a dirt road
Grade: easy; 3 or 4 days (including rest day); distance 36 miles/58km; altitude gain 2821ft/860m (1771ft/540m extra to Gasa Dzong); altitude loss 2821ft/860m (1771ft/540m extra after visiting Gasa Dzong); open

12   **Gangte Trek + southern variation**
Note: original trek might be affected by a feeder road: grade: easy–moderate; 3 days; distance 24.2 miles/39km; altitude gain 3234ft/986m; altitude loss 7554ft/2303m; open
Southern variation: easy–moderate; 4 days; double check if open

13   **The Nabji–Korphu Trek (Black Mountains or Jigme Singye Wangchuk National Park)**
Grade: easy–moderate; 6 days; distance 38.2 miles/61.5km; altitude gain and loss unknown; open

14   **Nubi–Chutey Trek near Trongsa**
Note: Incomplete details
Grade: easy–moderate; 5 days; double check if open

15   **Trongsa–Kasiphey–Dur Taschhu (hot springs)**
Note: Nearly ready in 2007
Grade: moderate; 4–5 days one way; double check if open

16   **Bumthang–Lunana (including trek to Dur Taschhu)**
Grade: strenuous; 8 days; distance 64.5 miles/104km; altitude gain: 15,764ft/4806m; altitude loss 11,385ft/3471m; open

17   **Gankar Punsum Base Camp below the South Ridge of Gankar Punsum – via Dur Tsachu**
Grade: demanding; 6–7 days one way; details – more research needed; double check if open

18 **Gankar Punsum Southeast Face–Thole La–Bumthang**
Grade: demanding–strenuous; 10 days; distance 41.5 miles/67km to southeast face + 47.7 miles/77km return to Bumthang = 89.3miles/144km; altitude gain 9059ft/2762m; altitude loss 9141ft/2787m; double check if open

19 **Gankar Punsum Southeast Face to Gankar Punsum Base Camp**
Grade: strenuous; 7 days to base camp; distance c56 miles/90km; altitude gain c8325ft/2538m; altitude loss c764ft/233m; double check if open

20 **Bumthang: Ngang–Tang Valleys and extension to Ura**
Grade: easy; 3 days; distance 25.1 miles/40.5km; altitude gain 3378ft/1030m; altitude loss 2772ft/845m; open
Extension to Ura – grade: moderate; 2 days; open

21 **Bumthang: Tang Valley–Rodang La–Lhuntshi–T(r)ashi Yangtse**
Grade: demanding; 10 days; distance 88 miles/142km; altitude gain 18,420ft/5616m; altitude loss 18,099ft/5518m; open

22 **Royal Heritage Trek: Bumthang–Kiki La–Tungi La–Kuenga Rabten–Trongsa**
Grade: moderate–demanding; 3–4 days, distance 28 miles/45km; altitude gain c8100ft/2470m; altitude loss c10725ft/3270m; open

23 **Ura–Buli/Zhemgang**
Grade: easy–moderate; 7 days; distance 52.1 miles/84km; altitude gain 7544ft/2300m; altitude loss 11,539ft/3518m; double check if open

24 **Bumdeling Wildlife Sanctuary Trek**
Grade: easy–moderate; 7 days; details incomplete; double check if open

25 **Migoi (Yeti) National Park (Merak–Sakteng Trek)**
Grade: moderate; 5 days; details incomplete; double check if open

26 **Kharungla Apeman Trek**
Grade: easy; 5 days; details incomplete; double check if open

27 **Manas National Park trek**
Grade: easy; 5 days; details incomplete; double check if open

APPENDIX 3

BIBLIOGRAPHY

The titles below represent a fraction of those consulted in the course of researching background material for this book.

Ashi Dorji Wangmo Wangchuk, Her Majesty The Queen of Bhutan. *Of Rainbow and Clouds: The Life of Yab Ugyen Dorji as told to his Daughter* 1999 New Delhi

Ashi Dorji Wangmo Wangchuk, Queen of Bhutan. *A Portrait of Bhutan. Treasures of the Thunder Dragon* 2006 New Delhi

Atlas of Bhutan. *Land Use Planning* Ministry of Agriculture, Thimphu, 1997 Bhutan

Beek, Martijn van, K., Bertlesen, Brix and Pedersen, P. (eds). *Ladakh, Culture, History, and Development between Himalaya and Karakoram* 1999 Aarhus, Delhi

Bhutan Lonely Planet Guide 3rd edition 2007

Bonn, Gisela. *Bhutan – Kunst und Kultur im Reich der Drachen* 1988 Köln, Germany

Cameron, Ian. *Mountains of the Gods* 1984 Bristol

Chapman, F. Spencer. *Helvellyn to Himalaya, including an Account of the First Ascent of Chomolhari* 1940 London

Dompnier, Robert. *Bhutan, Kingdom of the Dragon* 1999 New Delhi

Dorje, Gyurme. *Footprint Bhutan* 2004 Bath (1st edition)

Driem, George van. *Languages of the Greater Himalayan Region Vol 1 Dzongkha* 1998 Leiden, The Netherlands

Föllmi, Olivier. *Bhoutan, Le Temps d'un Royaume* 1993 Paris

Gansser, Augusto. *Geology of the Bhutan Himalaya* 1983 Basel/Boston/Stuttgart

Gerner, Manfred. *Bhutan, Kultur und Religion im Land Der Drachenkönige* 1981 Stuttgart

Gilchrist, Thomas R. *A Trekker's Handbook* 1996 Milnthorpe

Goldstein, Melvin C. and Beall, Cynthia M. *Nomads of Western Tibet, The Survival of a Way of Life* 1989/90 London

Neate, Jill. *High Asia: an illustrated history of the 7000 metre peaks* 1989 London

Peissel, Michel. *Lords & Lamas. A solitary expedition across the secret Himalayan kingdom of Bhutan* 1970 London

Peissel, Michel. *The Last Barbarians* 1998 London

Penjore, Dorji. *On the Mule Track from Dagana* 2003 Thimphu

Poel, Piet van der and Gruys, Rogier. *Mild and Mad Day Hikes around Thimphu* 2006 Thimphu

Pommaret, Françoise. 'On local and mountain deities in Bhutan' in *Reflections of the Mountain: Essays on the history and social meaning of the mountain cult in Tibet and the Himalaya* A. M. Blondeau & E. Steinkellner (eds), Österreichische Akademie der Wissenschaften, Wien, 1996

Pommaret, Françoise. *Bhutan* 6th edition 2007 Odyssey publs, Hong Kong

Razzetti, Steve. *Top Treks of the World* 2001 London

Schicklgruber, Christian and Pommaret, Françoise. *Mountain Fortress of the Gods* 1997 London (paper: *Gods and Sacred Mountains*)

Steele, Peter. *Two and two halves to Bhutan: A family journey in the Himalayas* 1970 London

The Bhutan Cookbook (4th edition) 2000 VSO/VSA

Vas, Lt. Gen. E. A. *The Dragon Kingdom. Journeys through Bhutan* 1986 New Delhi

Ward, Frank Kingdon. *Riddle of the Tsangpo Gorges* 1926 London

Ward, Michael. *In this Short Span* 1972 London

Wilhelmy, Herbert. *Bhutan* 1990 München

Zheng, Zhou and Zhenkai, Liu. *Footprints on the Peaks, Mountaineering in China* 1995 Seattle

Zurick, David and Pacheco, Julsun *Illustrated Atlas of the Himalayas* 2006 The University Press of Kentucky'

Medical references

Bezruchka, Stephen MD. *Altitude Illness, Prevention & Treatment* 2nd edition 2005 The Mountaineers, Seattle

Carline, Jan and MacDonald, Steve and Lentz, Martha. *Mountaineering First Aid: A guide to Accident Response and First Aid Care* 5th edition 2004 The Mountaineers, Seattle

Duff, Dr Jim and Gormly, Dr Peter. *Pocket First Aid and Wilderness Medicine* (10th edition) 1st edition with Cicerone 2007

Hackett, Peter H. MD. *Mountain Sickness, Prevention, Recognition and Treatment* 2nd edition 1980 The American Alpine Club

Steele, Peter. *Medical Handbook for Walkers & Climbers* 1999 UK

Tilton, Buck. *Backcountry First Aid and Extended Care* Guilford, Connecticut 2002

Wilkerson, James A. *Medicine for Mountaineering & Other Wilderness Activities* 5th edition 2001 The Mountaineers, Seattle

Articles/reports

Many articles were provided by many different libraries (see Acknowledgements)

JDNP–ICDP fieldwork report 2001 Thimphu, Bhutan

ICIMOD report regarding glaciers

Doug Scott in *Mountain Magazine*

Flora

Fletcher, Harold R. *A Quest of Flowers. The Plant Explorations of Frank Ludlow and George Sherriff* 1975 Edinburgh

Flora of Bhutan by the Royal Botanic Garden Edinburgh. Several volumes, several authors

Gurung, Dhan Bahadur *An Illustrated Guide to the Orchids of Bhutan* 2006 Thimphu (with 423 species described)

Hellum, Dr A. K. *A Painter's Year in the Forests of Bhutan* 2001 Canada

Mierow, Dorothy and Tirtha Bahadur Shrestha. *Himalayan Flowers and Trees* 1987 Kathmandu

Nakao, Dr. Sasuke and Nishioka, Keji. *Flowers of Bhutan* 1984 Tokyo

Negi, Dr S. S. and Naithani, Dr H. B. *Oaks of India, Nepal and Bhutan* 1995 Dehra Dun, India

Parker, Chris. *Weeds of Bhutan* 1992 Thimphu-Bhutan/Germany/UK

Pradhan, Rebecca. *Wild Rhododendrons of Bhutan* 1999 Thimphu, Bhutan

Stainton, Adam and Polunin, Oleg. *Concise Flowers of the Himalaya* 1978 Delhi

Stapleton, Chris. *Bamboos of Bhutan* 1994 Royal Botanical Gardens Kew, UK

Thukral, Gurmeet and Bond, Ruskin. *Himalayan Flowers* 1998 USA/New Delhi

Tsarong, Tsewang J. *Tibetan Medicinal Plants* 1984 Kalimpong/India

Fauna

Ali, Sálim. *Field Guide to the Birds of the Eastern Himalayas* 1999 Delhi

Flemming, Robert L. Sr and Jr., and Lain Singh Bangdel. *Birds of Nepal with references to Kashmir and Sikkim* 2000 Delhi

Gardner, Dana and Nature Tourism – Bhutan tour operator. *Birds of Bhutan* 2005 (a very handy laminated folding guide helping to identify nearly 100 common birds of Bhutan)

Grewal, Bikram and Pfister, Otto. *A Photographic Guide to Birds of the Himalayas* 1998 London

Inskipp, Carol and Tim, and Grimmett, Tim. *Birds of Bhutan* 1999 London

Kazmierczak, Krys and van Perlo, Ber. *A Field Guide to the Birds of India, Sri Lanka, Pakistan, Nepal, Bhutan, Bangladesh and the Maldives* 2000 East Sussex, UK

Poel, Piet van der and Wangchuk, Tashi. *Butterflies of Bhutan. Mountains, hills and valleys between 800 and 3000m* (to be published in 2007)

Spierenburg, Peter. *Birds in Bhutan: Status and Distribution* Oriental Bird Club 2005 ISBN 0952954516

Wangchuk, Tashi and others. *A Field Guide to the Mammals of Bhutan* 2004 Thimphu (with information on the 200 or so mammals of Bhutan)

Films and documentaries on Bhutan

Into the Thunder Dragon – A mountain unicycle odyssey in the Himalayan kingdom of Bhutan! by Sean White, starring Kris Holm & Nathan Hoover 2002 Outside Television

The Cup by Dzongsar Khyentse Rinpoche – 2000 Bhutan

Travellers and Magicians by Dzongsar Khyentse Rinpoche – 2003 Bhutan

School among glaciers by Dorji Wangchuk – 2005 Bhutan (a documentary film on a school in the village of Lhedi, located in remote Lunana)

APPENDIX 4

GLOSSARY

ABTO	Association of Bhutanese Tour Operators
anim	Buddhist nun
Ashi	title for a queen and/or princess
aum	term used for addressing a married woman
ba (or jha)	yak herders tent
banchung	small bamboo basket
bangchang	local beer
bharal	blue sheep
BHU	Basic Health Unit
Bhutan Observer	private newspaper in Bhutan
Bhutan Times	private newspaper in Bhutan
Bodhisattva	spiritual incarnate or emanation of Buddha who cares for all sentient beings
Bön (or Bon)	animist (shamanic) religion from the Himalayas practised before the arrival of Buddhism, still practised in Bhutan and other areas of the Himalayas
Brokpa	small group of people in central and eastern Bhutan, mainly above 3000m
bura	wild silk (raw silk)
BWS	Bumdeling Wildlife Sanctuary
caterpillar fungus	*Cordyceps sinensis* ('dbyar-rtsva-dgun-'bu'; yartsa goenbu). The rare combination of a fungus and the larvae of a caterpiller is also called 'sum mer grass – winter worm'. *Cordyceps* is found above 16,400ft/5000m. Clinical trials show an immune system enhancing effect.
chang	beer made of rice, millet or barley
chhu (chu)	river, water
chilip	foreigner
choeku (rimro)	Bhutanese Buddhist ritual, often wrongly referred to as puja
chogo metho	Bhutanese name for the plant *Rheum nobile* (see 'Flora' section)

choogo (or chugo)	chunks of smoked hard, dried yak cheese
chorten (stupa)	small, religious structure of brick or stone, consisting of a dome, a box, a spire and a plinth, sometimes containing relics (found all over Bhutan)
chungkay	porridge made out of fermented rice and cooked with butter and eggs
Dakpas	small group of people of Merak and Sakteng, mainly above 3000m
dapa	wooden bowl or cup made out of a gnarled burr
Dasho	honorary title given by the King to Government officials (= knighthood)
datse	traditional archery
doma	mixture of areca nut and lime wrapped in betel leaves
DoT	Department of Tourism
drey	unit of measurement in Bhutan
dri (or jim)	female yak
Druk Yul	in Dzongkha the name for Bhutan, meaning 'Dragon Kingdom' or 'The Land of the Dragon'
dungpa	(chief of) a sub-district
dzo	male cross between a yak and regular cow
dzomo	female cross between a yak and regular cow
dzong	fortress, monastery, administrative centre
Dzongkhag	national language of Bhutan
ema datse (or da(t)shi)	chillies cooked with cheese, sometimes mixed with cooked potatoes or vegetables; Bhutan's national dish
gang	mountain/hill (in Bhutanese; in Tibetan 'kang')
gangri	snow mountain
garuda	mythical bird in Hindu and Buddhist traditions
gewog	block, the lowest administrative level
ghechu	straight knife used in Bhutan
gho	national dress for men
gompa/goemba	monastery
gup	elected head of a gewog or county
JDNP	Jigme Dorji National Park
Je Khenpo	spiritual leader in Bhutan

Jib	fireplace, the heart of the nomad tent, made from turf and clay
Jops	small group of people in western Bhutan, living above 3000m
JSWNP	Jigme Singye Wangchuk National Park (formerly known as Black Mountains)
kabney	scarf for men, wrapped in a complicated matter around the upper body and shoulders when entering a *dzong* or meeting government officials, and at special ceremonies
kaddar (or kata)	ceremonial scarf; a traditional, good-luck present
katsup	opening between the fabric in the middle of the tent roof, allowing smoke from the fire to escape
khemar	red-bronze painted border high up around religious buildings
khenja	a jacket worn by Laya women
khonying	arch *chorten*
kira	the national dress for women
koma	decorated clips used to hold women's dress together at the shoulders
Kuensel	the national newspaper of Bhutan
la	pass
Lakhaps	small group of people in west-central Bhutan, living mainly above 3000m
lam	road
lama	Buddhist teacher or priest
langdo	Bhutanese farmers measure their land in *langdo*; a section of land that can be ploughed by a pair of bulls in one day
laptse	pile of stones with payer flags attached to sticks placed in it
lapza	a cold-resistant tough grass growing high in the mountains
lhagyelo (or lha gelo; or ha gyello)	a word(s) exclaimed on top of a mountain pass, meaning 'May God always win over evil' or 'The gods are victorious'
lhakhang	Buddhist temple
Lhotsampa	'the southerns': people living in the south of Bhutan with Nepali origin

Lunaps	group of people living in the Lunana area
lungdar	a set of five flags, put up on mountain passes, in five different colours: blue = space; white = water; red = fire; green = air; yellow = earth
Lyonpo	Minister's title
mandala	religious drawing
mani wall	a wall of stones inscribed with prayer texts
marcchu	butter
migoi (or yeti)	yeti
momos	traditional Tibetan dish of steamed or fried dumplings filled with meat, cheese or vegetables
NCD	Nature Conservation Division
NEC	National Environmental Commission
ngad-ja	black tea with milk and a lot of sugar, normally served with lots of biscuits
Ngultrum	Bhutanese currency equivalent to the Indian rupee (1US$ = 41 ngultrum [2007])
Om Mani Padme Hum	the mantra (oral prayer) of the Bodhisattva of Compassion: 'Hail to the jewel in the lotus'
poori (with alu dum)	fried chapattis with fried potato curry
prayer flag	pieces of cloth in various shapes, printed with prayers and found in all kind of places through out the country; the wind blows the flags and spreads the prayers
puja	ritual – Indian word, used in English (incorrectly) by some Bhutanese and others. In any Bhutanese language it is *choeku* or *rimro*
PWS	Phibsoo Wildlife Sanctuary
rachu	same function as the kabney for men, but more decorated and easier to put on
RBA	Royal Bhutan Army
RBG	Royal Body Guard
RBP	Royal Bhutan Police
RGOB	Royal Government of Bhutan
Rinpoche	title known to reincarnated lamas
rimro (or choeku)	Bhutanese Buddhist ritual, often wrongly referred to as puja
RMNP	Royal Manas National Park
RNR	Renewable Natural Resources

Rougimsee (or drong gimtse)	local name for the animal Takin
RSPN	Royal Society for Protection of Nature
Shabdrung	title for a spiritual leader of Bhutan
Shabdrung Ngawang Namgyal (1594–1651)	first spiritual leader of Bhutan and founder of the nation Namgyal
Sharchop	people of eastern Bhutan
Sharchopkha	language of the Sharchops
stupa	Sanskrit equivalent of a *chorten*
sudja	buttered and salted tea (also in Tibet and elsewhere in the Himalayas)
swastika	a Buddhist symbol of protection. In Bon Buddhism the symbol is used in reverse
SWS	Sakteng Wildlife Sanctuary
Tashi delek	an auspicious and versatile Bhutanese expression, meaning 'good luck', 'wishing you well', 'good wishes', 'cheers'
terma	sacred texts, found for example in lakes, hidden in the 8th century by Guru Rinpoche
thongdroel	enormous than(g)kha filling the front of a big building, and shown during religious festivals
TNP	Thrumshingla National Park
tsach(h)u	hot springs
tsampa	ground barley flour
tsechu	yearly religious festival in every *dzong* throughout the country
tsho	lake
Tulku	title for reincarnated high lamas
utse	main tower in the centre of a *dzong*
yak	long-haired relation of the ox family; kept for dairy and as a beast of burden
yathra	hand-woven woollen textile produced in Bumthang, central Bhutan
yartsa goenbu	dialect for caterpillar fungus
yeti	abdominal snowman (local name migoi)
zam (zampa)	bridge
zao	toasted rice snack served with tea
zi	an etched agate or striped chalcedong, highly valued throughout the Himalayas
zow (or zaw)	rice that has been boiled and then fried, making it puffed and crunchy

LISTING OF CICERONE GUIDES

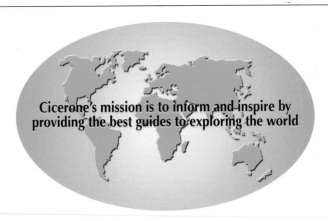

Cicerone's mission is to inform and inspire by providing the best guides to exploring the world

Since its foundation over 30 years ago, Cicerone has specialised in publishing guidebooks and has built a reputation for quality and reliability. It now publishes nearly 300 guides to the major destinations for outdoor enthusiasts, including Europe, UK and the rest of the world.

Written by leading and committed specialists, Cicerone guides are recognised as the most authoritative. They are full of information, maps and illustrations so that the user can plan and complete a successful and safe trip or expedition – be it a long face climb, a walk over Lakeland fells, an alpine traverse, a Himalayan trek or a ramble in the countryside.

With a thorough introduction to assist planning, clear diagrams, maps and colour photographs to illustrate the terrain and route, and accurate and detailed text, Cicerone guides are designed for ease of use and access to the information.

If the facts on the ground change, or there is any aspect of a guide that you think we can improve, we are always delighted to hear from you.

Cicerone Press
2 Police Square Milnthorpe Cumbria LA7 7PY
Tel:01539 562 069   Fax:01539 563 417
e-mail:info@cicerone.co.uk   web:www.cicerone.co.uk

CICERONE